AN OFFICIAL MENSA® BOOK

10-minute crossword puzzles

By Fred Piscop

WORKMAN PUBLISHING • NEW YORK

Copyright © 2011 by Fred Piscop
Design copyright © by Workman Publishing

All rights reserved. No portion of this book may be
reproduced—mechanically, electronically, or by any
other means, including photocopying—without written
permission of the publisher. Published simultaneously
in Canada by Thomas Allen & Son Limited.

Library of Congress Cataloging-in-Publication Data

Piscop, Fred.
Mensa 10-minute crossword puzzles / by Fred Piscop.
p. cm.
ISBN 978-0-7611-6322-0 (alk. paper)
1. Crossword puzzles. I. Title.
GV1057.5.P57 2011
793.732–dc23   2011023698

Workman books are available at special discounts
when purchased in bulk for premiums and sales
promotions as well as for fund-raising or educational
use. Special editions or book excerpts also can be
created to specification. For details, contact the
Special Sales Director at the address below, or
send an e-mail to specialmarkets@workman.com.

WORKMAN PUBLISHING COMPANY, INC.
225 VARICK STREET
NEW YORK, NY 10014-4381

workman.com

Printed in the United States of America
First printing August 2011

11 10 9 8 7

CONTENTS

INTRODUCTION

We often find ourselves in situations where we're passing the time: waiting at the dentist's or doctor's office, commuting to work on the subway or train, or stuck on the runway at the airport. It's those 10 minutes here or there that can be made more enjoyable with a puzzle.

But fast doesn't necessarily mean easy. A 10-minute puzzle still requires a balance of challenge and solvability—so whether you're a seasoned solver or a novice looking to hone your skills, these clues should tune your mind as you fill in the blank grids.

The puzzles I've assembled here first and foremost are meant to be enjoyed. I constructed them to include minimum trickery (obscure entries are rare, and lively cluing is the rule) for pleasurable solving. Which means they're neither trivial to the point of boredom nor brain-busting to the point of frustration—rather, they're *just right*.

This book contains a selection of some of my favorite crossword puzzles, as well as 100 brand-new, never-before-published ones. I hope you enjoy them.

Happy solving! —Fred

ABOUT MENSA

Mensa, the international high I.Q. society, has more than 110,000 members worldwide, with 57,000 in the United States. Mensa has only one requirement for membership: a score in the top two percent on a standardized, supervised intelligence test or the accepted equivalent thereof. Through its many local groups and international contacts, Mensa offers a rich variety of experiences to its members. Mensa also provides scholarships, a research journal, and educational outreach to gifted youth through the Mensa Education & Research Foundation. For a free brochure about American Mensa, call toll free 1 (800) 66-MENSA, or visit us on the Web at www.us.mensa. org. For additional information, call 1 (817) 607-0060, or write to Mensa, 1229 Corporate Drive West, Arlington, TX 76006. In Canada, call (613) 547-0824.

Puzzles

AT THE AIRPORT

Across

1 *Kon-Tiki* wood
6 "Agreed!"
10 Triangular sail
13 Statesman Sharon
14 Back 40 units
16 22-Across promise
17 Wearer of the latest fashion, perhaps
19 Grazing ground
20 Honest one
21 Drapery fabric
22 Ring exchange site
24 "Promise her anything . . ." perfume
26 One of a famous sailing trio
28 Landmark near the Arno
33 Strung along
36 Report card ruiners
37 Praiseful poem
38 Battling fiercely
39 The 24 in 36-24-36
41 *The Dukes of Hazzard* boss
42 Beehive State Indian
43 Immunology prefix
44 Sidewalk umbrella sites
45 Computer monitor with no intelligence
49 Took public transportation
50 Perfumes with a joss stick
53 No-no
56 Street slickener
58 Co. in *The Aviator*
60 Feller in a forest

61 Uninvited guest
64 Informal top
65 "Maria ___" ('40s hit)
66 Poet Stephen Vincent ___
67 Politico Landon
68 Stage item
69 Milk run's many

Down

1 Vamp Theda
2 Tourist mecca off Venezuela
3 Lid or lip application
4 Use a Singer
5 Support group for young people
6 Demonic child in *The Omen*
7 Environmental sci.
8 Battle of the Bulge site
9 Poe's Annabel
10 Send a Dear John letter to
11 "The very ___!"
12 Tusked animal
15 Factors in handwriting analysis
18 Discipline with a "warrior pose"
23 Mekong Delta dweller
25 Schemer's creation
27 "___ a Kick Out of You"
29 "In the doghouse," e.g.
30 Doghouse sound
31 Add fringe to
32 Rules, for short
33 Shower with praise
34 Ides of March rebuke
35 Carpe ___
39 Do a garden chore
40 Perp apprehender
41 Dutch portraitist Frans

43 Moe, for one

44 Cambridge University students, for short

46 Sis's sibling

47 Polar cover

48 __-do-well

51 Prefix meaning "race"

52 Remove dust bunnies

53 "Toodles"

54 Ice Capades jump

55 Burrito filler

57 Late-night Jay

59 Literature and music, etc.

62 Chalet site

63 Broadway background

HEAD STARTS

Across

1 Breaks in relations
6 Send forth
10 Pompous sort
13 For the birds?
14 Rudolph's high beam
15 Vogue rival
16 '20s political scandal
18 Tickled pink
19 Space rock
20 Playing marble
21 "Mazel __!"
22 Behaviorist B.F.
24 Hippie's two-finger sign
28 Pre-euro Portuguese money
30 State positively
32 Wee bit
33 __ podrida
37 Marsh bird
38 1836 siege site
40 Dire fate
41 In two parts
42 Hole goal
43 Do some film editing
45 Uses TNT
48 Fine china name
49 Most trite
52 Start for fix or mix
54 Race marker
55 Bit of ballet
60 Grand in scope
61 Skin-and-bones sort
63 Chicken part
64 MP's quarry
65 Spiral-horned critter
66 China's Lao-__
67 A jillion
68 Some are kosher

Down

1 Pro __ (proportionately)
2 Oscar winner Burl
3 Via Veneto car
4 Sticky strip
5 Bull, at times
6 Salad veggie
7 Ellington's "__ Indigo"
8 Doctrine
9 Pipe joint
10 Comedian Sherman
11 Pool table material
12 Meal with matzoh
15 Pasta strip
17 To boot
20 Handouts
22 Shell game, e.g.
23 Congratulations
24 Cowpoke's pal
25 Genesis twin
26 Where the Lena flows
27 Attica structure
29 Windows icon
31 Spanish munchies
34 Pork purchase
35 Bughouse
36 NYSE counterpart
39 Hang in there
44 Made a promise
46 Football's Dawson
47 Victor's share

49 Pooped out
50 Pounds an Underwood
51 Trixie's sitcom pal
53 Stimpy's buddy
55 Home run gait
56 Up to the job
57 *Hud* Oscar winner
58 "___ quote you?"
59 Some may split
61 Erie Canal mule
62 Eagle on a par four

INNER SELVES

Across

1 Tinker to ___ to Chance
6 Scratch up
9 Until now
14 Hold dear
15 Court feat
16 State one's views
17 Excuse givers
19 Captain's superior
20 Without delay
22 Actress Lupino
23 Following closely
26 Santa ___, Calif.
27 Claim against property
28 Most ill-humored
30 Club fees
32 Jump on one foot
33 MTV viewer, most likely
35 Clean kind of energy
38 Better-than-thou sort
41 In the distant past
43 More cunning
44 Kingly address
46 Gun-rights org.
47 Tide type
49 One of eight in a V-8
52 Mouse surfaces
54 Miner's strike
56 Degrades
57 Singer DiFranco
58 Performed surgery
60 ___ raving mad
62 World champion figure skater of 1989

66 Salon color
67 Suffix with opal or glass
68 Monte of Cooperstown
69 Analyze 54-Across
70 Classic Jaguar
71 Balance sheet plus

Down

1 Sister of Zsa Zsa
2 Actor Kilmer
3 Yalie
4 Red gems
5 Anglers' nets
6 Shark variety
7 Overlay material
8 Pine exudation
9 A handful of
10 ___-Locka, Fla.
11 Abel Tasman discovered them
12 Battery terminal
13 Showed again
18 Places to moor
21 Neuman's magazine
23 Post-workout woes
24 Fad doll with spiky hair
25 Pueblos of Arizona
27 Many August babies
29 Tennis units
31 Put into play
34 ___ a soul (nobody)
36 See eye to eye
37 Sounds from Simba
39 Pro shop bagful
40 Nest egg letters
42 Trattoria dessert
45 Place to play hockey

48 Rice Krispies sound
50 Spain's peninsula
51 Low points
52 Old Turkish title
53 Starting stakes
55 Modify, as a soundtrack
58 Thumbs-up
59 "Zip-___-Doo-Dah"
61 Genetic letters
63 ICU hookups
64 Deadlock
65 Ottawa's prov.

PHONING IN

Across

1 Popular mints
6 __ *Steverino!* (Steve Allen book)
10 Pond gunk
14 Be of use
15 Bloodhound's clue
16 It's chopped liver
17 Place setting piece
19 Toiling away
20 Like a pleasant aroma
21 Avoid court
23 __ out (just make)
24 Farm bundler
25 Aplenty
29 *In Cold Blood* author
32 Pile up
33 Quite the expert
34 Pac-12 school, briefly
37 Beats it, in dialect
38 One who's underage
39 Travel before takeoff
40 Orange or lemon drink
41 Nation once known as Dahomey
42 Pepper grinders
43 Noted Big Apple restaurant
45 Deadly missile
46 Addlebrained
48 In a blue funk
49 Spring arrivals
51 Dorm dwellers
56 Heavy load
57 Radio control
59 Minnelli of *Cabaret*
60 Vivacity
61 Moon surface feature
62 Like a sluggard
63 Politico Gingrich
64 Spirited horse

Down

1 Chaplin prop
2 __ *Almighty* (Steve Carell movie)
3 Fully absorbed
4 *Kon-__*
5 Deli gadgets
6 Mezzo-soprano Marilyn
7 Beatnik's "Understood"
8 Sweetums
9 Assns.
10 Showed one's contempt for, maybe
11 Open audition
12 Of service
13 Cabbie's ticker
18 Adidas rival
22 Black, in verse
25 Madly in love
26 Surrounded by
27 Up-to-the-minute gossip
28 CIA forerunner
29 __ Major (southern constellation)
30 Bell-ringing company
31 According to
33 __ Cooper (car)
35 Wheel shaft
36 Santa checks it twice
38 Avg.
39 Up to, in ads
41 __ Mawr, Pa.

42 Rainy day racetrack favorites

44 "Do ___, not . . ."

45 *Oz* creator L. Frank ___

46 Like Parker's wit

47 Ancient land near Lydia

48 Bit of daredeviltry

50 Cinematographer Nykvist

51 Picnic dish

52 Rework, as a story

53 Khartoum's river

54 O. Henry product

55 Malamute's tow

58 Córdoba cheer

SO CLUMSY OF ME!

Across

1 Cooperstown charter member Ty
5 Contracts, as an illness
9 Porker's meal
13 Baltic Sea feeder
14 Jazzman Chick
15 Transport by truck
16 Soldiers who drop into battle areas
18 Grid great Graham
19 *Atlas Shrugged* author Rand
20 Martini's partner
21 Cast a ballot
22 Maine politico Olympia
24 *The Biggest Loser* contestants
26 Whodunit plot element
28 Phone listing abbr.
29 Castle of the ballroom
30 Goya's *Naked* __
33 Thirty minutes of football
37 Not of the clergy
38 Googol's hundred
39 __-Day (vitamin brand)
40 Cornerstone word
41 Off-ramp
42 "__ a million years!"
43 Prefix with lead or fire
45 Earth tones
46 Road to conflict
50 Ump's broom
51 Troy, to Homer
52 Run __ of the law
54 "There's __ in 'team'"
57 Disney's __ & Stitch

58 Toucan Sam's cereal
60 Seemingly bottomless
61 Gems from Australia
62 Plot unit
63 Wraps up
64 Roly-__
65 Hebrides island

Down

1 Barry Manilow song locale
2 Anita who sang with Krupa
3 *West Side Story* composer
4 Playtex product
5 Christmas bird
6 Cupid, to Plato
7 Not so hot
8 Carrier to Oslo
9 Plays b-ball
10 Coffeeshop order
11 External
12 Walks wearily
14 Russell of *Gladiator*
17 Treasure store
21 Neckline type
23 Knuckleheads
25 S&L offerings
26 Uris's __ *18*
27 Seaport of Algeria
30 Tex-__ cuisine
31 Meyers of *Kate & Allie*
32 Scribble down
34 Gasoline additive
35 *Star Wars* princess
36 Autograph seekers
38 Tabasco quality
42 Noel who played Lois Lane

44 Fleming who created 007
45 Locks up
46 *An Ideal Husband* playwright
47 *Star Trek* extra
48 Rubbed the wrong way
49 Mute Marx
50 "__ Bully" (1965 hit)
53 Stable babe
55 C&W mecca, with "the"
56 Words of understanding
58 Stylish dresser
59 Intl. group since 1948

SMALL STUFF

Across

1 Big flop
5 Sacred bird of the Pharaohs
9 __ out (examine, slangily)
14 Familiar OPEC figure
15 Alaska gold rush city
16 Welcome words to a hitchhiker
17 La __ (weather worry)
18 Heroic deed
19 Blunted blades
20 Smallish NBA Hall of Famer
23 Ambulance letters
24 Vote against
25 Proper to a fault
29 Letters on a Cardinal's cap
31 Belted one out
35 Feared mosquito
36 Mad Magazine feature
38 "Get my point?"
39 Nightgown wearer of rhyme
42 NASA "walk"
43 Kunta Kinte's story
44 Year-end songs
45 Shoulder muscle, briefly
47 Middling grade
48 Play a reel, say
49 Neighbor of Mex.
51 Daddies
52 "Long Tall Sally" singer
59 Like a dryer trap
60 Portable dwelling
61 Gen-__ (post-boom babies)
63 Run __ of the law
64 Savvy about
65 Giant hop
66 Al __ (not too soft)
67 Koh-i-__ diamond
68 On pins and needles

Down

1 Jerry's partner in ice cream
2 Forget to include
3 Short skirt
4 Fiber source
5 FDR word about 12/7/41
6 Afrikaners
7 Apple product
8 Clockmaker Thomas
9 Biblical queendom
10 Some patients' outlays
11 Kadett automaker
12 Like Hamelin's piper
13 USNA grad
21 Polite affirmation
22 How a trucker might go up a hill
25 Handled roughly
26 Superman player
27 10 out of 10, e.g.
28 Give a darn?
29 Treat maliciously
30 Tot's "piggies"
32 "Since you __"
33 *Jurassic Park* star Sam
34 Formation fliers
36 Gin flavoring
37 Maze goal
40 Milk train, e.g.
41 Tacit assent
46 "That's hardly proper"
48 Contributing element

50 What's in, in fashion
51 Spotted horse
52 Long prison sentence
53 A party to
54 Rival of Harrow
55 Gambling mecca
56 Auto shaft
57 Papyrus plant, e.g.
58 Bummer
59 Terhune title character
62 007, for one

ON THE SET

Across

1 Seizes firmly
6 Brit's baby buggy
10 Rent-___ (security guard)
14 Taxpayer's fear
15 Suffix for the well-off
16 "Uh-uh!"
17 Paris's nickname
20 Time line segment
21 Innie buildup
22 Winter hazard
23 "A ___ bagatelle!"
24 Gives back to a borrower
26 Pay tribute to
29 Ushers' rentals
30 Flying high
31 Word with fire or white
32 Stick up
35 Clown with the photog
39 Ambulance letters
40 Where the boyz are
41 Runway strutter
42 Risked getting bleeped
44 Hastert's successor as Speaker
45 Infant's rite
48 Tackle box item
49 Pale as a ghost
50 ___ Valley, Calif.
51 Harper Valley org.
54 Get busy
58 Margarita need
59 Colorful horse
60 "You ___ kidding!"
61 Monopoly stack
62 Meal for an echidna
63 Increase in troop strength

Down

1 Modern-day scandal suffix
2 Essen's area
3 Think tank nugget
4 Snapshot, for short
5 Heel style
6 *Miracle on 34th Street* actor John
7 Situation for rubber bullets
8 Comics bark
9 Gibson of *Braveheart*
10 Protractor measurements
11 Skater Sasha
12 ___ out (declined)
13 Bedbugs, roaches, etc.
18 Get pooped out
19 Many a resort locale
23 Misplay, as a fly ball
24 Like much notebook paper
25 Co. bigwig
26 ___ day (delivery option)
27 Homecoming attendee
28 Snorers saw them
29 Chevy SUV
31 Attack en masse
32 Make over
33 Compounds ending in "-ite," often
34 Island near Java
36 Greek P's
37 ___ Cup (yacht race)
38 Lawn burrower
42 Surgical blockage relievers
43 KFC piece

44 Powerful feline
45 Low man in the choir
46 The Nile's ___ Dam
47 Suffix meaning "lover"
48 Colosseum combatants
50 Baseball card tidbit
51 Place to moor
52 Chinatown gang
53 Pay to play
55 One of the Gershwins
56 "Smoking or ___?"
57 Play about Capote

PINT-SIZE PUGS

Across

1 Some tuskers
6 Overthrow plotters
11 Super, to a Beatles fan
14 Disney World attraction
15 Biscotto flavoring
16 Latvia's cont.
17 Paperbacks name
19 Hoopla
20 A hydrogen atom has one
21 Barbecue site
23 Fired up
24 Helped out with Little League
26 Carbines and Winchesters
30 Public esteem
31 Freud contemporary Alfred
32 Runway strutter
33 Target of Senator McCarthy
36 *Hopalong Cassidy* star William
37 Cavity site, often
38 Popular auction site
39 Chicago Loop loopers
40 Apple gizmo
41 A *Canterbury Tales* pilgrim
42 Exuberant cries
44 Pub crawler's spree
45 Peach-fuzz removers
47 Et ___ (footnote abbr.)
48 Tribal emblem
49 Thoroughly soak
54 Oxcart's track
55 A tad tipsy
58 "___ as directed"
59 Kate's chum

60 Knight mare?
61 Debussy's "La ___"
62 Like the stereotypical ditz
63 *Driving Miss Daisy* Oscar winner

Down

1 *Cheers* actress Neuwirth
2 October's stone
3 Teenager's woe
4 Campus military org.
5 Hotelier Ellsworth Milton ___
6 Explorer Sebastian
7 "Author unknown," for short
8 Dust-cover blurb, perhaps
9 Start of a JFK quote
10 Electric guitar pioneer
11 Require firemen on diesels, e.g.
12 Bemedaled Murphy
13 Be bummed out
18 Hosp. diagnostics
22 Do something
24 Chest wood
25 Telephone abbr.
26 Broccoli ___
27 Teen fave
28 Bug dispatcher
29 Assumed command
30 Credits listings
32 Philippine Muslims
34 Mansard overhang
35 Batik artisan
37 Tie securely, as a vessel
38 Poetic nightfall
40 High school experimenter's place, for short
41 Petition

43 Salutation for Caesar
44 One of the Little Women
45 Play a banjo
46 Monopoly buy
47 Full, and then some
49 Kick target, maybe
50 Pro ___ (in proportion)
51 Yemeni city
52 ___ up (prepared to drive)
53 MacDonald's partner
56 Bedridden
57 Day-___ paints

DEUCE

Across

1. Gossip, slangily
5. Port of Israel
9. Newswoman Zahn
14. Bill of Rights defender, for short
15. Colorado skiing mecca
16. Williams of *Happy Days*
17. Controlled research study
20. *Taking Woodstock* director Lee
21. First name in courtroom fiction
22. Wears away
23. Pyramid part
24. Lender's claim
25. Give consent
28. "O," in love letters
29. Business subj.
33. Cobbler's inventory
34. Tourist attraction
36. Bard's before
37. 1962 Mitchum/MacLaine drama
40. ___ publica
41. Santa-tracking org.
42. Marble type
43. City near Provo
45. Body art, slangily
46. Goal maker
47. Like desert climate
49. Scale of mineral hardness
50. Ancient Rome's ___ Way
53. Adriatic port
54. Spot for a rubdown
57. Multiple allegiance
60. Ewing matriarch
61. Pub orders
62. By oneself
63. Vegas signs
64. Hatchling's home
65. Commentators' page

Down

1. Early baby word
2. PC pic
3. Counterfeit coin
4. Wheel's center
5. Disinclined
6. Internet access means
7. Really bug
8. Quarterback Manning
9. San Diego baseballer
10. San ___ (Texas city, familiarly)
11. Took advantage of
12. Blow, as a game
13. Tiny colonists
18. Steers astray
19. Paddock sounds
23. Make a stink
24. Raced in a chute
25. 9-Down foe
26. Cringe in fear
27. Go out of business
28. Part of a drum kit
30. Actor Romero
31. Speak like Bryan
32. More modish
34. Fine violin, for short
35. Forum on a political issue, perhaps
38. Corkscrew pasta
39. Swelled heads
44. Submit via USPS

46 Most achy
48 Indy 500 et al.
49 Pencil-and-paper puzzles
50 Arabia's Gulf of __
51 Be a whiner
52 __ Alto, Calif.
53 Ill temper
54 Work area
55 Air freshener scent
56 Copied
58 Treat, as hide
59 __-mo replay

PEDIPULATION

Across

1 Egg holder
5 "__ Joe's" (classic sign)
10 Enjoy brandy
13 Scopes Trial org.
14 Ham spicer-uppers
16 Play about Capote
17 Flub a grounder
19 Long, long time
20 __ roll (winning)
21 Classic theater name
22 Tedious account
24 Dwarf tree
26 Ring insert
27 Quit smoking, e.g.
34 Gimme on the green
37 "Looks __ everything!"
38 Lines from Shelley
39 Dismounted
40 Tie up tightly
41 *The Lion King* heroine
42 Bucket go-with
43 Pork and mutton
44 Eton boy's father
45 Get a move on
48 "Who __?" (slangy query)
49 Shaggy apes
53 Steamy, as a love affair
56 Talk back to
58 Excellent bond rating
59 Fruity drink
60 Pay for dinner, say
63 *Prelude __ Kiss*
64 Calm as can be
65 NYC's Park and Lex, for two
66 Radius's place
67 Attach, as a patch
68 Badlands sight

Down

1 Big wheel
2 Low-budget prefix
3 *McSorley's Bar* painter John
4 King in 1922 headlines
5 Resounding, as a canyon
6 Michael J.'s *Family Ties* role
7 Shakespeare's Sir __ Belch
8 Gardner of *Mogambo*
9 Spill the beans
10 "Fulton's Folly"
11 Anemic one's need
12 Pint-size
15 Cold shoulder
18 Show the ropes to
23 Afternoon affair
25 Comic bit
28 The "K" in 24K
29 Firm fact
30 *Steppenwolf* author
31 USNA grad: Abbr.
32 Just lying around
33 Salty drop
34 Highland toppers
35 Oodles
36 Unrealistic idea
40 End of a ring count
41 Canaveral org.
43 Recurrent themes
44 Analyze grammatically
46 Something to try to shoot

47 "Land o' __!"
50 Easily conned
51 High winds
52 Zesty dip
53 "Ciao!"
54 Wavy lines, in comics
55 Bucks' mates
56 Ratatouille or ragout
57 "__ extra cost"
61 Miner's find
62 Emeril's catchword

XQ-SE ME!

Across

1 Co-conspirator of Brutus
6 Apple debut of 2010
10 Genesis figure
14 Waikiki greeting
15 Gamblers' mecca
16 Stereo forerunner
17 Entree to the Internet
18 Pisa's river
19 "Render __ Caesar . . ."
20 Some NFL reserves, collectively
22 Newspaper ad meas.
23 Wahine's offering
24 In __ of (rather than)
26 Playing hooky, say
30 Shopaholic's problem
34 Soft, brimless hat
35 Treat with contempt
36 Gen-__
37 Clock division
38 Has an edge
39 Old Chevy model
40 White Monopoly bill
41 Reverse, drive, etc.
42 Vladimir of Russia
43 Reel from a blow
45 Most recent
46 Utah national park
47 Raleigh's title
48 December air
50 Revenue-collecting part of government
56 French clergyman
57 Very expensive
58 Madison's sitcom roomie
60 In two shakes
61 "This round's __"
62 Mystery writer's award
63 Sermon passage
64 Breakfast area
65 The Home Depot selection

Down

1 Video maker, for short
2 More than enough
3 Grape or cream
4 Cereal used in party mix
5 Pooh's creator
6 Basra resident
7 Major silver exporter
8 Pavlova of ballet
9 Makers of margin markings
10 Brought a smile to
11 Man of La Mancha
12 "Nay" sayer
13 Phobos, to Mars
21 Play place
25 Bed-and-breakfast
26 One of Dumas's Musketeers
27 Trailblazing Daniel
28 Concertina, informally
29 Where Lux. is
30 Surgical souvenirs
31 Escape vehicles
32 Neighbor of St. Kitts
33 Scholar's backing
35 Affix a brand on
38 Was supported by
39 Kook
41 Classic muscle car

42 Inlaid floor
44 Like the "k" in "knee"
45 Witness-stand no-no
47 Animated ogre
48 Thomas who lampooned Tweed
49 Plaintive woodwind
51 Alien: Prefix
52 Hunter's garb, for short
53 Bring to ruin
54 Frozen waffle brand
55 Not virtual
59 $200 Monopoly properties: Abbr.

GETTING THE MESSAGE ACROSS

Across

1 Fumigation targets
5 Jay and the Americans' "__ Mia"
9 Animal husbandry major, say
14 Toe the line
15 Many a moon
16 Nostradamus and others
17 One way to get the message across
19 Goody two __ (prig)
20 Do lacework
21 Lhasa __
22 SSE or NNW
23 Political asylum seekers
25 Ceases
29 One way to get the message across
31 __ Girls (Kelly musical)
32 Hamelin casualty
33 Extinct New Zealand bird
34 Who's position
37 Take a whack at
38 Static __
40 Eddie Rickenbacker, for one
41 Icky stuff
42 Honor society letter
43 One way to get the message across
48 Moved en masse
49 Swit, who played "Hot Lips"
52 Mug filler
53 Actress Rowlands
54 Article on a rack
55 __ Gras
58 One way to get the message across
60 Creature from outer space
61 Calliope or Clio
62 __ Mary Robertson "Grandma" Moses
63 Baby bringer
64 Makes a patsy of
65 Motels may ban them

Down

1 Lenya or Lehmann
2 Construction piece
3 Larry Bird or Bob Cousy
4 Cyclone center
5 Quibbling sorts
6 Rival of Sampras and Edberg
7 Bank takeback
8 Grate stuff
9 Home of St. Francis
10 Ripken surpassed him
11 Name on some GM cars, once
12 High dudgeon
13 Snaky curve
18 Room at the top floor
22 Corp. section
24 Guys' partners
25 Heavy cart
26 Teamster's wheels
27 Character on a cel
28 Negotiations hang-up
30 Fielder's flub
34 It's true
35 Cupcake finisher
36 Change cities, in Realtor-speak

37 Onetime tadpole
38 Written for voices
39 "Love your nails," e.g.
41 Tickled-pink feeling
42 Hypocritical sorts
44 Dump truck filler
45 Data path to a satellite
46 "The magic word," to tots
47 Simple hydrocarbon
50 Make impure
51 Burdened Titan
53 Bearded antelopes

55 Bell and Rainey
56 Cockpit abbr.
57 Cruise destination, briefly
58 Dallas sch.
59 Where X marks the spot

AT THE ARCADE

Across

1 Pack animal
6 Job for a plumber
10 "What time ___?"
14 Bagel choice
15 The life of Riley
16 Aborted mission words
17 Super harvest
19 Ladle out clumsily
20 Hook's henchman
21 Dander
22 Gaze stupidly
23 ___ of one's existence
25 *My Name Is ___ Lev*
27 Fast-food worker, informally
31 Eligible for Mensa
33 Corey of *The Lost Boys*
34 Jackie O's man
35 Gain deservedly
36 Pint-sized
38 Swarm member
39 Former Russian space station
40 Part of DNA
41 Bel ___ cheese
42 January 20, 2009 gala
46 Franklin's bill, slangily
47 Flying start?
48 UCLA player
50 Inexact fig.
51 Planning detail
55 Decorate anew
56 Popular carnival ride
59 ___ instant
60 Decorative window shape
61 Prefix meaning "five"
62 Give the heave-ho to
63 Hard to hold onto
64 Part of FAQ

Down

1 Short haircuts
2 "E pluribus ___"
3 Frosty coating
4 Phys. Ed. abrasion
5 Binary digit
6 Order from the top
7 Still pink
8 Prefix with metric
9 Get-up-and-go
10 Marching to the rhythm
11 Energy-harnessing device
12 Frankenstein's helper
13 Hit the bottle
18 World Series prize
22 Leveling wedge
24 Mosaics or topiary
25 From a distance
26 Sexy skirt opening
27 Ferocious swimmers
28 Valerie Harper sitcom
29 Chapters in history
30 Marriage, for one
31 Round before the final
32 Water conduit
36 Bunny's tail
37 Take on
38 Rainy-day footwear
40 1957 Stravinsky ballet
41 It's usually 3, 4, or 5
43 Locals' organizations

44 In conclusion
45 Software test version
48 Telly watcher
49 Former Attorney General Janet
50 Line to Tel Aviv
52 Flamingo color
53 One-named designer
54 Decked out
56 Corn locale
57 "__ had it!"
58 New Deal org.

WHO'S COOKING

Across

1 Robin Cook thriller
5 Taxi's ticker
10 Boston music makers
14 Fall birthstone
15 Beyond's partner
16 Cleveland's lake
17 Cooking "Mr. Television"?
19 Freshwater duck
20 Recites, in a melodic way
21 767 departure
23 Discontinue
24 Spud
25 Cakedom's ___ Lee
28 Hammed it up
32 Pork cut
36 Insignificant
38 VCR button
39 Westernmost Aleutian
40 Seven-time Daytona 500 winner Richard
42 Break under strain
43 Mimics rudely
45 July 4, 1776, e.g.
46 Tight as a drum
47 Gazed upon
49 Croaking voice
51 Clara Barton, notably
53 Love to death
58 Coin-op eatery
61 Goes up against
63 "If We Only Have Love" composer Jacques

64 Cooking Robin Williams portrayal?
66 In the cellar
67 Upper crust
68 Steinbeck migrant
69 "What ___ is new?"
70 Aired again
71 HS seniors' exams

Down

1 *Blondie* or *Beetle Bailey*
2 Have one's say
3 Mediterranean nation
4 Some saxes
5 Mare's hair
6 Recedes
7 Word with a pair of common homophones
8 Role for Madonna or Patti
9 Have a connection
10 Cooking all-time hit leader?
11 Cookie often eaten inside-out
12 Edith, the "little sparrow"
13 Narcissist's love
18 Change for a fin
22 Dole's 1996 running mate
24 Raw, like steak
26 Fuse rating unit
27 Hoops great Willis
29 Melt ingredient
30 Jacob's twin
31 Cabinet div.
32 Souvlaki meat
33 Siouan speaker
34 Bug bite consequence
35 Cooking *Cape Fear* star?

37 Blues singer James
41 "Why, certainly!"
44 Squalid digs
48 Dealer in cloth
50 One of three bears
52 Got a five-finger discount
54 Critters extinct since 1681
55 Honshu port
56 Send, as payment
57 Serpentine shapes
58 Up to the job
59 River to the Caspian Sea

60 Tracy's Trueheart
61 Twice tetra-
62 Fen-___ (controversial diet drug combo)
65 Radial filler

USE YOUR HEAD

Across

1 Doves' homes
6 Jellied dish
11 Dance like Hines
14 St. Theresa's town
15 Hard-to-find character in a book
16 Ex of Frank and Artie
17 Ice cream flavor
19 Hobbyist's purchase
20 Like some glances
21 Trifled
22 Crayola color renamed Peach
24 Evil computer in *2001*
25 Ball game delayer
26 Part of a toy construction set
32 Engraver Albrecht
34 Oodles
35 Place for a ring
36 Athenian H's
37 Does not mention
38 Like a slick road
39 Rode the bench
40 Seeks favor with
41 Atahualpa's people
42 Popular Campbell's variety
46 Castle material?
47 "Yoo-hoo!"
48 Nametag word
50 Relaxing gym amenity
53 Has permission
56 NASA spacewalk
57 Roof over Congress
60 Give the gas
61 Kevin of *Dave*
62 Italian ice flavor
63 Neolithic ___
64 Splinter groups
65 Sentence units

Down

1 Cleveland cagers, briefly
2 Horse course
3 Itsy-bitsy
4 Y sporter
5 Seaside aroma
6 On vacation
7 Kemo ___
8 Said "Not guilty!," e.g.
9 Mount in Crete
10 Casual talk
11 Observe intently
12 Rent-a-car giant
13 Maze solution
18 Lounge around
23 Mae West's *Diamond* ___
24 Emerald and ruby
25 Army units: Abbr.
26 Slovakia's capital
27 Runyon or Wayans
28 Troy, as it's also known
29 "Au contraire!"
30 Mixer for rum
31 Florida islets
32 Family tree listing: Abbr.
33 Bryce Canyon locale
37 Had liabilities
38 Nothing but
41 In a perfect world
43 Iron man Ripken Jr.
44 Bad-mouths

45 "It can't be!"

48 "___ goes!"

49 Happily-after link

50 ___ and Span

51 "___ No Sunshine" (1971 hit)

52 Beehive State Indians

53 NYC cultural institution

54 Love, personified

55 Cravings

58 Oktoberfest order

59 Not-so-hot grade

CRACKERS

Across

1 Martial arts schools
6 Not quite right
11 Bummed out
14 Everything included
15 Take over
16 Publican's pint
17 It may address academic dishonesty
19 Five-spot
20 Railroad support
21 Most past the shelf date
23 License prerequisite, often
25 Poet with a "fanatic's heart"
26 Traveled like Huck Finn
30 Actor Borgnine
33 Like some college walls
34 Kennel club classification
35 Pizza ___
38 Run out of gas
39 Ajax competitor
40 Tiniest bit
41 Vitamin C source
42 Go bad
43 Rice or Gantry
44 Police accompaniment
46 Most washed out
47 Baseball cap part
49 Causes of personality clashes
51 Vatican City, to Rome, e.g.
54 Pseudo-fat
59 Introducer of a color TV in 1954
60 Sagacious elder
62 Gullible one
63 Bounded along
64 Entertainment's "Great Dane"
65 *A Chorus Line* hit
66 With subterfuge
67 San'a's land

Down

1 Part of OED: Abbr.
2 ___ about (roughly)
3 Greenish gem
4 Corrida cheers
5 Like some serving spoons
6 Flu symptoms
7 Bossy's call
8 They can be indicated by a + or −
9 Good name for a Dalmatian
10 Left the flock
11 Scoring a run
12 Elite group
13 Body shop jobs
18 Hightailed it
22 ___ *Miz*
24 Orkin target
26 Meter maid of song
27 Like diehard fans
28 Emergency exit of sorts
29 Pigskin's perch
31 ___ off (recite)
32 Court divider
34 Vulgar sort
36 Salt Lake City athletes
37 Lip-puckering
39 Navy noncom
40 "___ treat!"
42 Sloppy signatures
43 Passed with care

45 Pine-___ (disinfectant brand)
46 Roper survey, e.g.
47 Left-hand page
48 Early Peruvian
50 "Oh, boy!"
52 Fretted fiddle
53 Set eyes on
55 Loafer, for one
56 Contract stipulation
57 Hit the ceiling
58 Mideast's Gulf of ___
61 Sushi fish

SLIPPERY

Across

1. Fuzzbuster's detection
6. Got 100 on
10. Kid's pie stuff
13. Well-tuned
14. Cowgirl Evans
15. It's no light reading
16. It's slippery
18. Hamburg's river
19. Toy train purchase
20. Greek consonants
21. Traveled on a float
23. Egyptian snake
24. Alters to fit
25. Marbles, so to speak
29. Affectionate term of address
30. Tiny bit
31. Something to whistle
32. "Very cool!"
36. Curmudgeonly Rooney
37. Doesn't hoof it
38. One of the Three Bears
39. Feathery scarves
40. "I" problems
41. Perp subduer
42. What "x" may stand for
44. "Om," e.g.
45. Pack rat
48. In place of
49. Line of trousers
50. Opening for a coin
51. Sellout sign
54. Dietary, in ads
55. It's slippery

58. "That's an order!"
59. Cheese in a ball
60. One sans permanent address
61. Novelist Radcliffe
62. Go ballistic
63. Mooring spots

Down

1. Tramp's attire
2. 1/640 square mile
3. The Everly Brothers, e.g.
4. ___ good clip
5. Put in other words
6. Total
7. Toy gun ammo
8. Brother of Peyton Manning
9. Humiliates
10. Very, on a score
11. Reddish-brown shade
12. Scouts do good ones
15. It's slippery
17. Word before "come" and "go"
22. CARE packages, say
24. Trident's three
25. Wild guess
26. The New Yorker cartoonist Peter
27. Zilch
28. It's slippery
29. Word of praise
31. Hank Greenberg or Al Kaline
33. Toward dawn
34. Rich Little, e.g.
35. Scarlett's place
37. Keep in mind
41. Clans' patterns
43. Rhoda's mom, in '70s TV

44 It turns the tide
45 *Broom ___* (comics witch)
46 Kremlin dome shape
47 Patty Duke's son Sean
48 Moth attractor
50 Hosiery mishap
51 Long-haul vehicle
52 Collect, as rewards
53 The "o" in Reo
56 Palindromic Oklahoma town
57 Vote seeker, for short

LIQUID LUNCH

Across

1 Plain, in Spain
6 Free from frost
11 Half-___ (coffee order)
14 Ship from Valdez
15 Grain disease
16 Grand ___ Opry
17 Hearty soup
19 Axis, once
20 Start of a hole
21 Weepy
23 "Not to mention . . ."
25 Lacking lucre
26 Pop-up-producing program
30 Brought to naught
33 Santa Claus feature
34 Building material
35 Intimidate
38 Likely to miss the bus, say
39 *Laugh-In* co-host
40 Spelunker's setting
41 Before, to a poet
42 More desperate
43 Did a fall chore
44 *Pulp Fiction* actor Ving
46 "Lucky" dice rolls
47 In the work cited: Abbr.
49 Word before bag or board
51 Bed-sheet fabric
54 Two-deck game
59 Singer Corinne Bailey ___
60 Soup toss-in
62 Ninny
63 Root or Yale
64 Beat the pants off
65 The Crystals' "___ a Rebel"
66 Subject of Khan
67 Abounds

Down

1 The ___ Boys of *Peter Pan*
2 Wingless parasites
3 Tissue softener
4 Butterfly catchers' needs
5 Site for an apple press
6 They're outstanding
7 Bobble the ball
8 Jim Croce's "___ a Name"
9 ___ d'Azur (French Riviera)
10 Gasoline additive
11 Sweet breakfast treat
12 Orally
13 Touchy-___
18 19th ___ (golf-course pub)
22 Stimpy's cartoon pal
24 Where many American pioneers settled
26 Having the resources
27 Letter opener
28 Salad ingredient
29 Old TV's *You ___ There*
31 Within reach
32 La-Z-Boy spot
34 Needing liniment
36 Bread baker's need
37 Ties the knot with
39 What a tire fits around
40 Cleveland hoopster, briefly
42 Computerized records
43 Simulate, as an old battle

45 Drunk's utterance
46 Lower-left phone button
47 Longtime name in talk TV
48 "__ Porridge Hot"
50 Take place
52 Kinks classic
53 Get to work on Time?
55 Fair-sized plot
56 __-Ball (arcade game)
57 There's no "I" in it
58 Equips for war
61 Detective's cry

BARBERISM

1 Alley Oop's weapon
5 "And away ___!"
9 Starbucks serving
14 Artful dodge
15 Fast-shrinking sea
16 *The Woman* ___ (Wilder movie)
17 Great job, to a barber?
19 Metro entrance
20 Russian space station of old
21 Stinkard
23 Black cat, maybe
24 Brave's babe
26 Ear-related
28 Fireworks-show exclamation
29 Distrust, and then some
33 Lhasa ___
36 Many stools' lacks
37 Homer Simpson exclamation
38 Average job, to a barber?
40 Rat-a-___
41 Go into detail
43 Capital on a fjord
44 *The Guns of* ___ (1961 movie)
45 Opposite of FF, on a VCR
47 Lodge members
48 Tug's rope
52 "Later, alligator!"
54 Go over the wall
57 Beantown ballplayers, for short
58 ___-garde
60 Newsworthy job, to a barber?
62 Present, as a grievance
63 Partner of anon

64 ___ doble (Spanish dance)
65 Mooring site
66 Gets hitched
67 "Rag Mop" brothers

Down

1 Swimmer's problem
2 Donizetti heroine
3 Take forcibly
4 $2 on the nose, e.g.
5 Terre Haute's river
6 Chip away at
7 Was charitable
8 Fashion's Cassini
9 Fleur-de-___
10 Physicist Becquerel
11 Economize, to a barber?
12 Intro to marketing?
13 Shangri-la
18 Peek-___
22 *The Lower Depths* dramatist Maxim
25 Unlikely tic-tac-toe win
27 Ground crew's rollout
29 Cut's partner, in word processing
30 Teen tribulation
31 Type style: Abbr.
32 Concerning
33 ". . . ___ of thieves" (Matt. 21:13)
34 Negri of the silents
35 Conclusion of a job, to a barber?
36 Muffin choice
38 Some home-district appropriations
39 Cropped up
42 Aerialist's forte

43 Critter on a potato chip bag
45 Rodeo entrants
46 Decorative pitcher
48 Mended temporarily
49 Belief of more than a billion
50 Hubbub
51 Former Montreal ball team
52 "Rikki-Tikki-___"
53 [ding-dong] "___ calling"
55 Disgorge
56 Spelunker's milieu
59 Hanoi holiday

61 Apr. workhorse

ETY-MOLOGY

Across

1 AAA handout
4 Israel's Eban
8 Go hungry
14 Munched on
15 Timely benefit
16 Rack-and-___ steering
17 Lee or Grant: Abbr.
18 Touch down on the tarmac
19 Play opener
20 Chew the fat
23 Home to most Turks
24 Health setback
29 Archaeologist's find
31 Big ___, California
33 ___ Island Immigration Museum
34 Stein's *The Autobiography of Alice B. ___*
37 Almanac tidbit
38 Gosh-darned
42 Gather up
43 Butter or margarine
44 Old anesthetic
46 Wee bit
47 Strip mall unit
52 Italian sports car
54 Air force heroes
55 Big cheese
60 Relative of C major
64 Sizable plot
65 Waikiki souvenir
66 Thin layer
67 Crazy bird?
68 USN VIP
69 Part of USPS
70 Runs out
71 Vintage auto

Down

1 Hungarian
2 "Relax, soldier!"
3 Crossword solver's need
4 Up to the task
5 Skiff or scow
6 Scrawny
7 TV's Rooney
8 "The final frontier"
9 Cause to giggle
10 Industrious bug
11 Carnival city
12 ___ *Ryan's Express*
13 Suffix with ethyl
21 Chiang ___-shek
22 In formation
25 ___ Romeo (Italian auto)
26 Prepare for the future
27 Under the weather
28 NY clock setting
30 10 pks., maybe
31 Doubting Thomas
32 Extremist
35 Says "yes" to
36 Entrepreneur-aiding org.
38 ___ noire (bugbear)
39 Bert of *The Wizard of Oz*
40 Imitative sort
41 Mormons, in brief
42 Ring official, briefly
45 1936 Loretta Young title role
48 Scotsman's cap

49 Eye-related
50 Many hairlines do it
51 Igloo dweller
53 From the country
56 Crinkly vegetable
57 Bus. major's study
58 Crushed underfoot
59 Cravings
60 Yodeler's perch
61 Onetime Chinese chairman
62 Real-time AOL exchanges
63 Coll. hoops event

SNOOZING

Across

1 Timber wolves
6 George Michael's old musical group
10 Poke with an elbow
13 Be wild about
14 Astronomical ring
15 Region containing modern-day France
16 Mild, white cheese
18 With 31-Across, *Ripostes* poet
19 Mistake catcher
20 "The Star-Spangled Banner" quartet
22 Start of long-distance dialing
23 Brittany seaport
24 Hoofing it
28 Picnic carrying case
31 See 18-Across
32 French textile city
33 Trucker's place
36 Auto executive Ferrari
37 Spitting mad
38 Owls' prey
39 Baker's no.
40 *Going Rogue* author
41 The younger Obama daughter
42 Ali or Ray
44 Something to vent
45 Taters
47 Fold, spindle or mutilate
48 Put forth as fact
51 Goes up
56 Quartet member

57 Brig structure
59 Swarm
60 *Each Dawn __* (Cagney film)
61 Far from windy
62 Be mistaken
63 Coventry containers
64 Be a busybody

Down

1 Street fixture
2 "P-U!" inducer
3 Old TV clown
4 Pasta served in soups
5 Scungilli, calamari, etc.
6 Info on an invitation
7 Linden of *Barney Miller*
8 Shakespeare title start
9 Zoo barrier
10 Fitness industry giant
11 Vibes
12 Do demolition work
15 Cinema vérité, e.g.
17 Broadway musical with the song "Will I?"
21 Highly adroit
24 Newspaper page for essayists
25 Forbidden thing
26 Radar detector
27 Yoko __
28 Honda with a palindromic name
29 Chemicals giant
30 Like MacDonald of song
32 1953 Leslie Caron film
34 Suffer from a charley horse
35 Noodle
37 Drink dog-style

38 Prefix with content
40 From pillar to ___
41 Some track and field events
43 Regional phrase
44 With the exception of
45 Sudden gush
46 Gondola guide
47 Place mat puzzles
49 Give off, as light
50 Actress Conn
52 Congregation's assent
53 Hawaiian tuber

54 "Happy Motoring" gas brand
55 Interval on a scale
58 California wine, for short

LATER!

Across

1 A whole bunch
5 Egyptian metropolis
10 Part of an orange
14 Halo, e.g.
15 Sharp-smelling
16 First name in scat
17 Castor or Pollux
18 Like an old cigar
19 Radar signal
20 Over the hill
23 Give a razzing to
24 Went carefully
25 Consider again
28 Some assaults from Moe
31 Tel ___
32 Stack-serving eateries
33 ASCAP counterpart
36 Unimpeachable
40 NOW's cause
41 Castle of the ballroom
42 Youngest 600-homer man, familiarly
43 Initial stage
44 Hang on the line
46 Québec's ___ Peninsula
49 Toiling away
50 Sort of
55 Complainer's sound
56 Literary Bret
57 Word from a klutz
60 One-named artist
61 Supped at home
62 ___ Helmer (Ibsen character)
63 Portland, Ore., college
64 Yogi and Boo-Boo
65 TV reception problem

Down

1 The Shangri-___ ("Leader of the Pack" group)
2 No longer fashionable
3 Police sting, e.g.
4 1984 Winter Olympics city
5 Furniture wheel
6 Oscar contender
7 Part of Bush's Axis of Evil
8 Stir up
9 Some works for heroes
10 Serengeti equines
11 Immigrants' island
12 *Ghostbusters* goo
13 Recorded, in a way
21 Baltic, e.g.
22 RC competitor
25 Broccoli ___
26 In perpetuity
27 "Howdy!"
28 Surgical bypass
29 Meet one's Waterloo
30 "Killer" PC program
32 "The More ___ You" (1945 song)
33 Badminton projectile
34 Othello, for one
35 Annual racing classic, for short
37 Forty-___
38 AMA members
39 TV fare for kids
43 Went into business
44 Where St. Paul preached

45 Super Bowl in which Namath starred

46 More plucky

47 Prior to, old-style

48 Feature of many quarters

49 Moving about

51 Whaler played by Peck

52 Kismet

53 Neck of the woods

54 Factory-whistle time

58 Voting yes

59 Tree surgeon's tool

ANTZ

Across

1 Nasal partitions
6 Healthful retreats
10 Barely edible fare
14 About the line of rotation
15 Guitarist's effect
16 Take cover
17 Prefix with fluoride
18 Paris-area airport
19 Heaps
20 Best Picture of 1981
23 Youth hostel, e.g.
24 Annual b-ball shootout
25 Antiaircraft fire
29 Be organized, in a way
31 ___-Mex cuisine
34 Part of USS
35 Princess's accessory
36 Pindaric work
37 Colonial force headed by Washington
41 "___ we there yet?"
42 Regatta crew leaders, for short
43 Sugar source
44 Pricing word
45 Abbr. on a city limit sign
46 *Tristram Shandy* author
48 Crusty treat
49 "___ 'nuff!"
50 "Close to You" vocalist
58 Fateful March date
59 Bridge master Sharif
60 "Understand?"
62 Took a turn

63 Hirschfeld hid her
64 Appetite stimulant
65 Really liking, informally
66 On tenterhooks
67 Forty-___

Down

1 Held a session
2 Company VIP
3 Essential part
4 Gold medalist Lipinski
5 He sacked Rome in 410
6 Faint, like a Sinatra fan
7 Hair division
8 Pointy tools
9 "Toodle-oo"
10 Arrow part
11 1953 Leslie Caron film
12 Gas leak clue
13 Tennis ace Sampras
21 Sign, as a deal
22 Student's worry
25 Tin Pan Alley org.
26 Ironing, for one
27 '40s-'50s slugger Ralph
28 Not out of place
29 Felt nostalgic
30 Back muscles, for short
31 Apple preparer
32 Madison Avenue workers
33 Philippine invasion site
35 It's dangerous to do while driving
38 Make housebound, say, in winter
39 Rocket's payload holder
40 Prez on a fiver
46 ___ *Hate Me* (2004 Spike Lee film)

47 Friendly Islands native
48 Sauce made with basil
49 Waterfall effect
50 Fuzzy fruit
51 Middle East seaport
52 Jonathan Larson musical
53 In the center of
54 Made a jingle
55 Polo of film
56 Rival of Harrow
57 Frosty coating
61 It's found in pits

ACCIDENTALS

Across

1 Totally screw up
6 Stand by for
11 Photo ___ (campaign events)
14 Be nuts about
15 Hobbyist's knife brand
16 Prized possession
17 Oil or coal
20 Looks over
21 "___ whiz!"
22 Toughen, as glass
23 In the past
25 Theology sch.
27 "Money ___ everything"
28 Ballpark snacks
32 Take a siesta
34 Cheroot residue
35 Dumpster deposit
37 ___-Locka, Fla.
40 1983 ZZ Top tune
43 Back end of a bray
44 Chip away at
45 Wasn't upright
46 Oscar Madison, notably
47 It may be exacted
49 Kotter portrayer Kaplan
52 Potpie spheroid
54 Gym iteration
55 Makes amends
57 ___ de plume
59 La ___ Tar Pits
63 Some cargo haulers
66 Notes after mis
67 Industry bigshot
68 Ladder parts
69 Ballpark fig.
70 *Funny Girl* composer Jule
71 ___ Hall University

Down

1 Cause of ruin
2 Anita of jazz
3 Mall bag
4 Person with a cause
5 Part of HMS
6 Wheel shaft
7 Goods for sale
8 Star pitcher
9 "The situation looks bad"
10 Any of TV's Simpsons
11 Cruel dudes
12 Praline nut
13 Silvery fish
18 Bug-eyed
19 Mil or mile
24 Preacher's delivery
26 Mistake remover
28 Greasy spoon fare
29 Workplace-monitoring org.
30 Take out of the freezer
31 Discotheque light
33 Put on hold
36 Deficit color
37 Muscat's land
38 Hunger twinge
39 Start the pot
41 Capacity increaser, in a taxi
42 IBM's chess-playing computer
46 Faxed or FedExed
48 Humorist Bombeck

49 Campaigner's slip-up
50 Rand's ___ *Shrugged*
51 Blowhard's claim
53 Playwright Chekhov
56 Falls back
58 Writer Sarah ___ Jewett
60 It's $50 for Boardwalk
61 Descartes's "therefore"
62 Org.
64 Selling no alcohol
65 E-file org.

AT THE A&P

Across

1 Test for a sitcom
6 Lettuce variety
10 Physics calculation
14 Pipe unclogger
15 Bibliog. shorthand
16 Wine city near Turin
17 Tank's exterior
19 Losing streak
20 Drudge online
21 Toward the summit
23 Peep show attendees
27 Zellweger of *Chicago*
28 Fur for a stole
29 RoboCop, e.g.
32 Party attendee
33 Censor's sound
34 UK heads
37 Decent-sized plot
38 Song of tribute
39 Face-to-face test
40 Luau gift
41 Jazz great Vaughan
42 Fiction genre
43 Alligator cousin
45 Came in second
46 "2, 4, 6, 8 . . .", e.g.
48 Pluto was once among them
49 Pre-Easter
51 Golfer's pocketful
52 Montreal player, once
53 Ventilation duct
59 Sinn ___
60 Bikini tops

61 Lop-___ rabbit
62 Nursery purchase
63 Final Four game
64 Besmirches

Down

1 Palm Treo, e.g.
2 Like "to be": Abbr.
3 On the ___ (fleeing)
4 Lennon's second wife
5 Pick on endlessly
6 Whacks hard
7 "Let's leave ___ that"
8 Club for Casey
9 Chicken cordon ___
10 Potato preparer
11 Seller's hoped-for figure
12 Metro entrance
13 Move like a crab
18 Whittle away
22 Skull in *Hamlet*, e.g.
23 *Love Story* author Erich
24 Hatchet-burying event
25 Don McLean hit
26 Get up
29 Completely off drugs
30 Slangy assent
31 Gridder Roethlisberger
33 Vamp Theda
35 *Hoffa* screenwriter David
36 Inuit transports
38 Cooking spray brand
39 Algerian seaport
41 Webmaster's creation
42 Curriculum components
44 San ___ (Texas city, familiarly)

45 "Nolo contendere," e.g.
46 Kirk Douglas chin feature
47 Spell caster
48 "Gotta have it" soft drink
50 Catches red-handed
51 Bygone London transport
54 Ill temper
55 __ Paulo, Brazil
56 __ Ben Canaan of *Exodus*
57 Salon stuff
58 Mag. staff

HOOFING IT

Across

1 Blood fluids
5 Picket line crosser
9 Generic cow's name
14 Yemeni port
15 Suffix with million
16 Put on cloud nine
17 Covering it all
20 Played a role
21 Siberian herding dog
22 "For ___ a jolly ..."
23 Snaky shape
26 Dirt road feature
27 Desert's dearth
29 Rubbernecker
34 Home to most
37 Spirited steed
39 Top-drawer
40 Gallant sort
43 Bermuda or Vidalia
44 Many millennia
45 Scandinavian capital
46 Ignite
48 Everest is on its border
50 Org. in *Michael Collins*
52 China's Lao-___
53 ___ rule (generally)
56 Like most new drivers
60 Inflatable boats
62 Evoking recollections
65 Gold brick
66 "___ Excited" (Pointer Sisters hit)
67 Mold-ripened cheese
68 Archie's dense pal

Down

1 Skater Hughes
2 Draw forth
3 Gets a flat, maybe
4 *Green Gables* girl
5 ___ Ysidro, Calif.
6 Smoke, slangily
7 They may be fine
8 Original *The View* panelist Joy
9 Sired
10 Oil of ___ (skin care product)
11 All the ___ (immaterial)
12 Poker variety
13 "Is it soup ___?"
18 Inventor's start
19 Grounded birds from down under
24 Tennis great Smith
25 Suit material
27 "Whoopee!"
28 Fiber made from cellulose
30 Star in Perseus
31 Lens holders
32 List ender
33 Slots site
34 Commotions
35 Mentally sound
36 "But ___ art?"
38 Lisa of *The Cosby Show*
41 Immeasurably large
42 Snail mail org.
47 Drescher of *The Nanny*
49 Flight: Prefix
51 Texas A&M athlete

53 In flames
54 Oktoberfest vessel
55 Black-ink entry
56 __ avail (fruitless)
57 Frozen waffle brand
58 Swelled heads
59 Jane Austen classic
61 Some Wall St. traders
62 Morrison of the Doors
63 Attendance fig.
64 Calendar pgs.

WHERE YOU LIVE

Across

1 Handful for a baby-sitter
5 Cashless deal
9 Trod the boards
14 Mechanical repetition
15 Andrews of TV's *Mod Squad*
16 Tend to the five o'clock shadow
17 Caveat emptor phrase
18 Hand lotion ingredient
19 "Boxcars," in dice
20 Place for community events, maybe
23 Preserved, as sounds
24 Rubbed off
28 "Sweet as apple cider" girl
30 Corots, Monets and such
31 Org. with a noted journal
32 Church recesses
36 Polo or Hatcher
38 Bouillabaisse, e.g.
39 Presidential campaign event, perhaps
42 Flunked a polygraph test
43 Woman of distinction
44 A library does it
45 Botanist Gray
46 Piglet's mother
47 ___ Perignon
49 Provides with a blind date
51 Othello's lieutenant
56 It may include urban renewal
60 Tati's comic character
63 Yale Bowl players
64 General Bradley

65 Net mag
66 Iditarod terminus
67 Village Voice bestowal
68 Played like Pan
69 A ruler holds it
70 Hands on deck

Down

1 "Well done!" at the opera
2 Violin bow application
3 Like the Tower of Pisa
4 Electrical pioneer Nikola
5 Produced, as a play
6 Bit of cunning
7 Totally wowed
8 Social equal
9 State confidently
10 Canton's country
11 Price add-on
12 An original sinner
13 ___ Moines
21 Sillily imitative
22 Goosebump-raising
25 Audited a class, say
26 Make fixes to
27 Canines, slangily
29 Attorney-___
30 Partner of dangerous
32 Book with insets
33 Self-assurance
34 Work long and hard
35 Word after living or dead
37 "Slippery" tree
38 Sault ___ Marie
40 Take as one's own
41 Violinist Mischa

46 Appropriate

48 *Juno and the Paycock* playwright Sean

50 Teatime treat

52 Stuck-up sort

53 Lion in *The Lion King*

54 How some popcorn is popped

55 Mean dudes

57 Deep desires

58 Furrow former

59 Succotash bean

60 With it, slangily

61 Israeli arm

62 Bit of insolence

SCORE!

Across

1 Much junk mail
4 Fall into a radar trap
9 Rodeo rope
14 Busy mo. for the USPS
15 Half of octa-
16 "Step right in!"
17 Yucatán "yay!"
18 John of *The Addams Family*
19 P. T. Barnum exhibit
20 #1 hit for Dion
23 Put forth, as effort
24 "Of course"
25 "___ Daba Honeymoon"
28 Like a ghost town
32 Dispatched the dandelions, perhaps
34 New money in 1999
36 34-Across replaced them in Italy
37 Stereotypical "gut" course
42 In need of a massage
43 Like a haunted house
44 Daddy Warbucks's henchman
47 Pounded the stuffing out of
52 Big Band ___
53 Get-up-and-go
55 "Well done!"
56 Focused on an objective
60 North Dakota city
63 Celestial hunter
64 Gerund ending
65 Ward off
66 Gossipmonger
67 Wedding page word
68 "Winner" in a famous 1948 headline
69 Jerks' offerings
70 Horace's ___ *Poetica*

Down

1 Went gaga over
2 Loaded with options
3 Movie snippets
4 Show set in the 23rd century
5 Mexicali moolah
6 Ides of March rebuke
7 Ms. Brockovich
8 Jim-___
9 Stuff destined for the dump
10 Concerning
11 Dug in
12 New York's Russian ___ Room
13 Two-by-two vessel
21 *Men ___ From Mars* . . .
22 Use the Singer
25 Tennis edge
26 Glacier breakaway
27 Sidewalk stand offering
29 Wimpy's payback time: Abbr.
30 Art Deco notable
31 Woodworker's fastener
33 Yalie
35 Flu fighters
37 Atomic physicist Niels
38 Square footage
39 Poseidon's realm
40 Basketball center?
41 Showy flowers
42 Sault ___ Marie, Mich.
45 Lacking consistency

46 Stew spheroid

48 Decorative vase

49 The green stuff on copper

50 More uniform

51 Evades, as questions

54 Devious maneuvers

56 "It's My Party" singer Lesley

57 Cookie since 1912

58 Brie covering

59 Greek I

60 "What, me worry?" mag

61 "__ had it up to here!"

62 Partner of "improved"

FOR TY COBB

Across

1 Run easily
5 Santa ___, California
10 Place for cookies
13 Sailed through
14 Loud ruckus
15 Vow words
16 Often-spicy fare
18 Yale student
19 Metric land measure
20 *Unsafe at Any Speed* author
22 Bard's before
23 *House of Incest* novelist
24 Like venison's flavor
25 Robber's take
26 Most hectic
29 Avant-garde composer Erik
32 Rip-roaring time
33 One of the Jackson 5
34 Tabriz's land
35 Movie double's task
37 ___ instant
38 Golf positions
39 Take a powder
40 "Fever" singer Lee
41 Completely fooled
43 In this way
45 Nursery intruder
46 Time on end
47 Flow back
50 Dirt clumps
52 New Testament letter
54 She-lobster
55 Martial art form

Down

59 Ultimate point
60 Whirling currents
61 *Garfield's* pal
62 Seek the affection of
63 *The Cloister and the Hearth* author
64 Prell competitor

1 Rotating shop tool
2 Earthy pigment
3 What "shalom" means
4 Cut and paste
5 Fee payer
6 ___ Palmas
7 Ethel Waters's "___ Blue?"
8 Reagan who wrote *My Father at 100*
9 Gladiatorial sites
10 Hippie's artistic activity
11 On one's duff
12 Bet that's not rouge
14 Antiques shop item
17 Tippy craft
21 Friendships
24 Burst of wind
25 Oil from flax
26 Roll-on brand
27 Without a date
28 Broadway award
29 River buildup
30 Operatic showstopper
31 South Korea's national sport
32 Chicle product
35 Hit the dirt
36 Give a licking to

40 __ Wars (Rome-Carthage conflicts)

42 Home-building bird

43 [giggle]

44 Pueblo Indians

47 Chopin work

48 *The __ Witch Project*

49 "John Brown's Body" poet

50 Get one's teeth into

51 Lantern-jawed monologist

53 Craftsman's workplace

56 Soft drink

57 Mrs. McKinley

58 Spanish hero El __

GIVE 'EM A HAND

Across

1 Deere products
6 Captain's hook
10 Top-quality
14 Tax filer's dread
15 Soothing gel ingredient
16 Nose-in-the-air type
17 O. Henry literary device
18 Digit that may "stick out"
20 Skid Row bum
22 Romantic gift
23 Tax-deferring instrument: Abbr.
24 Like Aesop's grapes
26 Street tough's weapon
32 Bomb defuser, maybe
33 Tony-winning Tyne
34 iPhone download
37 Stratford-___-Avon
38 Libya's Gulf of ___
40 The "A" of San Francisco's BART
41 Pro ___ (for now)
42 Goalie's success
43 Well-behaved child
44 Klutz
48 Tot's "piggies"
49 Get busy
50 Song of praise
53 Act the sponge
58 Something to grease, so to speak
61 "Death Be Not Proud" poet
62 Nick's partner in crime-solving
63 "The More ___ You"
64 Source of strength
65 Worked like Rumpelstiltskin
66 Blacken on the barbecue
67 Postal card cost, once

Down

1 Bill stamp
2 Enticement on a line
3 Gorgonzola feature
4 Chablis or Chianti
5 Salon worker
6 Mower owner's need
7 Zillions
8 In place of
9 Finder's reward
10 On liberty, maybe
11 Albatross, symbolically
12 Norton Sound port
13 Falls back
19 "I kid you not!"
21 Really bug
24 Lingering emotional injury
25 Tex. neighbor
26 Very dry, as wine
27 Macramé medium
28 Focus of the Manhattan Project, briefly
29 III, to Jr.
30 Moo juice dispenser
31 Looie's underling
35 Jury member, in theory
36 Good buds
38 Fill beyond full
39 Currier's partner
40 *The Ice Storm* director Lee
42 Hardhearted
43 Paid to play
45 Provo resident

46 Dell dweller of song
47 Rocks in a bar
50 Wrestling finales
51 Straddling
52 Hosiery shade
53 Collar victim
54 Like a wolf, perhaps
55 Getting ___ years
56 Soon, to bards
57 Don't allow
59 E-mail attachment, for short
60 Timber wood

AGAINST THE GRAIN

Across

1 Peter of *Columbo*
5 Casino game with numbered balls
9 1965 King arrest site
14 Cartoon light bulb
15 Lander at Ben-Gurion
16 Turn away from
17 Title for a Harris rabbit
18 Poor dog's share
19 Brainy group
20 Worth a D, grainwise?
23 Cockpit announcement, for short
24 Actress ___ Dawn Chong
25 Took a sample of
28 Like bell-bottoms, nowadays
30 "Beat it!"
33 Psyche element
34 Sidewalk-stand quaff
36 Penalty caller, for short
37 Jason's vessel
38 Witty sort, grainwise?
43 Individually
44 Chicle product
45 Harden
46 Reduce-speed caution
47 Indus or Irrawaddy
49 One who doesn't put down roots
53 Nonstick surface
55 Seemingly forever
57 Lyrical lines
58 Achievement of fame, grainwise?
62 Golf course hazard
64 *The Nazarene* novelist Sholem
65 Prefix with plane, once
66 Words of wisdom
67 Fingerprints, e.g.
68 Hidden valley
69 Pieman, e.g.
70 Weed whacker
71 Get snippy with

Down

1 Truth stretcher
2 Classified cost
3 Eye salaciously
4 Bush adviser Rove
5 Nairobi's land
6 Weds on the sly
7 *Peter Pan* pooch
8 Bullring cries
9 "Do you like green eggs and ham?" speaker
10 Makes smooth
11 Extended
12 Prefix with fire or fortune
13 Toothpaste box inits.
21 Chip away at
22 Work forces
26 Frozen waffle brand
27 *Let's Make a Deal* choice
29 Too hasty
31 ___ de menthe
32 Vintage 37-Down
35 Web search tool
37 *Car Talk* subject
38 Take it easy
39 The Clintons' alma mater
40 Environmental extremist
41 Soccer mom's car, perhaps
42 Redhead's dye

47 Porch seat
48 Heroic deed
50 Early Ford
51 Is gaga over
52 Exorcism targets
54 Lord of the manor
56 Catchall category
59 RPM indicator
60 City on a fjord
61 Tatterdemalion's attire
62 Semi part
63 Vitamin label amt.

BOXING DAY

Across

1 Baseball's "Say Hey Kid"
5 Affectionate nickname
10 *Pygmalion* playwright
14 "__ Plenty o' Nuttin'"
15 Arctic, for one
16 Mexican snack
17 Sweet quaff
19 Sailors' saint
20 Guy, informally
21 Cause of hay fever
23 Jennifer Lopez title role
25 Frosted Flakes–pitching tiger
26 Butcher shop purchase
32 Back talk
36 Barbie's beau
37 Jack, master of the "double take"
38 Nabisco treats since 1912
40 Like Duroc hogs
42 Place for knickknacks
43 Cinema name
44 Brillo rival
46 Plays for a sap
47 Scrappy
51 Algerian port
52 Degraded
57 Word before clear or ball
61 Houston ballplayer
62 Smee's boss
63 Visa competitor
67 Sommer of film
68 Put a stop to
69 Bug-eyed
70 Move smoothly
71 April forecasts
72 One-named soccer legend

Down

1 Offends
2 Be in accord
3 "__ pay for this!"
4 Metro entrance
5 Keystone comic
6 Post-OR place
7 Scout unit
8 Wrinkle-resistant fabric
9 In stock
10 Stereotypical hobo fare
11 Patriot Nathan
12 High point
13 Whittler's material
18 Zingy taste
22 Greek sandwiches
24 Two-by-two vessel
25 Selects, on the radio
27 Bard's above
28 Honolulu's island
29 Luau strings
30 Khartoum's river
31 Dict. offerings
32 Screwup
33 Pakistani language
34 Have a hunch
35 April 1 victim
39 Uppity sort
41 Borzoi, for one
45 __ Na Na
48 Constitution drafter
49 Singer Lola
50 Skier's lift

53 Songwriters' org.
54 Thespian's milieu
55 Swashbuckling Flynn
56 Jump out of the way of
57 Julia Child, for one
58 Wiener holder
59 Ms. Ono
60 Slant unfairly
64 *Star Wars* letters
65 Kayo count
66 Mag. execs

CALLING EBENEZER SCROOGE

Across

1 Way onto an auto ferry
5 100-meter race, e.g.
9 A metronome marks it
14 Like the Sabin vaccine
15 Off-the-wall answer?
16 Terminus of many rivers
17 ___ podrida
18 Weaver's need
19 Friars Club fete
20 1973 De Niro movie
23 "This ___ shall pass"
24 Chang's twin
25 Give two thumbs down to
26 Scam online
28 *Peg Woffington* author
30 Evil Disney lion
32 Sing the praises of
35 SASE, for one
37 "Many moons ___"
38 Farm team coupler
39 Karl Wallenda, notably
44 Farming prefix
45 Game with Skip cards
46 Dallas sch.
47 Transvaal trekker
48 Dollywood's state: Abbr.
50 Speck in the sea
54 Put into law
56 Dim bulb
58 ___ G (Baron Cohen character)
59 Queen, in chess

61 What an amusement park ride might provide
64 Daisy lookalike
66 "Swoosh" company
67 Rework, as copy
68 Pointer's word
69 Go sprawling
70 Il ___ (Mussolini)
71 Gets wind of
72 Cackleberry producers
73 Essayist's page

Down

1 Boardinghouse resident
2 Dahl in *Jamaica Run*
3 Sweet Spanish wine
4 Marshall ___
5 Triangular letter
6 Squirrel's stash
7 Site of Maxwell Smart's phone
8 Website's starting point
9 Some sculpted forms
10 Prefix with friendly
11 Slaughterhouse hanger
12 El ___, Tex.
13 Wise to the tricks of
21 Shelled out
22 Warms up in the bull pen
27 Phonograph needle
29 Disarm, as a bull
31 Plumped fowl
33 Islands strings, for short
34 Three times, to a druggist
36 Post-surgery support, for some
39 Treater's pickup
40 "My turn!"

41 Chinese potable
42 Tither's contribution
43 Buggy-driving sect
49 Place setting item
51 In traction, maybe
52 __ Islands (Tuvalu, formerly)
53 On a slant
55 Plot measurements
57 AA's 12
59 "Do the __!"
60 Stadium named for a tennis great

62 Suffix with million
63 Spiff up the décor of
65 Drop an easy one

TOYING AROUND

Across

1 Clear wrap
6 Bowling pin wood
11 Some MDs
14 Tuned in
15 Novelist Le Sage
16 Homesick, perhaps
17 Opening need, at least
19 Lobster __ Diavolo
20 1/1 song ender
21 __ Gatos, California
22 Old-time wrestling great Kowalski
24 __-Pei (wrinkly dog)
26 Expert at stall tactics
27 Outer layer of gray matter
30 Venus's tennis-playing sister
31 Bassoons' little brothers
32 Stuffed to the gills
33 Josh around with
36 Pants-on-fire guy
37 Gave a silent greeting
38 Give as a reference
39 Choreographer Shawn
40 Old AMC model
41 Recurring theme
42 Bouillon cubes, after hydration
44 Maltreat
45 Fires 21 guns, say
47 Snapshot, slangily
48 Sandy or Roberto of baseball
49 "No seating," briefly
50 __ Club (retail chain)
54 Snapshot, for short
55 Hit the ceiling
58 "Ew-w-w! Gross!"
59 Mastroianni costar
60 Argentine plain
61 __ Plaines, Illinois
62 Everglades wader
63 Gin flavorers

Down

1 Easily duped sorts
2 Farthest from the hole
3 Game delayer
4 Cop, on occasion
5 Opposite of paleo-
6 Captain's superior
7 "Ah, me!"
8 __-Man (early video game)
9 __ up (pie-eyed, in dialect)
10 Stored, as fodder
11 "Get lost!"
12 Reduce to mush
13 Belle or Bart
18 Linseed oil source
23 Office PC linkup
25 Cock and bull
26 Dissuade
27 Revolver inventor
28 Big Apple stage award
29 Highway patrol setups
30 Goalie's stat
32 Investment firm Goldman __
34 Reply to "That so?"
35 Nimble-fingered
37 Totally saturate
38 Like some olives
40 Fit for drinking
41 Bon __ (clever remark)

43 Grog ingredient
44 Cow's hurdle, in rhyme
45 Full of flavor
46 Carroll heroine
47 Weather map item
49 __ 'Pea
51 Spherical opening?
52 Wear a long face
53 Sauna spots
56 Hockey immortal Bobby
57 Mini-albums, for short

PAY UP!

Across

1 Film snippets
6 "__ lively!"
10 Old ruler of Iran
14 City where Galileo taught
15 Ankle-length, maybe
16 __ stick (springy toy)
17 Bedeck with tinsel, say
18 Skater's jump
19 Cambodia neighbor
20 It's measured in coulombs
23 All the rage
24 Pillbox, e.g.
25 1974 grant to Nixon
29 Serb or Croat
31 Frequently, to bards
34 Keystone State port
35 Veep after Hubert
36 Story of one's life
37 Kind of attack, in chess
41 "Go ahead, shoot!"
42 3-Down worshiper
43 1975 Wimbledon champ
44 Guitar pioneer Paul
45 Breakfast-in-bed item
46 Vent one's __
48 Uris's *QB* __
49 Xbox 360 competitor
50 Reese Witherspoon's role in *Walk the Line*
58 Before long, to bards
59 Time for a bite
60 Work, as dough
62 Opera superstar
63 Boorish sort
64 Cry of surrender
65 Bibliographical abbr.
66 __ May Clampett
67 "For __ sake!"

Down

1 Tax preparer, for short
2 Put on, as cargo
3 Graven image
4 24-karat
5 __ Panza
6 Like a brainiac
7 It's hailed by city dwellers
8 Co. bigwig
9 Sardine, by another name
10 Pie-in-the-face sound
11 Frosty coating
12 Bug-eyed
13 Gardener's need
21 Cargo amount
22 Great devastation
25 Piano part
26 Come to mind
27 Stands to lose
28 Busy mo. for the USPS
29 Deodorant type
30 Property claim
31 Needing a seatbelt extender, say
32 Library storage medium, for short
33 Coin at an arcade
35 Dreamcast game maker
38 Fiber-__ cable
39 Special building permit
40 Falstaff's princely pal
46 Knight's title

47 Open-backed truck
48 Easily bribed
49 *Peter Pan* heroine
50 Green gemstone
51 The "U" in BTU
52 Variable star
53 Kayaker's maneuver
54 Unwitting stooge
55 *Green Gables* girl
56 Split-off group
57 In fine fettle
61 Synthetic estrogen

"WELL, ISLE BE!"

Across

1. Persian Gulf port
6. Rocketry's Wernher von __
11. __ Tomé (island near the Equator)
14. Drama awards since 1956
15. Copy, briefly
16. Auditor, for short
17. Toast-and-cheese dish
19. Granola bit
20. Like many serving spoons
21. Abercrombie partner
23. Bronchitis symptom
25. Boston and Charleston
26. Inflationary path
30. Raised, as an anchor
32. "Hero" singer Mariah
33. Derisive look
34. Peach part
37. *Ars Amatoria* poet
38. Was partial
39. Producer De Laurentiis
40. Jazz's Montgomery
41. Judean king
42. '40s–'50s slugger Ralph
43. Pistol, slangily
45. Carefree
46. Metes out
48. Piedmont province
50. Do watercolors
51. Where Schwarzenegger was born
56. Barbarous one
57. Bassoon kin
61. Ill temper
62. Chattered incessantly
63. Strikeout king Ryan
64. Dapper fellow?
65. Movie double's job
66. Gladiator's workplace

Down

1. Fiddle sticks?
2. Genesis victim
3. Cylindrical building
4. Seventh day activity
5. Place for butts
6. Thin nails
7. Yank's foe
8. Police alert, for short
9. Spoon-bending Geller
10. Showing favoritism
11. Christmas tree choice
12. Zipping along
13. Solemn promises
18. Flesh-and-blood
22. Gerund suffix
24. Infamous box-opener
25. Scout's doing
26. Garbage hauler
27. Work on the street
28. Material for tablecloths
29. Unwelcome ink color
31. Work in the garden
33. Your Majesty
35. "Mockingbird" singer Foxx
36. British conservative
38. Solidifies
39. Fall flat
41. Fedora makers
42. Hare __

44 Long, long time
45 A/C measures
46 Rose garden pest
47 First Lady before Michelle
49 Francis or Patrick, e.g.
52 Norse hammer wielder
53 Thing to play
54 1979 hostage site
55 Pulitzer winner Quindlen
58 DC baseballer, for short
59 Animal seen on safaris
60 Ban-___ (shirt material)

NOT SO HOT

Across

1 Titled ladies
6 Beach scavengers
11 Airline to Stockholm
14 City in central Florida
15 Shake an Etch A Sketch, e.g.
16 Thermos topper
17 Hanging in the hammock
19 Wolfed down
20 Ethiopia's Haile __
21 Eagle's gripper
23 Go __ (flip out)
24 Most saintly
26 Common Seattle forecast
30 "Fabulous!"
31 "Can you dig it?" response
33 Heavy reading
34 Attorneys' org.
37 Completely unperturbed
40 Uncanny ability, for short
41 Aquarium structures
42 Moby-Dick ship co-owner
43 Naval slammers
44 Keyboard slip
45 "Yay!"
48 Suffix with riot or ruin
51 End of a fable
52 "You're on!"
57 "What a good boy __"
58 Lacking compassion
61 Skirt edge
62 Fred's dancing partner
63 With __ breath
64 Assent at sea
65 "Message received"
66 Book-lined room

Down

1 Rx writers
2 Reason to see a dentist
3 Letters and such
4 __ Enchanted (2004 comedy)
5 Tortilla chip dip
6 One to rub out?
7 Arm-twist
8 Thai's neighbor
9 Shaq's alma mater: Abbr.
10 Squares away a debt
11 Union minimum wage
12 Things in jams
13 Plumb tuckered out
18 AOL, for one
22 Inner tube filler
24 Rich part of soil
25 Oil letters
26 Orzo is shaped like it
27 Radio role for Freeman Gosden
28 Flapjack-selling chain
29 Nada
30 Knee-highs, e.g.
32 Vehicle with a "cherry top"
33 Sharp-tasting
34 With adroitness
35 Sound heard during gridlock
36 Cornstarch brand
38 Put into words
39 Tom Seaver was one
43 Feathered scarf
45 Missouri River city
46 Warm and comfy

47 Tough laundry problem
48 Significant one?
49 Be hooked on
50 "Born from jets" 12-Down
52 Killing time
53 "Dang!"
54 Westernmost of the Aleutians
55 ___ off (irate)
56 Whirling current
59 René Auberjonois's *Star Trek* role
60 Regatta unit

HOOT AND HOLLER

Across

1 Cookiedom's Famous ___
5 Mariner's peril
9 Timetable: Abbr.
14 Place to drop anchor
15 Catchall abbr.
16 Take to the stump
17 Public uproar
19 Hot Lips Houlihan, for one
20 Cash in Kyoto
21 Circusgoers' sounds
22 Betrayer
23 Garment with a supporting role
24 In a cluster
28 Raffle prize with bottles
31 Chain unit
33 Lash of oaters
34 The D'backs, on scoreboards
35 Java dispensers
36 Dynamic Duo's garb
37 Take a fall
38 "Society's Child" singer Janis ___
39 More like a wallflower
40 Hangs on a line
41 Isley Brothers hit covered by the Beatles
44 Take higher
45 More than impress
46 Windy City trains
47 Peace advocate
49 Joplin genre
52 Monthly bill, for many
55 Confederate battle cry
57 *Waiting for Lefty* playwright Clifford
58 Clickable image
59 Prefix with bellum
60 Bit of dogma
61 Porter's *Anything* ___
62 One of Mars's two

Down

1 "___ Breaky Heart"
2 Pouty look
3 The witch's demise, in *Hansel and Gretel*
4 Poseidon's realm
5 State tree of New Jersey
6 Inscribe permanently
7 Large features of African elephants
8 Elapse quickly
9 Sound quality
10 Post-surgery support
11 Raucous laugh syllable
12 UFO crew
13 Ruby of film
18 Bergen-born, say
22 ___ T. Firefly (Groucho role)
23 Captain's insignia
24 Destructive insects
25 ___ from the horse's mouth
26 Like *Goosebumps* stories
27 Faucet problems
28 Clyde's partner in crime
29 May who directed *Ishtar*
30 Not live
31 Furniture ensemble
32 Shrimper's net

36 Shoots the bull
37 In alignment
39 Most trite
40 Cylindrical fastener
42 Slim and graceful
43 Safe harbors
47 Like Erté's style
48 Slender woodwind
49 City near Lake Tahoe
50 Deep-voiced, for a woman
51 Country crooner Campbell
52 Motel extra

53 Suffix with many fruit names
54 Jerry's partner in ice cream
55 Offshore apparatus
56 Candied vegetable

DUFFERFEST

Across

1 Crosby's longtime record label
6 *Mod Squad* member
10 Henry Higgins's creator
14 Has a yen
15 Treat with a creamy middle
16 Dispense, as milk
17 Beef cut
19 Bicycled, say
20 Backpacker's stops
21 Sharp reprimands
23 Refusing to listen
25 Quitter's cry
26 Canine tooth
30 Way past ripe
33 Sweater synthetic
34 Smooth link, musically
35 Cry accompanying a head slap
38 "What time ___?"
39 *Hägar the Horrible's* dog
40 Eshkol of Israel
41 Fond du ___
42 Take by force
43 Theater lobby
44 Heir's concern
46 Like Nixon's "majority"
47 Pop singer Apple
49 Painful place to be kicked
51 To begin with
54 Jackie's "O"
59 Dogpatch cartoonist
60 Letterman show feature
62 *Night* author Wiesel
63 The munchies, e.g.

64 ___ du jour
65 Like batik fabrics
66 "Sounds fair"
67 English Derby town

Down

1 100-meter, e.g.
2 Canyon comeback
3 Cartoonist Addams
4 Indian-head coin until 1909
5 Invited for coffee, say
6 "___ luck!"
7 High dudgeon
8 Getting warm, in a way
9 Rum's partner
10 Coniferous tree
11 Clothing fastener style
12 Poet W.H. ___
13 Extract by force
18 Winter toy
22 Take the bait
24 Stops in one's tracks
26 Slinky's shape
27 Celestial bear
28 Common dessert order
29 Chili holder
31 Big brute
32 Egyptian boy-king, for short
34 Hissy fit
36 Place to wear a mitt
37 Dixieland jazzman Al
39 Mermaid's realm
40 Online guffaw
42 Badge shape
43 Pay for, as a project
45 Took potshots

46 Trig ratio
47 Batted against
48 Geographical "boot"
50 Concierge's place
52 Five-card game
53 Hotfooted it
55 Prelude to a duel
56 Knights' titles
57 Analogy words
58 Rose part
61 Links org.

DE-COMPOSING

Across

1 Celt or Highlander
5 In pieces
10 In fine fettle
14 Raines of film
15 More certain
16 Reunion attendee, for short
17 Composer's fee?
19 Cartoon bear
20 Took the helm
21 First-born
23 At the same time
26 Dog in an Inge play
30 Seeming eternity
31 Sight-related
35 Reef builders
37 Pasture call
39 Director Wertmüller
40 Ear-related
41 Frigidaire rival
43 Border on
44 PC support pro
45 Seal group
46 "Let's be honest"
48 Thick hunks
50 Cheeseheads' state: Abbr.
52 Not worth the bother
53 Order before setting sail
56 Indian cotton fabric
59 Lindbergh or Post
64 Squared away
65 Composer's watering holes?
68 Silent performer
69 Glowing coal
70 Stat for a mt.
71 Dumpster emanation
72 Gazillions
73 Vacationer's fill-in

Down

1 Salon supplies
2 Reached the ground
3 Choice word
4 Hang in the hammock
5 Forest quaker
6 Home of the Boilermakers
7 The D'backs, on scoreboards
8 ___ room (place to play)
9 Grove components
10 Composer's house?
11 Skin lotion ingredient
12 Lummoxes
13 Throw off
18 Court event
22 John, abroad
24 Given to wandering
25 Informed about
26 Ayr natives
27 Monopoly buy
28 *Fear of Flying* author Jong
29 Composer's stove part?
32 Land that's home to yaks
33 Native of Alaska
34 Slyly spiteful
36 Maple output
38 Lummox
42 Like a trim lawn
47 Filing month, for many
49 Mudbath locale
51 Under a parasol, e.g.

54 Cigar residue
55 Once-___ (quick checks)
56 Office note
57 Gung-ho
58 Audition CD
60 Aid in crime
61 Chaucer offering
62 Utah city
63 Invitation letters
66 Rambler mfr.
67 Celtics' org.

ACID CONTAINERS

Across

1 Boat skippers, familiarly
6 Dutch cheeses
11 Pharmaceutical-approving org.
14 Stan's pal
15 Salk's conquest
16 Dory propeller
17 Where hygiene is taught
19 Dad's bro
20 Beat at the rifle range
21 Like a crow's call
23 Amtrak map pts.
24 NFL tiebreakers
25 Danced recklessly
26 Choose
28 Lose one's cool
29 Failed to
32 Porter's regretful Miss
34 Talk like a tosspot
37 Actress Meyers
38 Military diplomat
41 Merkel of moviedom
42 Reply to a schoolmarm
44 "___ boy!"
45 Treble clef lines
47 *Little Iodine* cartoonist Jimmy
49 Actress Arthur
50 Type of pear
52 "___ you nuts?"
54 Caron title role
58 Buoyed up
59 Makes privy to
61 Slo-___ (type of fuse)
62 Certain church officer
64 Back muscle, for short
65 Martini garnish
66 ___ Haute, Ind.
67 Addis Ababa's land: Abbr.
68 Basic principle
69 Marked a ballot

Down

1 Pacific salmon
2 Eskimo's cousin
3 "Oro y ___" (Montana motto)
4 "Everybody's Talking" singer Harry
5 Son of Adam
6 ___ Theme Park (Disney World attraction)
7 Knuckleheads
8 In the style of
9 Hodgepodge
10 "Already?"
11 Department of Agriculture–sponsored youth group
12 Saint-Saëns's "___ Macabre"
13 Rainbow-shaped
18 Owl's call
22 Tag sale caveat
27 School org.
28 Typewriter type
29 Calendar page
30 Wrath
31 Kitchen worker's rag
32 Director Preminger
33 Tit for ___
35 Sturm ___ Drang
36 UK airmen
39 Whopper of a story

40 Shoebox letters

43 Big shark

46 Classic Italian astronomer

48 "I'm a Little ___"

49 *Little Women* woman

50 Luxurious fur

51 D sharp equivalent

52 Still kicking

53 Bowling alley button

55 Like helium or neon

56 *Casablanca* actor Peter

57 Signed, as a contract

60 '70s–'80s Canadian comedy show

63 ___ Tin Tin

THE ROYALS

Across

1 Cremona violin-maker
6 Turn, as pancakes
10 Nordic runners
14 Copier company
15 440 or 10K
16 Salon job
17 Ebbets Field great
19 ___ Eleanor Roosevelt
20 Held tightly
21 Scorpion's weapon
23 Rotisserie League stats
25 Something to settle
26 Agcy. with Goodwill Ambassadors
30 Following close behind
33 Went airborne, briefly
34 One getting one-on-one help
35 Beer buyers' needs, for short
38 ___ a one
39 Fleshy-snouted beast
40 Lionel layout, perhaps
41 Pull an ___-nighter
42 Mercury and Saturn, e.g.
43 This puzzle has one
44 Pollster's projection
46 Tied to the pier
47 Old-time rejoinder to "Shall!"
49 Totally gone
51 Silverware stains
54 Mine vehicles
59 ___ of invincibility
60 "One O'Clock Jump" composer
62 Part of an agenda
63 To boot
64 Reason to take bicarb
65 Artist Magritte
66 Boo-Boo of cartoons
67 *The Maids* playwright Jean

Down

1 Flexible, electrically
2 Rough up
3 "My Way" lyricist Paul
4 Tot's "piggies"
5 Do a spot check on
6 Mexican artist Kahlo
7 Young kiltie
8 Nails down, as a victory
9 Smart-alecky
10 Golfer's concern
11 Mentor of Louis Armstrong
12 Word before ear or tube
13 "Can you believe this?" look
18 *Quo Vadis* emperor
22 Psychiatrist's response
24 Dazed states
26 Bone near the radius
27 *Hud* Oscar-winner Patricia
28 Chief Justice, 1953–69
29 Bug planter
31 Mayberry toper
32 Ship's pronoun
34 ___ Modern (London gallery)
36 Title for Myra Hess
37 Downhill runner
39 Vintner's vessel
40 Cry of surprise
42 Voting no
43 Fund-drive premium
45 ___ only (titularly)

46 *Beetle Bailey* creator Walker
47 Flight segment
48 ___ cuisine
50 Military medal, e.g.
52 Natural bandage
53 Gopher's creation
55 Wrestling extravaganza enclosure
56 Z ___ "zebra"
57 Baptism or bris
58 Ticket datum
61 *Dos Passos* trilogy

CATCH!

Across

1 "That's a lie!"
6 "__ is an island . . ."
11 FB's scores
14 Burger topper
15 "I give!"
16 __ polloi
17 Talk trash
19 Monopoly foursome: Abbr.
20 Left Bank river
21 Gardener's sackful
23 __-eyed (naive)
25 Passage between buildings
26 Confections on sticks
29 Goldie of *Laugh-In*
31 Color TV pioneer
32 Prefix with form or cycle
33 He was thrice the champ
34 Inedible oranges
37 "Tsk!"
39 Pave over
41 Bid farewell, in a way
42 For no profit
44 IRS form expert
45 Soccer star Hamm
46 "Say what?"
47 Put an edge on
48 Clobber with snowballs
49 Mother-of-pearl source
52 __ Valley, Calif.
54 Go wild
56 Cartoon mirages
59 Bio bit
60 Sleep fitfully

63 Max. opposite
64 Have __ for news
65 Vital vessel
66 Windsor's prov.
67 Barbershop quartet member
68 __-Kettering Institute

Down

1 Japanese theatrical style
2 Heavy load
3 Poop out
4 Cubes, spheres, and the like
5 Cat-__-tails
6 Greek N's
7 "Movin' __" (*The Jeffersons* theme)
8 "American Pie" singer Don
9 Hitching post?
10 Birds, at times
11 Lose on purpose
12 Backs, anatomically
13 Wuss
18 Sitcom set at the Stratford Inn
22 Colorful parrot
24 Where the Clintons met
26 Onetime larva
27 Words after "sit" or "step"
28 Set up camp
30 Coven member
34 Stemwinder
35 Ungodliness
36 Membership on Wall Street
38 "__ pay for this!"
40 Bronx Zoo houseful
43 Attempt to hit
47 Cooking oil name

48 .45-caliber, e.g.
49 Last stand of 1836
50 Sadat's co-Nobelist
51 Nary a soul
53 ___ a wet hen
55 Gas brand in Canada
57 Cash on the Continent
58 Sp. miss
61 ___ Lingus
62 One of the Bobbseys

THE MEDIA

Across

1 Betty of cartoons
5 Galvanometers measure them
9 Oncologist's treatment, for short
14 Kon-Tiki Museum city
15 Links cry
16 Make fun of
17 Broadcaster to Iron Curtain nations
20 1952 and '56 campaign name
21 Donkey's cry
22 What tenants sign
23 "Dunno"
25 "O.K., why not?"
26 "You there!"
27 Statehouse VIP
28 Tool repository
32 Like some lingerie
35 Jobs for mechanics
37 Hosp. area
38 Start of a series, hopefully
41 Historical period
42 "Holy Toledo!"
43 O. Henry technique
44 ___ sci (coll. major)
46 Beehive State tribe
47 School org.
48 "Jabberwocky" starter
50 Fez features
54 Get hold of
57 Sub ___ (in secret)
58 Compete
59 It'll stop the presses

62 Carroll's tea party visitor
63 ___ facto
64 Object of gossip
65 Grandmothers, affectionately
66 Hockey heavy
67 Cub Scout groups

Down

1 ___ acid (mild antiseptic)
2 City near Kobe
3 Of a bygone era
4 Hawaiian dish
5 Free-for-all
6 Voracious eel
7 The hunted
8 "Now ___ here!"
9 Salad oil holder
10 Bother persistently
11 Ids' counterparts
12 Wear a long face
13 Snake eyes
18 Keep an eye on
19 A craps natural
24 Quaker pronoun
25 "La Bamba" band Los ___
27 Tourist's aid
29 Hawaiian seaport
30 Business subj.
31 Scout's pledge word
32 Process part
33 Dragon slayer, e.g.
34 Airline to Tel Aviv
35 Hurdles for future attorneys: Abbr.
36 Shows contempt for
39 Galápagos lizard

40 Savers' options, for short
45 Lake source of the Mississippi
47 Deliver, as information
49 Wet naps, e.g.
50 Armless sculpture, e.g.
51 Modern party notice
52 Equate, in a way
53 "It __ to me . . ."
54 __ even keel
55 Composer Bartók
56 Chang or Eng

57 Bank takeback
60 Corkscrew-tailed animal
61 Unburden

SIGHT RHYMES

Across

1 Drain problems
6 Thick hunk
10 Open mike performer, perhaps
14 Decorated Murphy
15 Vacuum feature
16 Part of an ancient inscription
17 "The Thrilla in Manila" was one
19 Kett of old comics
20 Capitol Hill group
21 Miss Prynne of *The Scarlet Letter*
23 Pizza __
24 '60s guru Timothy
25 Dutch artist noted for optical illusions
29 Jack and wife, of rhyme
32 Red Cross supply
33 Like an alley cat
34 "Take me as __"
37 Tooth part
38 Spotted cat
39 Like quiche or custard
40 Done, to Donne
41 Group of quail
42 Figure skater Sasha
43 Buffy, vis-à-vis vampires
45 "Om," e.g.
46 Place to get a tan
48 Small dog, for short
49 Label whose parent company is Sony
51 Poor folks
56 Fixes, as an election
57 See 12-Down

59 Court great Arthur
60 Coffee grown on Mauna Loa
61 See eye to eye
62 Veil fabrics
63 Trumpeting bird
64 Quickie ghost costume

Down

1 Toy gun ammo
2 Fisherman's fly, e.g.
3 God who rode an eight-legged horse
4 Sphinx site
5 Did a slow burn
6 Polo, e.g.
7 Cabin-builder's materials
8 Airborne particulates
9 *Little Women* woman
10 Like car-radio buttons
11 "Awesome!"
12 With 57-Across, direction to an actor
13 Visibly upset
18 Teatime, perhaps
22 Carrier to Ben-Gurion
25 Tortosa's river
26 __ gin fizz
27 Low-calorie brew
28 Recently stolen
29 Cut off
30 The hunted
31 Stool pigeon
33 Quitting time, often
35 Word with New or golden
36 Mimicking bird
38 Shy, in a flirtatious way

39 Seemingly forever
41 Quitter's contraction
42 Features of iPhones
44 Second number in a team's record
45 "Outta my way!"
46 Kitchen wrap
47 Begin a revolt
48 Idol worshiper
50 Queries
51 Tennis ace Mandlikova
52 Close at hand

53 Mean dude
54 Quaker's "you"
55 Proofer's mark
58 Marooned motorist's need

ROUND AND ROUND

Across

1. *SportsCenter* cable channel
5. Starbucks size
9. Genies' homes
14. __ 'Pea (*Popeye* kid)
15. __ gin fizz
16. Like neon or krypton
17. Get pooped
18. Fine-tune
19. They're taboo
20. Auto spec sheet figure
23. Lode output
24. Beach shade
25. Half of "Who's on First?" team
29. Catch on to
31. Item on a to-do list
35. Actress Garbo
36. Goof off
38. Wire service inits.
39. Charge account feature
42. Time of anticipation
43. Cat's nine
44. Formal proclamation
45. Slithery swimmers
47. Gen-__ (boomer's kid)
48. Burdens of proof
49. Go hastily
51. Rainbow's shape
52. Thread-making device
59. Thrash about
60. Zoo home
61. Witch's concoction
63. Line from the heart
64. Diabolical
65. __ IRA
66. Scatter about
67. Walk like a sot
68. __ buco (veal dish)

Down

1. Body shop fig.
2. Loretta of *M*A*S*H*
3. Andean land
4. __-do-well
5. Souvenir garment
6. On one's own
7. Like a Hail Mary pass
8. Grouchoesque look
9. Yorba __, Calif.
10. Consecrate with oil
11. Cafeteria list
12. Old hands
13. Paul and John: Abbr.
21. Most
22. Storage spot
25. See eye to eye
26. Alla __ (2/2 time)
27. Cut at an angle
28. Ear: Prefix
29. Doomed one
30. Bacon's partner
32. Many Autobahn autos
33. Cumin or coriander
34. Saint __ and Nevis
36. Deliberate loss
37. Battlefield furrow
40. Female fox
41. University URL ending
46. Certain Muslim
48. *1984* author George

50 Spouse's sibling
51 Farming major
52 Place for mail
53 Henry VIII's sixth, Catherine ___
54 Cake decorator
55 Basilica center
56 River through Aragon
57 Cupid counterpart
58 Reply to "Shall we?"
59 Mi followers
62 The ___ ("Tommy" band)

THREE-D

45 Crooner Vic
46 Cultural: Prefix
47 Grafter's need
48 "Hold the rocks," at a bar
49 Stuck in Pamplona?
50 Loses, as weight
51 Crack from the cold
52 Stir up
53 They occasionally clash
54 Wine area in Italy
57 Slangy refusal
58 Word before dance or bride

CORPS OF ENGINEERS

Across

1 Scaled back
6 Brat's talk
10 "The Purple Cow" rhyme scheme
14 *Butterfield 8* author John
15 Cocoon's content
16 Repetitive routine
17 Some denims
18 Genesis locale
19 Petri dish filler
20 Ride in a country bar
23 Bring to a halt
24 Seating option
25 Reroute, as traffic
29 Mell Lazarus comic strip
32 Blue-pencil
33 First Lady after Bess
34 PC's "brain"
37 Lightning producer
41 ___ Plaines, Ill.
42 Shoot-'em-up
43 On the peak of
44 Fictional champ Apollo ___
45 Cause of burnout
47 Back forty's forty
50 Gulped down
51 Fe, for iron
58 Home with hexagonal cells
59 Run ___ (go wild)
60 Left Bank locale
62 In a dead heat
63 Regal address
64 Send to seventh heaven
65 Shoulder muscle, for short
66 Had down cold
67 CSA notable

Down

1 Campaign pro
2 "Beg pardon . . ."
3 Talk like a psycho
4 Hoss Cartwright's given first name
5 One of Santa's team
6 Act the high roller
7 Car with a four-ring logo
8 On ___ (with no guarantee)
9 Yemen's capital
10 Yemen's peninsula
11 Like a $3 bill
12 "Any Time ___" (Beatles tune)
13 Early TV's "Uncle Miltie"
21 Carpenter ___
22 Glittery fabrics
25 Scout's action
26 Off the job
27 Is in contention
28 "Yada yada yada"
29 Sprayed, or clubbed, in a way
30 General Bradley
31 "Cool" sum of money
33 Dust critter
34 Dove's home
35 Thumbs-up voters
36 Mgr. ejectors, at times
38 Upper bodies
39 Northwest Passage seeker John ___
40 Feathers adhesive
44 Dental adhesive
45 Porker's place

46 It's easily lost when short
47 Had a yen
48 Potato skin garnish
49 Party hearty
50 Out of whack
52 Vintner's barrel
53 Despot played by Whitaker
54 Passed-on tales
55 Barn bundle
56 Like much testimony
57 Lo-cal
61 "I told you!"

SHOE!

Across

1 Hawks and doves
6 Picket line crosser
10 Poker winnings
14 To no ___ (fruitlessly)
15 ___ podrida (spicy stew)
16 "E pluribus ___"
17 Fragrant tree
19 Denver elevation
20 V-8, e.g.
21 Pea's place
22 Gallup or Roper undertaking
23 Shooting marble
25 Trawler's gear
27 Promo package
32 The Big Band ___
33 Fab Four film of '65
34 Trim to fit, maybe
36 Quick bite
40 Surrealist Salvador
41 Voice an objection
43 De Matteo of *The Sopranos*
44 Quench, as thirst
46 Actress Russo
47 Mardi Gras follower
48 Ending with rocket or racket
50 Make over
52 Link together
56 ___ v. Wade
57 Dairy aisle purchase
58 FYI part
60 Least amiable
65 ___ Bator, Mongolia
66 One from the prairie
68 Get pooped
69 Doily material
70 Act segment
71 Dame Myra ___
72 One-named New Ager
73 1989 Oscar winner Jessica

Down

1 Morally low
2 Court star Lendl
3 Summoned the butler
4 Actress Conn
5 Italicizes, e.g.
6 Boar's mate
7 Horse's footfall
8 Standoffish
9 No-goodnik
10 Water drawer's fistful
11 Bermuda or Vidalia
12 Veil fabric
13 Refine, as ore
18 Needed a patch
24 Dentist's order after "open," perhaps
26 Many AARP members
27 Professors' degs.
28 "It's been ___!"
29 Cinders of old comics
30 Music's "King of Corn"
31 Oven accessory
35 Piano pro
37 Plane measure
38 Euro fraction
39 Winslet of *Titanic*
42 Rifle's kick
45 Fair-hiring letters

49 Thumb through
51 Assign new actors to
52 Refinement
53 Stan's partner
54 Closes in on
55 Ryan in Cooperstown
59 Off-color
61 Ancient Peruvian
62 Genesis garden site
63 FedEx, say
64 Deuce beater
67 Mad Hatter's drink

HERE COMES THE JUDGE

Across

1 Mel Ott, notably
6 NYC gallery
10 Lasting impression
14 Arctic or Antarctic
15 Acknowledge frankly
16 Wear out the carpet
17 Knight's protective garb
19 Connors opponent
20 Caspian feeder
21 Shopping binges
23 Chef's collection
27 Away from the center
28 Made amends
29 Like a skinhead's head
32 Ignores
33 Parasol's offering
34 Letter after upsilon
37 Resurfaces, in a way
38 Donny's singing sister
39 Bump off
40 Aardvark's morsel
41 Cut off
42 Render impure
43 Left at the altar
45 Shrink in fear
46 Shorthand taker, for short
48 Coffee-table protector
49 Works on a scrapbook
51 "___ way, please"
52 Mandolin kin
53 Champ's opponent,
   in a workout

59 Rich Little, e.g.
60 Ages on end
61 Devilish doings
62 Gull-like bird
63 Sonnet, e.g.
64 Wooden shoe

Down

1 Hi-tech dash attachment,
   for short
2 Debtor's letters
3 Noted 1964 convert to Islam
4 Cole who was "King"
5 Road-show givers
6 Cass and Michelle, in '60s pop
7 Stadium shape
8 Miss Piggy's "Me?"
9 Hole-making tools
10 Like trees on a prairie
11 Illustrative example
12 Needed aspirin
13 '40s–'50s Dodger star
18 I Love Lucy landlord
22 Do roadwork
23 Dreadlocked Jamaican
24 Actor Hawke
25 Yorick was one
26 B&B's
29 Destroy, as classified
   documents
30 Stylist's concern
31 Fruity quencher
33 Keep in reserve
35 Door part
36 Prefix with act or play
38 Ran into

39 Place for a roaster
41 Tart plumlike fruit
42 Speaks disparagingly of
44 On-the-job learner
45 Rattler's posture
46 Water balloon impact sound
47 Hosiery shade
48 Great divide
50 Part of an AA program
51 Pitchfork part
54 Friend of Pooh
55 Fertility clinic cells

56 Barbecue morsel
57 __-mo
58 Biblical verb ending

HAVING A BAWL

Across

1 Not quite right
6 Africa's largest city
11 Mega-proportioned
14 Classic Milton Bradley card game
15 Nasty-smelling
16 Toothpaste-endorsing org.
17 Real pity
19 An LBJ dog
20 French capital, in song
21 Bogart's sleuth
23 Peloponnesian War side
26 Calendar box
29 Send out
30 Natives of Lima or Toledo
32 Nursery arrival
34 Guilty one, in copspeak
35 "Yum!"
37 Droopy tree
43 Stale from overuse
44 "Hear no ___ . . ."
46 Run-of-the-mill
50 Dinosaur, e.g.
53 Bank take-back
54 The limit, in a saying
56 Mind teaser
57 Online message to RSVP to
59 Cisco Kid, to Pancho
61 '59 Caddy feature
62 Jerusalem prayer site
68 Drink with a head
69 Tupelo's favorite son
70 Lint-trapping navel
71 Fourposter, e.g.
72 Driving hazard, in winter
73 Adlai's running mate in 1956

Down

1 ___ de Triomphe
2 Cover with graffiti, e.g.
3 Hardly hospitable
4 Play Double Dutch, e.g.
5 Beethoven opus
6 Job for Perry Mason
7 Had a yen
8 Portfolio part, for short
9 Lens holder
10 Works of Shelley
11 Grand ___ (island near Florida)
12 Cry of triumph
13 Egg, for one
18 The "G" of GTO
22 Fenced-in area
23 ___ up (absorb)
24 "That was close!"
25 Suffix with zillion
27 Respond to a knock
28 Abominable Snowman
31 Christmas gift giver, informally
33 Popeye's gal Olive ___
36 FBI worker: Abbr.
38 Org. that might meet at a school
39 Bearded bloom
40 Disappointments
41 Roman poet banished by Augustus
42 Executor's concern
45 Washington and ___ University
46 Assembly-ready
47 Speak badly of

48 Put in one's two cents
49 Pub crawler
51 Limerick's land, literarily
52 Porker, in tot-speak
55 Certain Ivy Leaguer
58 She sheep
60 Niagara's veil
63 The whole shebang
64 ___ *Got a Secret*
65 Doodlebug's prey
66 Lay it on thick
67 ___ *Miz*

TAKE NOTES

Across

1 Unmixed
5 Johnny-on-the-___
9 Gripping tools
14 Mother of Horus
15 South Seas food staple
16 Prefix with mural
17 Fare
19 Deck out
20 35 is the minimum one to be US president
21 Essay page, for short
22 Some interior workers
27 They pack stadiums
29 Represented visually
30 "Olé!" recipient
32 Bounce back
33 Promoted with gusto
34 Vitamin bottle info
37 Has a bug
38 Went white
39 Injure, as a knee
40 ___-cone (cool treat)
41 Ship from Valdez
42 It's alive
43 Least refined
45 Farmers' group
46 Kangaroo in motion
48 "___ than fiction"
50 Toiling away
51 Multivol. lexicon
52 Great buy, slangily
54 Laredo
60 Parts of bottles

61 Switch's partner
62 Liniment target
63 In a tough spot
64 Paths of pop-ups
65 Menial laborer

Down

1 Movie, slangily
2 Olympics chant
3 Chest protector
4 Computer key, for short
5 Not impromptu
6 KP tool
7 Alternative to .com
8 Bath water tester
9 Itinerary word
10 Like most plumbing nowadays
11 Retire
12 Blew it
13 Does a woodworking chore
18 Concubines' place
22 Type size units
23 At full speed
24 Sofa
25 Self centers
26 Surgical probes
27 Street ___ (urban acceptance)
28 Like a boiled lobster
31 Button between * and #
33 Dutch portraitist Frans
35 Shabby state
36 Cause of an outburst
38 Berth place
39 Mr. Connery
41 *How Sleep the Brave*, for one
42 Small nails

44 Slow on the ___ (thickheaded)
45 Hall of Fame members
46 ___ a clue (is lost)
47 Playful animal
49 Like some industrial waste
53 Leary's psychedelic
54 Awaiting scheduling, initially
55 Drum site
56 Upper limit
57 Italian ___
58 However, for short
59 Tokyo cash

WHAT'S YOUR SIGN?

Across

1 An arm and a leg?
6 Atlas section
10 Newsman Bernard or Marvin
14 *The Tempest* sprite
15 Fourth of July sound
16 Ersatz butter
17 Road sign
19 Map out
20 Pay to play
21 Closed in on
23 St. crosser
24 Balaam's beast
26 Chewed on the furniture, maybe
28 Molls' men
33 Morning deposit
34 Common street name
35 Coloraturas' tunes
37 Walleyed swimmers
41 Road sign
44 Stuffed to the gills
45 Whopper topper
46 Tap choice
47 Drum site
49 Will-___
51 Namby-pamby
55 Wordsworth work
56 Incense
57 Head shop purchase
60 On the main
64 Basilica center
66 Road sign
68 Measured amount, in hospitals
69 Psychiatrist's reply
70 Raising goosebumps
71 The deadly seven
72 Took a gander at
73 Stallone's *Judge* ___

Down

1 Singer Cantrell
2 Mesabi Range deposit
3 Morning haze
4 Dispose of, Tower of London-style
5 ___-mo
6 Equal to the task
7 Actress Thompson
8 Nonreactive
9 "It's a deal!"
10 Sennett lawman
11 Shi'ite's deity
12 Swab's time off
13 Like a filet
18 Requiring a coin flip, maybe
22 Dredged out, perhaps
25 Done in haste
27 American Leaguer since '61
28 Petroleum name
29 It's a crock
30 Skip over
31 Surrealist Joan
32 Issue a refusal
36 Houlihan portrayer
38 River in a 1957 movie title
39 Bioelectric critters
40 "___ right up!"
42 Cheat at pin-the-tail-on-the-donkey
43 Santa's exclamation
48 Dorm companion

50 Not as alcoholic

51 -

52 Farsi speaker

53 *Deathtrap* playwright

54 Metrical composition

58 Patella's place

59 Bowled over

61 The King of Id, to Rodney

62 Author Bagnold

63 Like much fine wine

65 Tabloid aviators

67 Bloodshot

CHOP-CHOP

Across

1 Walden, for one
5 LL.D. holder
9 Seaside cities
14 Love personified
15 Pug's garb
16 Dickens's Heep
17 Scale down
18 Minuscule pest
19 Letter after gamma
20 Selfish motive
23 Had an edge
24 Dark times, poetically
25 Queen of mystery
27 Type of lily
30 Dazed and confused
32 Taking after
33 Finalizes, as a deal
36 Was in the red
40 Gulf War projectile
43 Merlin, e.g.
44 Dredge
45 Fudge the facts
46 Like some alleys
48 More off-the-wall
50 Inebriated
53 In alignment
55 "All the Things You __"
56 Thin, angular physiognomy
62 Cavity site, often
64 Yemeni, for one
65 Love personified
66 Writer Zola
67 Ancient letter
68 Hoof sound
69 More judicious
70 Do KP work
71 Former Twins star Oliva

Down

1 One of the Three Bears
2 Muscat's land
3 Role for Myrna
4 Philadelphia university
5 A noble gas
6 Ice picker-uppers
7 Lift for a skier
8 Hirsute Himalayan
9 Evidence of melting
10 Bonanza stuff
11 Lunar valley
12 Spud
13 Of ill repute
21 Emulate Mr. Kotter
22 Tabloids "monster"
26 Vietnam neighbor
27 Persian and Manx
28 Natural emollient
29 Poor, excuse-wise
30 Made inquiries
31 Office fill-in
34 Pretentious
35 Author Wister
37 Woolly partner
38 Nobelist Wiesel
39 Salt lick visitor
41 Wall St. whizzes
42 One end of a pig
47 Bush-Kerry debate moderator Jim

49 Switch sides
50 Arcade attractions
51 Java quality
52 Baseball exec Bud
53 Macbeth's title
54 One of Lee's men
57 Infield cover
58 Rock's Mötley ___
59 Woody's son
60 Critter for Crockett's cap
61 Catch sight of
63 Hoppy quaff

THE FAMILY JEWELS

Across

1 Greek odist
7 Lamarr of *Boom Town*
11 Get-up-and-go
14 Software thief
15 Two-tone cookie
16 In-flight announcement, for short
17 Rattlesnake variety
19 "__ longa, vita brevis"
20 Get the pot going
21 High __ (Western peaks)
23 Seaweed-filled sea
27 Shoppe sign word
28 Merciless
29 Attacked guerrilla-style
33 Priestly vestments
34 Stimulating quaff
36 Slinky or yo-yo
37 VCR button
38 Vein contents
39 *Kidnapped* monogram
42 Wearable souvenir
45 Sad news item
46 Like many autos
48 Sachet's quality
49 Yemeni port
50 Resin-yielding tree
53 Did a cobbling job
57 Slave away
58 Hallucinogenic initials
59 European land's nickname
64 Conductor __-Pekka Salonen
65 "Good shot!"
66 Competition judge, of sorts
67 "Whoopee!"
68 Metro map's dot
69 Heirs split it

Down

1 Remitted in advance: Abbr.
2 Super Bowl in which Namath starred
3 Heston was its pres.
4 Compensation for injuries
5 Musically keyless
6 Monopoly payments
7 Play __ with (do mischief to)
8 Hurling stats
9 Prefix meaning "tenth"
10 Symbol of oppression
11 Site of the USS *Arizona*
12 Much Wall Street activity, these days
13 Got a "D" on, perhaps
18 __ Plaines, Ill.
22 One of a dozen, often
23 "Amscray!"
24 He sang about Alice
25 '60s Rolling Stones hit
26 Butcher block wood
30 Tie up in the harbor
31 Convy or Lahr
32 Sport __ (versatile truck, briefly)
34 Mexicali moolah
35 Sonic bounce
37 Part of Roy G. Biv
40 City founded by Pizarro
41 Detached, in mus.
43 Cubic Rubik

44 Apr. addressee
45 Lip reader
46 Chris of *Beverly Hills Ninja*
47 Black Sea port
48 Reebok's acquirer
51 ___ snail's pace
52 *Lorenzo's Oil* star Nick
54 Monocle part
55 Give forth
56 Art ___
60 Public image, briefly
61 Penn or Grand Central: Abbr.

62 Tennis do-over
63 Before, to bards

FILLING THE BILL

Across

1 Reggae fan, maybe
6 Way up or down
11 Inexpensive pen
14 Hunter in the night sky
15 Two under par
16 Hosp. section
17 Handlebar attachment
19 SE or NW
20 Big name in pet foods
21 One with no hope of getting out
23 Foul-weather footwear
27 Fully attended
29 Locals' organizations
30 Two-dimensional
31 Cause to swell
32 Madrid gallery
33 Pollution control org.
36 Port side
37 Jotted down
38 Avian trumpeter
39 School web address ender
40 *Common Sense* author
41 Treasure holder
42 __ Islands (Tuvalu, formerly)
44 Ultimatum phrase
45 Put out leaves
47 Got a whiff of
48 Cagney's TV partner
49 Guinness measure
50 1950s campaign nickname
51 Early A-bomb test site
58 0, in soccer scores
59 Circular gasket

60 "Not a chance"
61 Hair preparation
62 Eastwood's *Rawhide* role
63 Jobs of Apple Computer

Down

1 Rip off
2 __ Ben Canaan (*Exodus* character)
3 [as printed]
4 Cracker Jack bonus
5 Way over the hill
6 Is apparent
7 Keep __ on (check)
8 Carbon dater's calculation
9 Flu-ridden
10 Chile __ (stuffed pepper)
11 Say a final goodbye
12 More standoffish
13 Spicy dish of India
18 Phyllis's sitcom husband
22 __ jiffy
23 Moscow money
24 Lacking guidance
25 User of organisms to produce electricity
26 Dinghy or dory
27 Yogi was behind it
28 Stow, as cargo
30 Lying facedown
32 Comparison shopper's concern
34 Behind the times
35 Chipped in
37 Bide one's time
38 Silverstein of children's literature

40 Hugh Hefner's magazine
41 King Minos's subjects
43 Tell a whopper
44 Prefix with potent
45 Highland dance
46 Jack of *The Great Dictator*
47 Acts the stool pigeon
49 Cleanser scent
52 A Gershwin
53 Scout Carson
54 Little one
55 Have creditors

56 W.C.
57 Caustic cleaning agent

GETTING NUTTY

Across

1 Sonora snacks
6 Whip-and-chair wielder
11 Maglie or Mineo
14 To the left, to a sailor
15 Dropped a line
16 Investment option: Abbr.
17 Kids' card game
19 Imprisoned Nobel Peace Prize winner __ Xiaobo
20 Nor'easters, e.g.
21 Put down roots
23 __, Pray, Love (Elizabeth Gilbert bestseller)
24 Bottomless pit
25 Render harmless, as a snake
29 Unjust accusation
32 Escape from
33 Kohoutek, e.g.
34 GIs' morale booster
37 Film composer __ Rota
38 The "S" in WASP
39 Dress shirt closer
40 Beachgoer's goal
41 Roof overhang
42 Prefix with dollars
43 Arafat of the PLO
45 Buffy, vis-à-vis vampires
46 Own up
48 Relaxing getaway
49 They're blue, in verse
52 Twin brother of Pollux
56 __ Arbor, Mich.
57 Warner Bros. cartoon series

60 Go out with
61 She played Lady L in Lady L
62 Business on the Internet
63 Take a shot at
64 Give a seat to
65 Like undercooked eggs

Down

1 Middle of XXX
2 Auto loan terms: Abbr.
3 Surface layer
4 Rice-shaped pasta
5 Liquid used in making plastics
6 '60s dance craze
7 Neighbor of Chile: Abbr.
8 Scale of mineral hardness
9 Diminutive ending
10 Do-over
11 Toy in a plastic egg
12 First sign of spring
13 Sings the praises of
18 Online periodical
22 Awaiting scheduling, initially
25 Subject of an insurance appraisal
26 Noted literary pseudonym
27 Counterfeit cash
28 Big commotion
29 Shorts style
30 Cookie maker Famous __
31 Place to hang out
33 Stalactite site
35 "You bet!"
36 Gorgonzola emanation
38 Carrier to Bergen
39 Ross, for one

41 Oscar winner Parsons
42 Cast material
44 Feel bad
45 Neuter
46 Sailor's "Halt!"
47 Beanery
48 Lavender quality
50 Labor-saving gadget
51 Like bad losers
53 Dancer's dress
54 ___ irregular basis
55 Mount's restraint

58 Japanese computer giant
59 Not easily tricked

BERG-ERS

Across

1 Big Mama
5 Belgrade native
9 __ tender
14 Sparkling wine center
15 Professor Plum's game
16 Slip past
17 Tartan-clad group
18 Word after "ye"
19 Genesis 1:1, for one
20 First Jewish baseball Hall of Famer
23 Come to a halt
24 Sportscaster Berman
25 "So's yer old man!," e.g.
28 No longer edible
29 New Haven collegians
31 Roll-call vote
32 Fall bloomer
35 Bunyan's Babe and others
36 Pizazz
37 *Jurassic Park* director
40 Hollywood's Grant
41 "Woe!"
42 Prone to back talk
43 Tattoo place
44 17-Across member
45 __ of hope
46 Sneeze cause, in cartoons
48 9-to-5 grind
49 Rest-cure facility
52 Beat Generation poet
56 Katmandu's land
58 Partner in war
59 School attended by 007
60 Cara or Castle
61 __ Alto, Calif.
62 Dunce cap shape
63 Apple-peeling tool
64 "You said it!"
65 Was positive

Down

1 Hidden repository
2 Narnia lion
3 Greet the judge
4 Swim's alternative
5 Made a basket, say
6 TV host DeGeneres
7 Lacking manners
8 "I've __ had!"
9 Flood barriers
10 Turn inside out
11 Grotesque carvings
12 PC pop-ups
13 Jeans brand
21 Icy look
22 Pickling need
26 Plays parent to
27 Sharp-tasting
28 Group of beauties or birds
29 Political exile, briefly
30 Mementos of Maui
32 Songwriters' org.
33 Icy look
34 Big writing assignment
35 1952 Winter Olympics site
36 Cyber-auction site
38 Mother-of-pearl
39 Hurdles for future attys.

44 eBay user
45 *Guys and Dolls* author
47 Carpentry tool
48 Valley of the moon
49 ___ Hall University
50 Flat on one's face
51 Nixon's running mate
53 California wine valley
54 David Bowie's rock genre
55 Tea Party favorite Glenn
56 Quick drink
57 Hurler's stat

BREW CREW

Across

1 Practices, as a trade
6 Pueblo Indian
10 Dropped, as in the polls
14 Feature of some quarters
15 Numbered composition
16 When tripled, a Seinfeld catch phrase
17 Capitalist tool
18 Small stream
19 Use a swizzle stick
20 Pro team's pick
23 Intense anger
24 Monopoly payments
25 Material thing
29 Witch trials site
32 Unexpected advantage
33 Farm measures
34 Cross shape
37 Repressed anger, et al.
41 ___-cone (icy treat)
42 Tourneys for all
43 Becomes inedible
44 False front
45 Plant sprayer
47 Cloak-and-dagger types
50 Hi-___ graphics
51 Sitcom sound effect
58 VW or BMW
59 Shuckers' units
60 Boozehound
62 "No contest," for one
63 Loretta of *M*A*S*H*
64 Place to fight

65 Pull down, as a salary
66 Harrison Ford film role, for short
67 Like an oboe's sound

Down

1 Get-up-and-go
2 Canned fat
3 Borodin's *Prince* ___
4 Cinders of old comics
5 Deem appropriate
6 Preakness entrant
7 Mayberry boy
8 Sign on a door
9 The Emerald ___
10 Word with solar or nervous
11 What Mr. Chips taught
12 Dimwit
13 Mends, in a way
21 The old college ___
22 Blue jay's topper
25 Tapers off
26 When shadows are short
27 The Wizard of Oz's exposer
28 Bankbook abbr.
29 Script division
30 Venus de Milo's lack
31 Baseball's Durocher
33 Fruity quenchers
34 Tugboat blast
35 Contribute to the kitty
36 Cold war inits.
38 Dirty rat
39 Prefix with center or cycle
40 Apr. payee
44 Columbus, by birth
45 Unit of RAM, for short

46 Hoffman/Beatty film bomb
47 Suffix with land or moon
48 Abdul or Zahn
49 Lay to rest
50 Out of shape
52 Ricky player
53 Croquet surface
54 Like Death Valley
55 Ran like heck
56 Guarded sword
57 Rip to pieces
61 Bit of hope

AERIAL SHOW

Across

1 Spinet or upright
6 Antlered critters
10 Crows' cries
14 Utah politico Hatch
15 Aide: Abbr.
16 Taj Mahal site
17 Star of the show
20 USNA grad
21 "Later!"
22 Least furnished
23 ___ I (speed of sound)
24 Runs into
25 Toiling away
28 Brazen woman
31 Bondsman's payment
32 M*A*S*H land
33 Alfred E. Neuman's mag
36 The star's sidekick
40 The Braves, on scoreboards
41 April 1st baby, e.g.
42 Map out
43 Religious devotion
44 Causing goosebumps
46 Runs a 10K
49 Any of TV's Simpsons
50 Heads-up notices
52 Some museum hangings
53 Belief system
56 The star's enemies
59 Tiny colonists
60 Sign gas
61 Oscar winner Burstyn
62 New Ager John
63 Like horror flicks
64 Like a bassoon's sound

Down

1 Sponge opening
2 Spinach is rich in it
3 Rainbow shapes
4 Suffix with beat or refuse
5 Like a modest garage
6 Big Indian
7 ___ buco
8 Atty.'s title
9 Well-worn pencil
10 Grinch player Jim
11 See eye to eye
12 Take forcibly
13 Deices, in a way
18 Clock sound
19 2001 Sean Penn film
23 Gangster's gal
25 "Mamma Mia" group
26 Stretched tight
27 What a codicil modifies
28 Corny
29 WWW addresses
30 "Get it?"
32 Make a sweater
33 Lawn burrower
34 "Make it fast!"
35 Refuse to believe
37 Cummerbund spots
38 Ill temper
39 Ready for business
43 Disappear forever
44 Fast food order
45 Yearbook listing

46 Morocco's capital
47 Lacking a partner
48 "Two mints in one" brand
49 Cheap-sounding
51 Performed an aria
52 Hint of a gas leak
53 Archipelago unit
54 Place for a mower
55 "__ are called . . ."
57 *The Matrix* hero
58 Home brewer's concoction

COUNTRY STYLE

Across

1 Spanish appetizers
6 Dr. No foe
10 Times patriarch
14 Drop off
15 Bow-wielding god
16 Honolulu-based detective
17 Road-sign ad sponsor of yore
19 Some flooring
20 Cut of beef
21 Capt. Ahab, or his ship
23 Virtuoso piece
27 Like a bump on a log
28 Rival of Sparta
29 Marching together
32 Perform well
33 He outranks the sarge
34 Wild Bill Donovan's org.
37 Bivouac shelter
38 ___ on (fusses over)
39 Pipsqueak
40 Memorable age
41 Fit for a king
42 Barrel race locale
43 Sour cream morsels
45 League of Nations seat
46 Museum artifact
48 Proposed Mormon state
49 Calls to mind
51 Cede the football
52 Detective's assignment
53 Ragtime dance
59 German border river
60 Tribe defeated by the Iroquois

61 "Out!"
62 Knicks' rivals
63 Parts of many Halloween getups
64 Violinist Mischa

Down

1 Caps Lock neighbor
2 ___ Dhabi
3 It's 2 for many minigolf holes
4 Convenience-store convenience
5 Shipping route
6 Sod grass
7 Arabian sultanate
8 Thanksgiving time: Abbr.
9 Took a straw
10 Pump figure
11 Piquant spice
12 More vigorous
13 *Hägar the Horrible's* dog
18 Habitual tipplers
22 Report issuer Shere
23 "Take a bite"
24 Catchall category
25 Dining room piece
26 Rapper 50 ___
29 Minimal quantities
30 Seasonal air
31 A sib
33 Opera house section
35 Spaghetti strainer
36 Not-so-prized fur
38 R&D part: Abbr.
39 ___ down (mute)
41 Paella need
42 Give a facelift to
44 Some park users

45 Trait maker
46 Scout's mission, for short
47 Dodge, as taxes
48 You may put 'em up
50 Brunswick, e.g.
51 Victorian sort
54 Swiss canton
55 ___ Aviv
56 PC capacity
57 Egg cells
58 Hamilton's bill

GOOD VS. EVIL

Across

1 Dizzy Gillespie's music
6 Box office hit, slangily
10 Sweep's heap
13 Sans friends
14 Say with assurance
15 *The New Yorker* cartoonist Peter
16 Highland fling, e.g.
17 Hoedown seat
18 Coward of the stage
19 World's highest cascade
21 Critic Greene
22 Mess up
23 Bar garnish
25 Poorly manufactured
29 Run __ of
31 Right-hand person
32 Beat, barely
34 Put to shame
38 Field wear
40 Ill temper
41 Singer Mariah
42 Take it all off
43 George Eliot's Adam
45 Drained dry
46 New car option
48 "__ home?"
50 Like carob or okra
53 TGIF part: Abbr.
54 Currency in Ireland
55 Serious trouble ahead, with "the"
62 Male-only
63 Evangelist Roberts
64 Get in touch, in a way
65 Yellow Monopoly bills
66 Luxor's river
67 Leave stranded in the Arctic, say
68 Sitcom planet
69 Garden store purchase
70 Small pies

Down

1 "__ bing!"
2 Spirited style
3 Sound from Big Ben
4 Tale starter
5 Took it all off
6 Kid-lit elephant
7 Track shape
8 Hit bottom
9 Painting on plaster
10 Loud, as the surf
11 Look of contempt
12 Some Christmas greenery
15 1960 Rosie and the Originals hit
20 *Punky Brewster* star Soleil Moon __
24 Red scare org. of old
25 Is weary
26 Saber handle
27 Telltale sign
28 Cream-filled cakes
29 Go along
30 Fill, as a parking meter
33 Claim-staker's call
35 Folk's Guthrie
36 "As __ on TV"
37 London's __ Park
39 Blade with a guarded tip
44 Marquis's inferior

47 House enlargements
49 Chowderhead
50 Pasta sauce with basil
51 External
52 Lapped up
53 Rounded the edges of
56 Niagara River source
57 Low-lying land
58 Boat in *Jaws*
59 Loading site
60 Keep ___ (persist)
61 Strong desires

TIEUPS

Across

1 Spring sound
6 Spring up
10 Hidden catch
14 Li'l one
15 Algeria's Gulf of __
16 Load of bull
17 Fireplace-user's buy
19 Islamic holy man
20 Bray starter
21 "It's News to Me" columnist Herb
22 Weightlifter's rep
23 ". . . leave no __ unstoned"
24 Did a doggie trick
26 Novel idea
30 Load of bull
32 Grub
33 Letters before an alias
34 Llama land
35 Penalizes for lateness, perhaps
37 Inventor Elisha
38 Critter in a hobby farm
39 Gaels' college
40 One iron, old-style
41 Mardi Gras souvenir
45 "All hope abandon, ye who __ here!"
46 Plot measure
47 Puts through a sieve
49 Workers' protection agcy.
50 Rock's __ Lobos
53 Evidence of decay
54 Occupation
57 Aviation word form
58 Pendulum paths
59 Cause to decay
60 St. Louis gridders
61 Bump into
62 Church council

Down

1 One of the musical Three B's
2 Cousin of the English horn
3 Concerning, on a memo
4 Composer Rorem
5 Produce seller
6 Ivanhoe's beloved
7 Anemic person's need
8 __ Paulo, Brazil
9 Not-so-desirable bread slice
10 Incite, as trouble
11 Items on some office doors
12 Word of woe
13 Tiara inlays
18 Paying passenger
22 Sch. groups
23 NO __ TRAFFIC
24 Enjoy a tub
25 Matinee times: Abbr.
26 Way to reduce health-care costs, it's argued
27 Joltless joe
28 "__ from Muskogee"
29 It's a piece of work
30 Sites of hot springs
31 Bivouac shelter
35 Old Venetian official
36 __ about (approximately)
37 Part of many "shoppe" names
39 Negative stats for a QB

40 Wine holders
42 Emcees' lines
43 Most contemptible
44 Sonic comeback
47 Fly high
48 Creative spark
49 Second word of many limericks
50 Bird on a Canadian dollar
51 Novus ___ Seclorum
(dollar bill phrase)
52 *TV Guide* chart, for short
54 On the ___ (fleeing)

55 Dander
56 Dryly humorous

FOR THE BIRDS

Across

1 Rat-___ (machine gun sound)
5 Like #1 pencils
9 ___ be tied (furious)
14 Fortune founder Henry
15 Pointless Olympic event?
16 Computer pix
17 Nose wrinkler
18 Baptism, e.g.
19 Machine guns' spots
20 Marx Brothers classic
23 Synthetic fiber
24 Batting average fattener
25 Tidal movement
28 Unruly crowds
32 PC flasher
34 No. cruncher
37 Santa's sackful
39 One of the Judds
40 Fails miserably
43 Madder than mad
44 Take to the sky
45 John, Paul, and George, but not Ringo: Abbr.
46 Fastening, in a way
48 Miss Clairol user
50 It may be served in pints
51 Letterman list count
53 Twangy, as a voice
58 Volcano emanation, perhaps
63 Buttinsky
65 Use the kiddie pool
66 To some degree
67 Hide-covered home
68 Lamb alias
69 Trattoria tubes
70 Follow-the-leader folks
71 Patronize U-Haul, e.g.
72 New York archbishop named a cardinal in 2001

Down

1 Hilo hi
2 Henry VIII's house
3 Squirrel's nugget
4 Sparing of words
5 Feudal servant
6 Andy's sitcom boy
7 Salty cheese
8 Comb projections
9 Adjust to perfection
10 Torte prettifier
11 Ejects
12 Blaster's need
13 CIA forerunner
21 Stately shader
22 Lush sound?
26 Flying Fortress's payload
27 Party cheese
29 Prefix meaning "ear"
30 Shows respect, in a way
31 Church council
33 *Peanuts* oath
34 Snorkeler's milieu
35 It's passed in friendship
36 Italian wine region
38 Stick it out
40 ___ monster (dangerous lizard)
41 Removable choppers
42 Charlemagne's domain: Abbr.

47 Item in a setting
49 They may administer IVs
52 Not so passé
54 Bowl over
55 Edna Ferber novel
56 Curly-tailed pooch
57 Admit, as to a club
59 Look like a lecher
60 Bait for shoppers
61 Valhalla bigwig
62 Remarkable achievement
63 School org.
64 Weight room unit

PACKAGE DEAL

Across

1 Krall or Rigg
6 Roller coaster feature
10 An older brother of Seth
14 Not fulfilled
15 Rob or Chad of film
16 Inventive Goldberg
17 Packing need
19 "S.O.S." pop group
20 Time with a psychiatrist, e.g.
21 Grabbed with a toothpick
23 Gentle firelight
25 Adorns expensively
26 Brewer Adolphus
30 Cry from an impatient diner patron
33 Fancy ties
35 "___ here long?"
36 Puns and such
39 Beijing air problem
40 Is sporting
42 Early James Bond foe
43 Where a rabbit may be hidden
44 Has to
45 Glacial period
47 Sour note
50 Really excited
51 Shorten again, perhaps
53 Audiotape holder
55 More pretentious
58 British upper crust
63 Tax deferral plans
64 Packing need
66 Hit the bottle
67 Hard precipitation
68 Roaring Camp chronicler
69 Hammock holder-upper
70 Air France destination
71 Attack like an eagle

Down

1 Recording studio tasks
2 With respect to
3 Old Testament book
4 Part of CNN
5 When bats fly
6 South American plains
7 *Alley* ___
8 Is in the red
9 Fresh-mouthed
10 Like our numerals
11 Packing need
12 Drew back
13 Tops the standings
18 Vote seeker, for short
22 Opposed to, in dialect
24 Dictionary name
26 Criticize harshly
27 DDE's alma mater
28 Packing need
29 Gear part
31 Model T alternative
32 "___, vidi, vici"
34 Avoid contact with
37 *Come Back, Little Sheba* playwright
38 Pigeon-___
41 "Don't ___ me!"
42 "___ Bums" (Brooklyn Dodgers)
44 *La Bohème* heroine

46 Islamic leaders
48 Rent payer
49 "For sure!"
51 "Nick of Time" singer Bonnie
52 Diamond flub
54 Suffix with ranch
56 Audio effect
57 Rise up, as a horse
59 *Saint Joan* playwright
60 Islands starch source
61 Knowing about
62 Leak out slowly

65 "___ Darlin'" (jazz standard)

WHAT'S YOUR TYPE?

Across

1 Shuckers shuck them
6 Devious Dickens clerk
10 Long-gone Mauritian bird
14 Elephant gone amok
15 "Back to you"
16 "Hear no ___ . . ."
17 1993 Robert De Niro movie
19 Fax or e-mail
20 Some disappearances below the horizon
21 Items in a round
23 School's e-mail suffix
24 Part of some locks
25 Primitive calculators
29 Ronald Reagan made many
34 Uses a letter opener on
35 Dull way to learn
36 Barley brew
37 Yellow Monopoly bills
38 Doublemint hucksters
40 Footnote abbr.
41 On Soc. Sec.
42 "Scram!"
43 Paycheck booster
44 Jessica Lange TV-movie based on a Willa Cather novel
47 Rear-___ (auto mishap)
48 Huge birds of myth
49 Pay-___-view
51 Spread out, in a careless way
54 *Bewitched* witch
59 Owl's call
60 Midsection-strengthening exercises
62 Capital on a fjord
63 Pirates' milieus
64 Gold purity unit
65 ___ *Gynt*
66 YOU ARE ___
67 Riyadh native

Down

1 Pull an all-nighter
2 Timber wolf
3 Farming prefix
4 Short-lived atomic particle
5 Martial arts masters
6 Place for a relaxing soak
7 Spacewalks, in NASA-speak
8 Sushi fish
9 Looks into the future
10 Ball/Arnaz studio
11 Pizza Hut fixture
12 Soft shot, in tennis
13 GM line until 2004
18 Marked, as a ballot
22 Assign stars to
24 "The Wanderer" singer
25 Ballplayer with a star insignia
26 Cussword cover-up
27 "___ a stinker?"
28 Euro divs.
30 Previous conviction, on a rap sheet
31 Like a mad dog
32 Beethoven dedicatee
33 Passover meal
38 "Rock the Casbah" band

39 Griper's list
40 "At Seventeen" singer Janis __
42 Frosty's makeup
43 Puts in a new order
45 Silver-tongued speaker
46 Few and far between
50 Bird that yields red meat
51 Seek bargains
52 Sit for a shutterbug
53 Patton, to Scott
54 Capone facial feature
55 March Madness sports org.

56 NO __ TRAFFIC
57 Noodle, so to speak
58 Source of Italian bubbly
61 Swarm member

BUGGING OUT

Across

1 Birch relative
6 Davis of *Thelma and Louise*
11 Train unit
14 Ethiopia's __ Selassie
15 Shaped into a sphere
16 Be in hock
17 Intelligent bug?
19 Lose, in sports headlines
20 "That's strange . . ."
21 Two-tone treat
22 Tend, as a furnace
24 *The Lion King* villain
25 Completely wrecked
27 Yellow River boat
30 Bridge maven Charles
31 Dingbat
32 Top-of-the-line
33 Home-run hitter's gait
37 Insect's tee shot?
40 Save in Tupperware
41 Gets the squeaks out of
42 Luau dances
43 Atlanta university
45 Good friends, in street lingo
46 macnamarasband.com, for one
49 Christmas trees
50 Stockpile
51 Bring home the bacon
52 PC's "brain"
55 Carol contraction
56 Insect party?
60 "Boola Boola" collegian
61 Rash action
62 Sweater synthetic
63 VCR button
64 Mary or John Jacob
65 1/1/94 treaty acronym

Down

1 Facetious "I see"
2 Sgt. Friday's employer
3 Fizzled out
4 Pipe bend
5 Move with one's job
6 Dead duck
7 Therefore, to Descartes
8 Fall back
9 Bridal bio word
10 "__ Fideles"
11 Early programming language
12 Came to
13 Take new vows
18 Caspian Sea land
23 Rug rats' outbursts
24 Clean enough to eat off
25 Awards named for Antoinette Perry
26 Galena and bauxite
27 Bro and sis
28 Together, musically
29 Kyocera __ (copier name)
30 "Gee whillikers!"
32 Like a house __
34 The Gipper, to Reagan
35 Not great
36 Tracy's Trueheart
38 Cry "rah!"
39 Novelist Wilder
44 Violin virtuoso Elman

45 Rent, as a limo
46 Cooler contents
47 Griffith of the ring
48 Having a high pH
49 Quack
51 Outer: Prefix
52 Bossy's baby
53 Novel's essence
54 Forearm bone
57 ___ Tafari
58 Suffix with final or fatal
59 Auto grille covering

IN CODE

45 Lower class in *1984*
46 Money in Abadan
47 Newsman Matthews
48 Johanna Spyri heroine
50 Like some talk or print
52 Like a change-up
54 Event not run in the Olympics
55 Author Oz
56 Conga feature
57 Leave be, editorially
60 Mendes or Longoria
61 Guy's date

IN THE SADDLE

Across

1 Nun's garb
6 PCs' "brains"
10 Campaign news
14 Please no end
15 Trunk fastener
16 Port on a lake of the same name
17 General who rode Traveler
19 Inflict corporal punishment on
20 Speak haltingly
21 Tot's transport
23 Headmaster's title
24 Cops' stunners
25 Beaded shoe, for short
28 "__ the season . . ."
30 Oregano, e.g.
31 Open-eyed
33 "__ me out!"
35 __ La Douce
39 Big rig
40 Org chart levels
41 Roller coaster feature
42 Muscle malady
43 __ Well That Ends Well
44 Garlic portion
45 Slinky's shape
47 Def Comedy Jam channel
49 Tex-__ cuisine
50 Horrify
53 Landers of advice
55 Woman with vision
57 A number of
61 Singing Mama

62 Revolutionary hero who rode Brown Betty
64 Choir voice
65 Making a hobby of
66 Go for another 12 issues, say
67 Feudal drudge
68 In apple-pie order
69 Tire feature

Down

1 Towel word
2 Oodles
3 Rummy cake
4 Tabloids twosomes
5 Home-wrecking bug
6 "Half-Breed" singer
7 Broadway's __ Joey
8 Plays for a sap
9 Ghostly apparitions
10 Legendary cowboy who rode Widow Maker
11 Mount the soapbox
12 Lid or lip application
13 Grouchoesque looks
18 Actress Polo
22 Crew implement
25 Halloween accessory
26 The Virginian author Wister
27 Hunter's garb, for short
29 Swindler's aide
30 Draconian
32 Wild West scout who rode Apache
34 Sinuous swimmer
36 Part of an accusation in the game Clue
37 Deep Blue decision

38 Very top
40 Dizzying dive
44 Adopt Judaism, say
46 Córdoba cry
48 1930s heavyweight champ Max
50 Tin Pan Alley org.
51 Positive thinking proponent
52 Marinara alternative
54 "When pigs fly!"
56 All there
57 Schedule opening
58 Actress Russo

59 Apartment listing datum
60 Like a dirty old man
63 Hagen of Broadway

CROSSES TO BEAR

Across

Across

1 Word before panel or battery
6 Bad time for Caesar
10 Urban woe
14 Witchy woman
15 Barbershop call
16 Castel Gandolfo resident
17 Cross-bearing Hall of Famer?
19 Kett of old comics
20 Hoist by one's own ___
21 Arthur of fish and chips fame
23 It may be hitched
25 Cowboy's moniker
26 MS reviewers
27 Crib users
31 Eye drop
33 Dory mover
34 Reason to reboot, maybe
36 Eliot's Marner
39 Tiny bit
41 Athenian lawgiver
43 Pug's wear
44 Pigskin feature
46 Crowbar, essentially
48 Rathskeller quaff
49 Sci-fi alien of '58, with "The"
51 Given a raise, perhaps
53 Erwin of early TV
55 Tolkien beast
57 Baptism or bris
58 They may be secret or silent
61 Lipton competitor
65 Lacking couth
66 Cross-bearer's request for a time-out?
68 Bronx Zoo houseful
69 Avenger ___ Peel
70 Not perfectly upright
71 Cravings
72 Organizational div.
73 Freshwater ducks

Down

1 Old English bard
2 Poet Sarah ___ Jewett
3 Boorish sort
4 Cochise player Michael
5 New draft
6 Gerund ending
7 Can imperfection
8 Bring to bear
9 Stickball "field," often
10 On ___ (as a gamble)
11 Cross-bearing prospector's find?
12 ___ out (declined)
13 Clock innards
18 Bookkeepers, at times
22 x and y, on a graph
24 Swashbuckling Flynn
27 Monk's attire
28 "Very funny!"
29 Cross-bearing singer with the Animals?
30 Cobbler, at times
32 Go public with
35 Generic pooch
37 Up to the job
38 Burpee bagful
40 Business card abbr.

42 Fairly recent
45 Any minute now
47 Machine gun's sound
50 Made beer
52 Connect, in a way
53 Apply graffiti, in a way
54 Hosiery shade
56 Oreo filler
59 Hardy lass
60 Lamebrain
62 Brunei's home
63 Compaq competitor

64 *Hamlet* quintet
67 Gangster's gun

CROSSING WORDS

Across

1 Clarinetist Artie
5 Current units
9 *Ghosts* playwright
14 RPM indicator
15 Chophouse order
16 GI's time off
17 Italian wine region
18 Genealogical chart
19 Shot in the foot, say
20 Newsman's dramatic cry
23 Tokyo's island
24 Turner or Cole
25 Dot-com's address
27 Prepare scrapple, say
28 Tree-planting New Deal org.
31 Play chords
35 Nobel Peace Prize city
37 Diamond Head isle
38 1957 John Osborne play
41 Look like a lecher
42 Angler's tempter
43 Borscht veggies
44 Campaigner, for short
45 Bosom buddy
46 Hydrotherapy site
48 Beaten by the tag
49 Coveted statuettes
54 "Be sensible!"
59 Corday's victim
60 Bee, to Andy Taylor
61 Christening, e.g.
62 Celebrity's concern
63 Machu Picchu resident
64 Dirty socks emanation
65 Not so nutty
66 Have a hunch
67 Geeky guy

Down

1 Hide away
2 Can't help but
3 Follow, as advice
4 Defeats handily
5 Dudley Moore title role
6 Stud's mate
7 Make ready, informally
8 Crystal-ball gazer
9 "You betcha!"
10 Beauty's admirer
11 The __ (ditto)
12 Holiday nights
13 Dime novelist Buntline
21 Solicit a ride
22 Company in a 2001 scandal
26 Not express
27 Floats like a butterfly
28 Place for batting practice
29 Guitarist Atkins
30 Mongrel dogs
31 Hardly-edible fare
32 Like some pizza orders
33 "__ Over Beethoven"
34 Luau instrument
36 Hit the slopes
37 Word on a penny
39 Taper off
40 Bring down
45 Minigolf club
47 Way in or out

48 Inedible orange

50 *Gigi* star Leslie

51 Line to the audience

52 Turbine part

53 Bergen dummy Mortimer

54 Dalai __

55 1979 hostage site

56 Babe in the woods

57 Bring to proper pitch

58 Years ago

59 Mal- relative

EEEEE!

Across

1 Clumsy ships
5 Corn eater's leftover
8 Current styles
13 Interview wear
14 Sharif of film
16 "You ___ kidding!"
17 Swiss artist Paul
18 Flat formation
19 Actress Scacchi
20 Big name in convenience stores
23 Chest muscle, slangily
24 Needing a note, perhaps
25 Conductor ___-Pekka Salonen
26 Potato morsel
27 Chowderheads
30 Early communications satellite
33 Forum greeting
34 "Toodles!"
36 Conger catchers
39 "Do the ___!"
41 Daughter of Lear
43 Belle's boyfriend
44 The NY Mets' div.
46 Blunted blade
48 CITY STATE ___
49 "Listen up!"
51 Rebellious time, maybe
53 Place for a tack
55 Gold: Prefix
56 Salt, symbolically
58 Sturgeon delicacy
59 Moon's makeup, in stories
64 Rile up

66 Genesis brother
67 Decked out
68 Michelangelo masterpiece
69 ___ out (ignore)
70 Tart taste
71 "Hit the road!"
72 Marked, as a ballot
73 Do in

Down

1 Is inquisitive
2 Occupy the throne
3 Ukraine capital
4 TV's *Remington* ___
5 Hale-Bopp, for one
6 Brunch entree
7 Morally low
8 Business bigwig
9 Bruins great Bobby
10 Intense cold
11 Sign up for
12 Actor Keach
15 "Bolero" composer
21 Tweed caricaturist Thomas
22 Dead Sea Scrolls scribe
27 Butler's expletive
28 Locket shape
29 "If I Had a Hammer" singer
31 Champing at the bit
32 Priest's garment
35 Dudley Moore title role
37 Drought ender
38 Has a late meal
40 Own, to a Scot
42 Italy's ___ Mountains
45 Big name in liquor

47 Draw with acid
50 Put up
52 Sends to the Hill
53 Where some tee shots land
54 Greek column type
57 Pimply
60 __ de cologne (scented liquids)
61 Line to Ben-Gurion
62 Yemen's capital
63 All wound up
65 Hellenic H

FRACTIONALIZATION

Across

1 Errant golf shot's destination, perhaps
6 Chap, in Chelsea
11 Sound of hesitation
14 Like wicker baskets
15 Decorated Murphy
16 Gardner on screen
17 Offering in bulk
19 Sportscaster Barber
20 Multiplied by three
21 Ranch employee
22 Event for scullers
25 Owens of track fame
26 WWII losers
27 Wrestling hold
31 Musician's job
32 Cut into
33 Stash overhead
35 Enjoy with relish
37 Tweed twitter Thomas
41 Item in *Poor Richard's Almanack*
43 Be less than candid
44 Developing nations, collectively
49 TV watcher's seat
50 Throws a fit
51 Aerie youngsters
53 Picnic intruders
54 *You Cannot Be Serious* tennis great
57 Presidential nickname
58 Ship part reserved for officers
62 Sardine holder
63 "What's it all about?" guy
64 White-plumed wader
65 Get firm
66 Dutch painter Jan
67 Does a casino job

Down

1 URL part
2 "How exciting!"
3 Ab ___ (from day one)
4 River mouth formations
5 *Hägar the Horrible's* dog
6 Nursery rhyme opening
7 Quiet time
8 *Garfield* dog
9 Warm-hearted
10 Brain-wave test, briefly
11 Bother no end
12 "Still, . . ."
13 Drive insane
18 Clockmaker Thomas
21 Lady of Troy
22 Poverty, symbolically
23 Illuminated sign
24 Computer acronym about faulty data
25 *The West Wing* president ___ Bartlet
28 Part of a voting machine
29 To's partner
30 Hide-hair link
34 ___ and all (as is)
35 Got an eyeful of
36 Back then
38 Skin lotion ingredient
39 Search carefully

40 Tetley products
42 Letters on a shingle
44 Geneticist's study
45 Tearjerker take-along
46 Firmly fixed
47 Pre-Easter
48 The brave do it
49 Heavy hammer
52 Wounded in Pamplona
54 Prefix meaning "many"
55 Place for espresso
56 Canal opened in 1825

58 __ in "queen"
59 Big Band __
60 Cartoon collectible
61 Some chess pcs.

WHAT'S YOUR BEEF?

Across

1 Diamond thefts
6 Commuters' towns, for short
11 Gentle __ lamb
14 Dance partner for Fred
15 Dizzying display
16 Taker of vows
17 Friars Club host
19 Oater "Scram!"
20 Ritzy homes
21 Piece of legislation
23 "I'm game!"
25 Combined, in a way
26 Short sock
30 Sylvester's would-be prey
33 Got on the ump
34 Fern leaf
35 Shale extract
38 Place for a stud
39 Sang the blues
40 Charlie of commercials
41 __ out (barely make)
42 Meat and potatoes, e.g.
43 Molds and mildews
44 Goren's game
46 Hang around
47 Recordholder before Bonds
49 Source of roe
51 Airport porters
54 Do business
59 Glass of public radio
60 Hotel lobby's locale, often
62 Put on
63 __ up (spoil)

64 Meriting a 10
65 Otoscope user, for short
66 Op-ed piece, e.g.
67 "My bad!"

Down

1 Without a stitch
2 Hubbubs
3 Trousers part
4 Supermodel Benitez
5 Avoided court
6 Blowhard's words
7 DHL competitor
8 Hamelin victims
9 One of the Mavericks
10 Attacked from the air
11 Knickers-clad AC/DC guitarist
12 High-end hotel option
13 Fed the kitty
18 Partner of greet
22 King discovered by Howard Carter
24 Big steps
26 Fit for duty
27 Place for a dinette
28 NBA star signed at age 17
29 Jeans brand
31 Sad sack's list
32 Draw the curtain on
34 Tadpole, eventually
36 *Picnic* playwright
37 Place of refuge
39 New England catch
40 Winery cask
42 Get by trickery
43 "Semper __" (Marines motto)
45 Fabulous flier

46 *Dragnet* force, for short
47 "All kidding ___ . . ."
48 Ohio rubber center
50 Food that doesn't easily spoil
52 "Aye" voters
53 ___-chef (kitchen #2)
55 Give a fresh look to
56 State firmly
57 Mad dash
58 ___ May Clampett
61 World Baseball Classic team

TERMS OF ENDEARMENT

Across

1 Say boo to?
6 Nash's "One-l" fellow
10 The other side
14 Rainbow-shaped
15 Teen fave
16 Cash on the Continent
17 Classic Mattel plaything
19 Sale tag caveat
20 "___ had it!"
21 Airline based in Stockholm
22 Gives the slip to
24 *Iliad* sage
26 Slangy "Sure!"
27 Available to rent
30 Under siege
34 Envelope part
37 Anesthetic of old
40 Puerto ___
41 Right-hand person
42 Pack away
43 Pack away
44 "It's been ___!"
45 Beetle's tormentor, in the comics
46 Madonna ex Sean
47 Gossiper's tidbit
49 Immediate purpose
51 Brewski topper
54 Sources of home fries, slangily
58 Manicotti filler
61 Botch a catch

62 Auction batch
63 De-wrinkle
64 Song from *Gentlemen Prefer Blondes*
67 Cut back
68 "Puppy Love" singer Paul
69 Join the jam session
70 Curmudgeonly Rooney
71 New driver, usually
72 Act segment

Down

1 Oral vaccine developer
2 Really, really want
3 Farm measures
4 One of Gen. Lee's men
5 Menlo Park inventor
6 Tupperware toppers
7 Commotion
8 Like spoiled bread
9 Kate's sitcom pal
10 Classroom favorite
11 "Pipe down!"
12 The "E" in HOMES
13 It doesn't gather on rolling stones
18 Like harp seals
23 Bar bill
25 1971 Van Morrison tune
28 Kett of old comics
29 Rose sticker
31 Place to build
32 Business school subj.
33 Crier's employer
34 Jamie of *M*A*S*H*
35 In ___ of (replacing)
36 Comic Sandler

38 "Cogito, ___ sum"
39 Shuttle flight return
48 Emeritus: Abbr.
50 Tender touch
52 Facing the hurler
53 Pop singer Taylor ___
55 Tickle pink
56 Maid Marian's man
57 *Funny Girl* composer Jule
58 Kelly of talk TV
59 Iraq foe of the '80s
60 Firewood purchase

61 Israel's Abba
65 ___ out (barely manage)
66 Big name in pens

LAUNDRY LIST

Across

1 *Batman* sound effect
4 Joe of cigarette ads
9 Dragon of song
13 One-on-one exam
15 Greek salad morsel
16 "Clinton's Big Ditch"
17 Launder trees?
19 Like hens' teeth, so to speak
20 Rudolph's master
21 Competed in Wrestlemania
23 Dead Sea Scrolls makers
26 Guy's partner
27 Launder heat?
33 Three-card monte, e.g.
37 Prefix with Chinese
38 Boot out of one's own country
39 ___ Major (Sirius's constellation)
41 In spite of, in short
42 Model airplane stick-on
43 Choice invitees
44 Steiger and Stewart
46 In need of dehumidification
47 Launder Harleys?
50 Chinese "way"
51 Had a life
56 "We, the People . . .", notably
61 Cleo or Frankie of songdom
62 Dagger handle
63 Launder lumber?
66 Twiddling one's thumbs
67 Trademarked cow
68 Smell something fierce
69 Cask dregs

Down

1 Outlaw-chasing group
2 Killer whales
3 Tips off
4 *Hill Street Blues* character
5 Clay, now
6 ___ vase (precious porcelain)
7 "Did you ___?"
8 Gil Blas's creator
9 In puzzlement
10 Caspian Sea feeder
11 Word before sale or door
12 Chicken dinner?
14 Pear-shaped instrument
18 Judge's seat
22 Sectioned, as a window
24 Biblical priest
25 "Who goes there?" asker
28 Like some committees
29 Soup morsel
30 Costa ___
31 Alluring, for short
32 Hammer-to-the-thumbnail reaction
33 Surgery reminder
34 Colombian city
35 Has ___ with (is connected)
36 Falsifies
40 Something to let off
45 Application datum
48 Bit of Halloween décor
49 Missile housing
52 Coal-rich region

53 Tuckered out
54 Wrapped up
55 Classroom furniture
56 Punxsutawney celeb
57 Coney Island attraction
58 Model Macpherson
59 Film composer Schifrin
60 Gas brand in Canada
64 Hotfoot it
65 Oyster's abode

ARBORISTS

Across

1 Cat calls
6 James ___ Garfield
11 Neaten the outfield
14 "I don't ___" (punchline follower, sometimes)
15 ___-mouthed (devious)
16 "Let's call ___ day"
17 *I've Got a Secret* regular
19 Cardinal cap logo
20 Serious risk
21 Pelé's game
23 Take the role of
26 One-named new age singer
28 India's first prime minister
29 Awfully long time
30 Hemmer-and-hawer's interjections
32 Highland miss
33 Neb. neighbor
34 Up the creek
38 Political asylum seekers
40 Nazareth's locale
43 Night crawler, e.g.
45 ___ de mer
46 Cupid, to the Greeks
48 Red or Coral
49 Ararat lander
50 Brings in, as harvest
52 H. Rap Brown's org.
55 Diarist Frank
56 Collect in abundance
58 Get a grip on
60 The whole shootin' match
61 Mrs. Trump #2
66 Word in a bridal bio
67 Double reeds
68 One iron, in old golf lingo
69 Have a go at
70 Requisites
71 Saxophonist ___ G

Down

1 Classic British sports car
2 Extra-wide, at the shoe store
3 Polo Grounds great Mel
4 Super-thin
5 Ocular woe
6 At full speed, on the briny
7 Bankrupt, slangily
8 It precedes the Bull, in the zodiac
9 Pub potables
10 Comic Cohen
11 Ukrainian-born violin virtuoso
12 Playful swimmers
13 Arctic tusker
18 ___-K (toddlers' school)
22 Bull fiddles' little brothers
23 Common lap dog, for short
24 Rich soil
25 Famed sharpshooter
27 Baja buddy
31 Surgery memento
34 Factory-reject tag: Abbr.
35 Trawler's gear
36 Hearth debris
37 Airline to the Netherlands
39 Québec's ___ Peninsula
41 Yield, as interest

42 Sommer of the screen
44 Got fraudulently
46 Off the mark
47 More genuine
51 Pal of Theodore and Alvin
53 Without couth
54 Pushrod pusher
55 Granny Smith, for one
57 Local theater, slangily
59 Big bag
62 ___ v. Wade
63 Spy novelist Deighton

64 Bard's nightfall
65 "Ole Buttermilk ___"

TOOL KIT

Across

1 Site of Iowa State
5 Confronted directly
10 "Howdy!"
14 Super star
15 Bring down
16 Port of Yemen
17 Precision marching group
19 Put salt on, maybe
20 Absorb, as a loss
21 Capitol Hill worker
22 Mexican dish
24 Popular tea brand
26 Tiny arachnid
27 Brenda of country music
28 Breathtaking view
32 Blood-related
35 Lessen in intensity
36 Prehistoric terror, informally
37 Tabriz's land
38 Brought on board
39 Make well
40 Air freshener scent
41 Toe the line
42 Chatter idly
43 Increase from 5 to 30, say
45 ___-Magnon
46 Words of understanding
47 Prying aid
51 Pizza portions
54 Counterfeit
55 One of Frank's exes
56 Clickable word on a Web page
57 Document holder
60 Years ago
61 Keats, for one
62 Fairy-tale fiend
63 Cop's patrol
64 Well-worn
65 Hoses down

Down

1 Aconcagua's range
2 Gangster Bugs
3 Madonna title role
4 Mule of song
5 Easily done
6 Home sweet home
7 Intl. relief org.
8 Clairvoyant's skill
9 Predetermined
10 Track and field event
11 Invention starter
12 Cheerleaders' routine
13 Starting stake
18 Carnation spot
23 ___ Z (the works)
25 Business traveler's purchase
26 Brit's buddy
28 "Gay" city
29 Neck of the woods
30 Venison or veal
31 Auto shaft
32 Elvis's swivelers
33 Pennsylvania port
34 Tailless feline
35 Oath taker's need
38 Dreams of
42 Free sample, say
44 Put to work

45 Cunningly evil
47 Place for valuables
48 Sheriff's star, e.g.
49 Stave off
50 ___ back (rises)
51 No neatnik
52 Singles bar come-on
53 Victim of Pizarro
54 Open, as an envelope
58 First Lady McKinley
59 Weather system

OOH, YOU!

Across

1 Freeway exits
6 Jillions
10 Telegram punctuation
14 Dickens's Mr. Heep
15 Run like heck
16 Get pooped out
17 Clinton shooting pool?
19 Boleyn or Heche
20 NYC trading hub
21 Sort
22 Give this for that
24 Sunbather's spot
27 "You're So Vain" singer Simon
28 Like some football kicks
29 *The Mikado* character sitting in church?
32 Playful chitchat
34 Prefix with gram or graph
35 Morse E
38 Bovine-feline hybrids?
41 Watch Junior
42 Circusgoers' cries
44 Swedish actress Anita
46 Interior decorators' concerns?
49 Monopoly buys
53 Boca ___
54 Humongous
55 Aquanaut's workplace
57 Tyler or Ullmann
58 UK reference
59 Furnish for a time
60 Skimpy Chinese meal?
64 *Bus Stop* playwright
65 Mariner's peril
66 "___ porridge hot . . ."
67 Like batik fabrics
68 Dick's Trueheart
69 Periodic table figs.

Down

1 In relaxed rhythm, musically
2 Sprung up
3 Some track runners
4 Buddy
5 Doo-wop's ___ Na Na
6 Discombobulate
7 Be deficient in
8 The Buckeyes' sch.
9 Egyptian of yore
10 Like a clear night
11 Old photos
12 Writer Sarah ___ Jewett
13 Use a spyglass
18 ___ Creed (statement of Christian doctrine)
23 Biblical floater
25 Eve's origin
26 Source of 25-Down
27 Chocolate substitute
29 Bony chicken parts
30 New Haven student
31 Freshly painted
33 10-, 11-, or 12-year-old
35 Homer's outburst
36 Debtor's marker
37 Deer and antelope playground, in song
39 "Yes, ___ No Bananas"
40 B'way hit signs

43 Burned with steam
45 Director Van Sant
47 ___ snail's pace
48 Steamboat builder Fulton
50 Amerindian language family
51 "Nevertheless . . ."
52 Marsh plants
54 Offends
55 Eluded the tag
56 Counting-out word
57 Some T-shirt sizes: Abbr.
61 "I didn't know that!"

62 New Deal org.
63 Up to this point

BIKE WEEK

45 Crude sort
46 All the world's one, to the Bard
47 Cabinet post
48 Pectoral's place
50 Do the crawl, say
51 Ollie's partner
52 Not that?
53 Fair-hiring org.
54 Sitcom about a Texas single mom
55 Toboggan, e.g.
58 *Exodus* hero

PRESIDENTIAL TIMBER

Across

1 March 17 honoree, for short
6 Pastrami purveyors
11 Barn hooter
14 Saudis and others
15 ___-garde
16 Actress Vardalos
17 "I'll Always Love You" singer
19 Bobble the ball
20 Falco of *The Sopranos*
21 Slithery swimmers
22 Architect Frank ___ Wright
24 Motion detector, e.g.
26 Synthetic fabric
28 *In Cold Blood* writer
33 Sot's malady, for short
36 SASE, e.g.
37 Concert sites
38 On the briny
40 A sib
42 Salsa quality
43 Kid in a dugout
46 Cleanser in old TV ads
49 Conscription org.
50 *Death of a Salesman* playwright
53 "___ luck!"
54 Takes as one's own
58 La Scala offering
60 Red-ink figure
63 *Quo Vadis* emperor
64 Columnist Marilyn ___ Savant

65 *The Mary Tyler Moore Show* coproducer
68 Psyche part
69 Two on a par four, e.g.
70 A moon of Saturn
71 "Smoking or ___?"
72 Doesn't budge
73 Gardener's packetful

Down

1 Fills to the gills
2 Deal between ball clubs
3 Ante up
4 Most capable
5 General on Chinese menus
6 Miami-___ County
7 Demo unit, for short
8 Applies, as a phony accent
9 Rural stopover
10 First-rate
11 Face-to-face meetings
12 Lean and muscular
13 Fat in a can
18 Any *Seinfeld*, now
23 *Selena* portrayer Jennifer
25 Bauxite, for one
27 ___ Victor ("His Master's Voice" co.)
29 Roast hosts, briefly
30 Suspect's story
31 ITAR-___ (Russian news agency)
32 Repairmen's figs.
33 "Aba ___ Honeymoon"
34 Old Russian ruler
35 Agrees to
39 Really can't stand

41 Mineo of *Exodus*
44 Power problems
45 Calendar units: Abbr.
47 Use dynamite
48 Brit. reference work
51 Sweet Spanish wine
52 Reagan, as Nancy called him
55 Orange ___ tea
56 What's in vogue
57 Achy spots
58 Pizzeria fixture
59 Walt Kelly's possum

61 "I'm ___ human"
62 Fr. holy women
66 Hamelin rodent
67 Driver's lic., et al.

SHOCKER

Across

1 Poker pile
6 Partiality
10 Fellers' tools
14 Draw a bead on
15 Red beans go-with
16 Military subdivision
17 High-fiber fruit drink
19 __ colada
20 Dress rehearsal
21 Christmas star's place
23 Helicopter pioneer Sikorsky
25 Stock market fear
26 Lofty standards
30 Bar, in law
33 Playful sprite
34 Sharon of *Valley of the Dolls*
35 Page with views, briefly
39 Wroclaw's river
40 Wall art
41 Cunning trick
42 Wink in tiddlywinks, e.g.
43 Follow orders
44 Past or present
45 Big-city
47 Postal machine
48 Lose one's amateur status
51 *Sleepy Hollow* actor Johnny
53 Pig out
56 Tire with new life
61 Cut into cubes
62 Assume control
64 __ even keel
65 Keatsian or Pindaric
66 PC chip maker
67 Campsite structure
68 *The Simpsons* creator Groening
69 Clay pigeon

Down

1 USN rank
2 Take on
3 Don of morning radio
4 Huff and puff
5 Germ-free
6 __ Magli shoes
7 Hour on a grandfather clock
8 Passbook no.
9 Visionary sort
10 USSR, until 1991
11 O'Day of jazz
12 Skid row denizens
13 Spherical bacterium, briefly
18 Moonshine holders
22 Prefix with system
24 Bump from behind
26 Gadget with earbuds
27 Conn of *Grease*
28 They're splitsville
29 Jet stream, e.g.
31 Collar stiffener
32 Address book no.
34 Hefty horn
36 Milk amount
37 Otherwise
38 Does and bucks
40 Teeming group
44 Hotdogger's challenge
46 Beluga or shad product
47 Job detail, briefly

48 Beckett no-show

49 Like lambs

50 Praline nut

52 Standing up

54 Cyclotron particle

55 Cry of achievement

57 Colonel or captain

58 *Harper's Bazaar* artist

59 *A Death in the Family*
  writer James

60 Shoulder muscle, briefly

63 Caboodle's partner

I'VE BEEN ROBBED!

Across

1 Pop's Lady __
5 "A __ pittance!"
9 Magic incantation
14 On the summit of
15 Victor's shout
16 City where Galileo taught
17 Offer encouraging words
20 Ginger __
21 Wear the crown
22 A-list folks
23 German pastry
25 Architects' annexes
26 Court divider
27 Warner __ (entertainment co.)
28 Arcing shot
31 Pet adoption org.
34 __-chef (kitchen #2)
35 Stuffing seasoning
36 Upstage the star, perhaps
39 KISS part
40 Male deer
41 Fare payer
42 Cardinal letters?
43 Animation frames
44 Put an embargo on
45 On the house
46 Thick soup
50 Like "hot" goods
53 Ruth or Didrikson
54 Tennis do-over
55 "Relax!"
58 Sills specialties
59 Lander at Ben-Gurion
60 Shot, for short
61 Ones in a gaggle
62 Leafy vegetable
63 Pirouette points

Down

1 Big dos
2 Listing
3 Coffee picker-upper, say
4 Fitting
5 Stately dance in 3/4 time
6 Tom of *The Seven Year Itch*
7 Come to the surface
8 PT boat crewman: Abbr.
9 Tanker mishaps
10 City on the Seine
11 __ out (expunge)
12 Cousin of a mandolin
13 Dundee miss
18 Tough time
19 Speaker before Boehner
24 Open, as a toothpaste tube
25 Blow one's lid
27 Afrikaners
28 Give kudos to
29 Grimm villain
30 Kegger quaff
31 Makes a request
32 Dele canceler
33 Lemon zest source
34 Oil-bearing rock
35 Time on the job
37 Famous last words?
38 Result of a meteor strike
43 Result of ironing
44 Fielder's muff

45 Canine woe
46 Of the Vatican
47 1836 battle site
48 "___ to the Church on Time"
49 Cultural mores
50 For the boys
51 Deli container weight
52 Tom Joad, for one
53 Lugosi of horror
56 Mouse fearer's cry
57 Graze in the meadow

TOO LATE

53 Winter hazard
55 Beyond plump
56 Run into
57 Out of town
58 Ferocious cat
59 Stable mother
60 Glassmaker's material
61 Leave the stage
62 Mailed
63 CD players
66 Mermaid's home

PRESIDENTIAL NICKNAMES

Across

1 Simile center
4 Enola Gay's payload
9 Ill-suited
14 Bad start?
15 Kitchen gadget
16 "Peachy-keen!"
17 Fish player
19 Actor Fernando or Lorenzo
20 Turned on an axis
21 Nosy sorts
23 Jewel's place
26 Sawbones
27 Baseball's "Iron Man"
33 Bellyacher
37 "You stink!"
38 Tonto's mount
39 Leeds's river
40 *Heidi* author Johanna
43 Muscular fitness
44 Acts the deejay
46 Dog days mo.
47 Teller's stack
48 Pianist with Benny Goodman
52 Trinity member
53 Gorge crosser
58 Disciplines
63 Poker player's initial investment
64 Flexible, like a ballerina
65 Tina's ex
68 Intense hatred
69 Author Shute
70 Gone by
71 "For __ sake!"
72 1988 Oscar winner Davis
73 "__ blu, dipinto di . . ."

Down

1 Rack up
2 Luxurious fur
3 Attu native
4 Having a low pH
5 Cranberry source
6 "__ y Plata" (Montana's motto)
7 Docs prescribe them
8 Soccer standout Chastain
9 Sets free
10 Tide type
11 Fortune's partner
12 __-TASS (Russian news agency)
13 Deposit in the "circular file"
18 Nov. 11 marcher
22 Alley __
24 Catches red-handed
25 Zero-star cuisine
28 Word before flush or jelly
29 Outer: Prefix
30 Factory whistle time, perhaps
31 Flag Day month
32 I-95 et al.
33 Start fishing
34 Like unwashed gym clothes
35 Like the Sahara
36 Reach for your toes
41 Fall color
42 Stereotypical lab assistant
45 Card counters' methods
49 Hand-wringer's word
50 Line score division

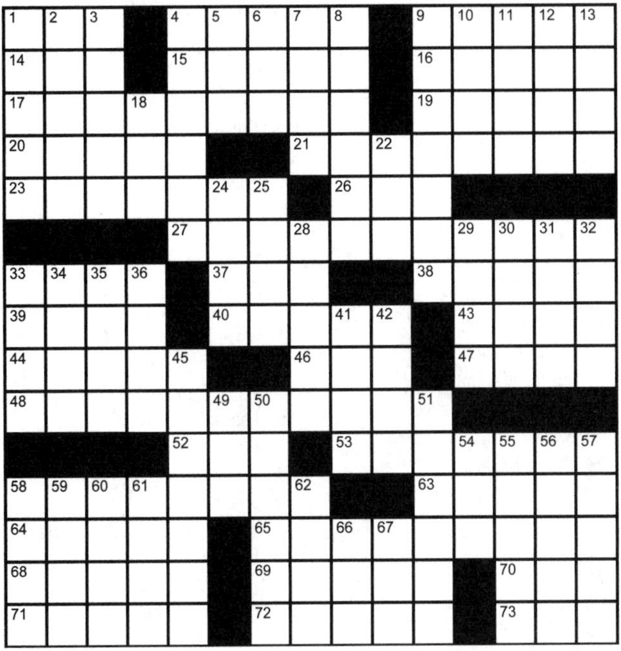

[Crossword grid]

51 Interstellar dust cloud
54 Kerouac's *Big ___*
55 Joe ___ (1979 Alda role)
56 Feudal lord
57 Sign up
58 Hoofbeat sound
59 Make oneself scarce
60 Working diligently
61 Elisabeth of *Soapdish*
62 ___-Ball (arcade game)
66 Eden evictee
67 Sardine holder

WHERE'S ED?

44 Buck's partner
45 Unit of yarn
47 Like some scents for men
48 "PG" or "X" assigner
49 Superior to
50 Less dotty
51 Quark's place
52 Taboo act
53 Mortarboard tosser
54 Tennis score after deuce
58 Bard's before
59 Sign before Virgo

BELLS

Across

1 "That's a laugh!"
5 Former press secretary Fleischer
8 Invited
13 Oxeye window shape
14 Emit coherent light
16 Drummer who replaced Best
17 One, for one
18 Sweet fruit of Washington and Oregon
20 Bloodhound's clue
21 Retort to 7-Down
22 Diana or Betsy
23 Sidi ___, Morocco
25 PC pic
27 Miss Frances's kiddie show
33 Cornhusker State city
34 Elevator name
35 Apollo vehicle
37 Attempted to score
38 Wall and 42nd: Abbr.
39 Stat for a goalie
40 Tool man Allen
41 Italian bubbly
43 More rational
44 Indoor racket
48 Looking down on
49 Road reversals, slangily
50 Be a blowhard
53 Moves like sludge
55 Run ___ (go crazy)
59 1963 Johnny Cash hit
61 Mindy of *The Facts of Life*
62 Create cuffs on, perhaps
63 Snow construction
64 Role for Welles
65 Trombone feature
66 Teachers' org.
67 Tuck away

Down

1 Nonpaying train rider
2 Driven by greed
3 Christmas pageant prop
4 "I'm game"
5 Lacking melanin
6 Cookie or bread morsel
7 "That's not true!"
8 Cigarette tip
9 Buffet table heater
10 Corn syrup brand
11 Boots the ball
12 Prohibition backers
15 "Me" types
19 Strep throat bacteria
24 Pharmaceutical-approving org.
26 Surprised cries
27 Verb with "thou"
28 "Got it, dude!"
29 Judd or Watts
30 Gained access
31 Chan portrayer Warner ___
32 Destroy completely
36 A ___ child
38 Pay a brief visit
39 Pathetic sorts
41 Actor's rep: Abbr.
42 *Mad* magazine specialty
43 "You don't ___!"

45 Acted shrewish

46 Nom de __

47 Coin of Toledo, once

50 Victoria's Secret buys

51 Small brook

52 Prefix with knock or lock

54 Utah national park

56 Castle's trench

57 "That's not good!"

58 Was familiar with

60 It needs refining

PETRIFIED FOREST

Across

1 Big name in wines
6 *Look __ Talking*
10 Nuisance
14 Give a wide berth to
15 Overly smooth
16 English essayist
17 Colorado River structure, originally
19 Laundry holders
20 Wind up
21 Fill beyond full
22 JFK's wartime vessel
24 Too hasty
25 Sheepherding breed
26 Romp about
29 Martin's "That's __"
30 Adventuresome story girl
31 Part of Bush's Axis of Evil
32 Underwater exhalation sound
36 Shirt measurement
37 Bookkeeping task
38 Rank above viscount
39 Co. bigwig
40 Set down
41 Beetle's comics superior
42 Mean dudes
44 Got ready to travel
45 *USA Today*'s publisher
48 "Do the __!"
49 Delphic shrine
50 Painter Chagall
51 Not worth a __
54 Heavy reading?
55 Neolithic mystery
58 Net surfer
59 Made a mad dash
60 Post with good etiquette
61 Smart-alecky
62 Floored it
63 Mandolins' cousins

Down

1 Comic Kaplan
2 Skin-So-Soft seller
3 Ear-shattering
4 __ Abner
5 "Most likely . . ."
6 Valued at
7 Lie low
8 Suffix with pay or play
9 Orchestral performance
10 PGA stop
11 Poet T.S. __
12 Moses' mount
13 Nibble on
18 Toward sunrise
23 Druggist's thrice
24 Fillmore East event
25 Sharp as a tack
26 Mr. Peanut prop
27 Slugger Rodriguez
28 Nasty habit
29 "Ars gratia __"
31 Place to moor
33 Merry antic
34 Egg on
35 Used leeches on
37 Audiologists' procedures
41 Paige in Cooperstown

43 Toothpaste style
44 Trim down
45 Started one's day
46 Started one's day
47 Finger-pointer
48 Coiffed like Leo
50 Oliver Twist's request
51 Peevish state
52 Gape at
53 One-eighties
56 Toy with a string
57 Cassowary's cousin

WRECKERS

Across

1 Dig deeply
6 Hiker's spot
11 "Well, lah-di-___!"
14 Saharan stopovers
15 Sonata movement
16 Hurler's stat
17 No friend of monopolists
19 Balloon filler
20 Butchers' measures
21 Party at a house-sale closing
23 Team batting first
26 With finesse
27 Camera card contents
28 Sermon deliverer
32 Place for a cappuccino
33 Country called Chosen by Japanese
34 Nosh on
37 Poet's preposition
38 Indiana native
40 Simile connection
41 [not my error]
42 Globe-shaped
43 LP problem
44 Horseshoes score
46 Give one's consent
48 Male ballroom dancer, traditionally
50 Led, as a meeting
51 "One more time!"
54 Most high-schoolers
55 Show curiosity
56 Cyclotron

61 Trial lawyer's advice
62 The "k" in 24k
63 Paper deliverer's assignment
64 The Beatles' "And I Love ___"
65 Kagan of the Supreme Court
66 Live in fear of

Down

1 Precise moment
2 Musical gift
3 Baton Rouge sch.
4 Faint trace
5 Elvis's Graceland, e.g.
6 More correct
7 Antarctica's ___ Sea
8 Tiny hill dweller
9 Bad time for Caesar
10 Oral tradition
11 Negotiations killer
12 The Little Mermaid
13 President after Franklin
18 Abbr. in many company names
22 Thai's neighbor
23 Nasty habits
24 Pottery from Japan
25 Fingertip filer, in cartoons
28 Model at work
29 Needing irrigation
30 "Get it?"
31 Feathers' companion
33 Port on Osaka Bay
35 "All kidding ___ . . ."
36 Mended temporarily
38 Sweetie
39 Assn.

43 Clip out, as a coupon
45 Altar affirmative
46 Throat-clearer's word
47 Baseless rumor
48 Fido's restraint
49 Come after
50 Jai alai basket
52 Fall tool
53 List-ending abbr.
54 Agt. under Ness
57 Excavation find
58 Rainbow component

59 LAX posting, for short
60 Sunburned

THE FICKLE FINGER

Across

1 Sow's mate
5 Fellers' needs
9 Daisy's cousin
14 Mrs. Krabappel of *The Simpsons*
15 Rock's ZZ Top, e.g.
16 Battleship in 1898 news
17 Home sites
18 Sorry situations
19 Ghana's capital
20 ___ economics (Reaganomics term)
23 Keystone lawman
24 Kitchen pests
25 Pastoral poems
27 Tapped trees
30 Traffic-stopping event
32 IRA-establishing legislation
33 Trevi Fountain city
34 Put the pedal to the metal
37 [not my mistake]
38 Most profound
41 Altar affirmation
42 Fifth Avenue retailer
44 Neckline shapes
45 Place to hit a bucket of balls
47 Places for pins or mikes
49 Saxophonist called "Bird"
50 King Minos, for one
52 Bubbly drink
53 Sot's sound
54 Spiny fish
60 Tummy troubles
62 It may be junk

63 Mineral in Geritol
64 One color on a barber pole
65 Up to the task
66 Start the pot
67 Flower part
68 Jell-O shaper
69 Winning margin, in a close race

Down

1 Boxer's prize
2 Sign of decay
3 Prefix with climax
4 Spanky, Alfalfa, and gang
5 Clown's props
6 City where Van Gogh painted
7 Like jokers, sometimes
8 Only fair
9 *Syriana* actress Peet
10 Cul-de-___
11 Please greatly
12 Sign up
13 Hauls in
21 Do a pizzeria chore
22 Cellular phones' lack
26 Gridiron distances: Abbr.
27 State of chaos
28 Bocelli delivery
29 Morsel on a fast-food burger
30 Benedict XVI et al.
31 "Rag Mop" brothers
33 Fiddler's tune
35 Beat, but barely
36 Active sort
39 Track meet part
40 Stock market transaction
43 Was in session

46 Graceful horse
48 Whole bunch
49 Solicited opinions from
50 Tobacco plugs
51 Nouveau ___
52 Expertise
55 Shia leader
56 ___ San Lucas, Mexico
57 River through Pisa
58 Shelter beds
59 ___-slapper (riot)
61 Hellenic H

I'M PUZZLED!

Across

1 Waste maker
6 Philatelist's item
11 Consumer protection agcy.
14 Fabric that travels well
15 Desert ruminant
16 Sigma preceder
17 Highway noise barrier, e.g.
19 Canon camera line
20 Suffix with Peking or Siam
21 Stout serving
22 On one's toes
24 Test news
26 Bowling alley button
28 Highland negative
29 In one place
32 ___-craftsy
35 Humorist Bombeck
36 Woody's boy
37 Tackle box item
38 ___ in (aware)
39 Trucker's amount
40 Jenny Craig plan
41 Late-night name
42 Gridiron series
43 Like an obsessive mind
45 Vessel in an alcove
46 Editorial bias
47 Mild currents
51 Motel posting
53 *Cosmo* and *GQ*, e.g.
54 ___ carte
55 Post-op locale
56 Weapon in the game Clue

60 LBJ, for one
61 Act the jester
62 Causing goose pimples
63 Mindreader' letters
64 By and by
65 Orchestra group

Down

1 Lout, in Canada
2 Came up
3 Turns on an axis
4 Trucker's amount
5 Bridge tactic
6 Some medical tests
7 President who sat on the Supreme Court
8 Bowling equipment mfr.
9 Sportscaster Allen
10 The "magic word"
11 NBA one-pointer
12 Hammer-wielding god
13 Damage, so to speak
18 Take the bait
23 Not to mention
25 Shake up
26 1996 DiCaprio role
27 "Zounds!"
29 Spare's place
30 Lively spirit
31 Lightning catchers
32 Film tough-guy ___ Ray
33 Bring to naught
34 Remains of a felling
35 Give a seat to
38 The Kennedys, for one
42 Bedroom furniture piece

44 Naughty one
45 Strong-arm
47 Farm bundler
48 Congo's name before 1997
49 Conqueror of Valencia, 1094
50 "For goodness __!"
51 Carnival attraction
52 Unreturnable serves
53 Retailer's gds.
57 Physicians' org.
58 Kook
59 Summer shirt, informally

CHUMP CHANGE

Across

1 *Dorian Gray* creator Oscar
6 Hawley's tariff act co-sponsor
11 Raises
14 *The Tempest* sprite
15 Make very dry
16 Singer/actor Peeples
17 It may be subject to a code
18 Hot under the collar
19 Inhabitant: Abbr.
20 Shoes with coin ornaments
23 Pisa's river
26 Half-wit
27 200-meter, e.g.
28 "Yer dern __!"
30 Skee-Ball locales
33 Livy's tongue
34 Supply-__ (certain economic theorist)
36 Gridiron formation
41 Aquafina rival
42 Dashboard array
44 Like a paid parking spot
48 On-off switch, e.g.
49 Dummy Danny
50 __ up (conclude)
52 Miami five
53 Ned Buntline, notably
58 Airport approx.
59 Musical about Sra. Perón
60 MDX automaker
64 Online chuckle
65 Breakfast fruit
66 Comic strip section

67 Men __ From Mars . . .
68 Ceaselessly
69 Fine English china

Down

1 Glob of gum
2 Like some sale clothes: Abbr.
3 Links position
4 Tyrannical
5 ". . . or __!"
6 Starts a *Wheel of Fortune* turn
7 *The Bells of St. __*
8 Word before hygiene or history
9 Eight: Prefix
10 "Take __ Train"
11 Like much junk mail
12 Fictional doctor Hawkeye
13 Gets smart with
21 Indian flat bread
22 Monk's title
23 NL East city
24 Equine shade
25 Words of denial
29 Worker on a comic book
30 Mideast's Gulf of __
31 Sports "zebra"
32 Words to live by
34 Lost traction
35 First lady McKinley
37 Adam's madam
38 Sip before bedtime
39 Like Solomon
40 First name in scat
43 Things that go together
44 Early Ford
45 Blue-pencil wielder

46 Burrito's cousin

47 Look over

48 __-night doubleheader

50 Mother __ (American saint)

51 Spiral-horned antelope

54 Verne skipper

55 Place to bake

56 Awful-tasting

57 Easy dupes

61 Mattel card game

62 "Curse you, __ Baron!"

63 Pub potable

GROUP THEORY

Across

1 Paddled at an initiation, say
6 Make-believe
10 __ of the land
13 In reserve
14 Andean land
15 Wound at the corrida
16 Wedding party member
18 Genesis brother
19 Miss World et al.
20 Strengthen by tempering
22 Switch positions
23 Dead heat
24 Smelter refuse
25 Murphy __
26 Painted with dots
30 Western plateaus
33 __ d'oeuvres
34 Zero, in tennis
35 Wharton School subj.
36 Mubarak's predecessor
37 Diva's performance
38 Like most workhorses
39 Jazz vocalist Anita
40 Mournful ring
41 Starts by short-circuiting
43 Suffix with neat or beat
44 Currier's partner
45 Swerve at sea
46 Word of advice
49 Ray-Bans, e.g.
52 Short Beethoven work
54 Libel, e.g.
55 Mule or burro
57 "To __ his own"
58 Wind ensemble member
59 Peace goddess
60 Paid player
61 Body decorations, slangily
62 Male and female

Down

1 Arthur Marx, familiarly
2 Like most Turks
3 Criticizes harshly
4 Sharp quality
5 Presidential campaign events
6 Sudden influx
7 Towel pronoun
8 "We __ the World"
9 Cave-wall painter
10 Earring site
11 Surface figure
12 Give a whoop
15 Ship-to-shore connection
17 Camelot lady
21 Carpet fuzz
24 Alley cat, e.g.
25 Range of radio frequencies
26 Fountain drinks
27 Handed-down stories
28 Wicked doings
29 Negotiation's end, hopefully
30 Fishnet stocking pattern
31 Off-the-wall response?
32 Santa suit soiler
33 Where the Styx flows
36 Touchy subject
40 Service club since 1915
42 "__ got a mule . . ."

43 *Peter Pan* dog
45 Oxen connectors
46 Casio and Swatch competitor
47 Totally absurd
48 Turns white
49 Aerobics move
50 Frosty coating
51 With the bow, in music
52 Dundee denizen
53 Get bushed
56 Lawyers' org.

PUT-DOWNS

Across

1 Fine rains
6 Mosque head
10 Half the checkers
14 Go gaga over
15 Triathlon, e.g.
16 Creative spark
17 1991 Oscar winner Foster
18 Seagoing predator
19 Dosage unit
20 Reckless one at a punk rock venue, perhaps
22 Editor's "leave it in"
23 Archery bow wood
24 Cut, as a log
26 Give this for that
30 Smashes into
32 Monopoly buy
36 Succotash bean
37 Mesabi resource
38 Post office employee
39 Tennis score after deuce
40 Beauty's beloved
42 Stadium section
43 Computer whiz
45 Museum-funding org.
46 Sailors' saint
47 Golf's "Slammin' Sammy"
48 Asian nation suffix
49 Virginia dance
50 Back of the neck
52 Record label absorbed by Geffen
54 Kind of herring
57 Informal chat
63 Place for polish
64 Post mortem bio
65 Spy novelist John Le __
66 "Ye" follower
67 Our Gang pooch
68 Cat-__-tails
69 Sow's mate
70 Burn a bit
71 Stun gun

Down

1 Capts.' superiors
2 Admired one
3 Scotch's partner
4 In good shape
5 Run-down
6 Pots and kettles
7 Painter Chagall
8 Means of entry
9 Stiller partner
10 Something remarkable
11 Cut and paste
12 22-Across's opposite
13 Pretzel topper
21 Oxygen-dependent bacterium
25 One of the five W's
26 Venetian blind parts
27 Add lanes to
28 Priest's vestment
29 Seeker of spare change
31 Had in mind
33 Serving a purpose
34 Note from the boss
35 Flynn of film
38 Batter's position
41 Tailor

44 Wyo. neighbor
48 Navy builder
51 Things onstage
53 Fancy tie
54 Nose-in-the-air type
55 Heavenly circle
56 Elton John Broadway musical
58 Bread for gyros
59 Yemen's capital
60 Pupil's place
61 Author Sarah ___ Jewett
62 At no time, to poets

TUNEFUL TETRAD

Across

1 Postgame show
6 Italian white wine
11 Danson of *Cheers*
14 Author Jong
15 Synthetic fiber
16 Suffix with serpent
17 CROSBY
19 Shriver of tennis
20 Indy 500 et al.
21 Spherical opening?
22 Foul odor
25 Stylist Vidal
28 Snapshot, for short
29 STILLS
32 Make amends
34 They're deep in study
35 Muscular fitness
36 Doves and hawks
37 Storklike creature
41 Mineral containing magnesium
43 Part of a drum kit
44 NASH
48 Hamelin evictee
49 Has in mind
50 Full of mischief
52 Square footage
53 Moses mount
55 Fenway team, on scoreboards
56 YOUNG
62 Long. crosser
63 Think the world of

64 Homeric epic
65 Mag. bigwigs
66 *Goodbye, Mr. Chips* Oscar winner
67 Aides: Abbr.

Down

1 ___ room (play space)
2 Drop the ball
3 AFL merger partner
4 Squirrel snack
5 Verve
6 In need of liniment
7 Spheres
8 "Rope-a-dope" pugilist
9 Wernher ___ Braun
10 A Siamese twin
11 Walk softly
12 Win the heart of
13 Exorcism targets
18 Bounce back
21 Invites to enter
22 Petty quarrel
23 Percussionist Puente
24 Galbraith's subj.
25 Etaoin ___ (Linotype line)
26 "Rag Mop" brothers
27 Patriotic org.
30 States one's views
31 Jazz pianist Chick
33 Snapple alternative
36 Home of football's Cowboys, familiarly
38 Adriatic seaport
39 Nest egg accts.
40 Third son of Adam

42 Give two thumbs down to
43 Mogadishu's country
44 Practicable
45 Encroachment
46 Blasts from the past?
47 Yothers or Majorino
51 Dose units
53 Blood fluids
54 "Yeah, right"
56 Good, in the 'hood
57 Fuss
58 Arlo, to Woody

59 A sib
60 Manx or Persian
61 HB's gains

ERRORS

Across

1 Love personified
5 Capone facial feature
9 Handed out
14 ___ Valley, California
15 Ashtabula's lake
16 Young conger
17 Dutch cheese town
18 Took a cab
19 Piece of Latin percussion
20 Breezy end of a classic palindrome?
23 "I didn't know that!"
24 Quaff with fruitcake
25 Take a gander at
26 Part of NIMBY
27 Rod-shaped bacteria
31 House Beautiful topic
33 "To a . . ." work
34 ___ Misbehavin'
36 Many-headed serpent
39 Inheritor's summer appliance?
43 U.S. Grant adversary
44 Cherry throwaway
45 Bowie collaborator Brian
46 Pakistan's chief river
49 Looked like Snidely
51 "Money ___ everything!"
53 Toga party vessel
55 Murcia Mrs.
56 Weapon in the game Clue
57 Crown prince, before?
62 As a joke
64 Here Is Your War author Ernie

65 Set straight
66 Goal-line effort
67 Nobelist Wiesel
68 Hoof it
69 "Look, Ma, no ___!"
70 Monopoly card
71 TV Guide listing

Down

1 Befuddled
2 Longish dress
3 Barbra's Funny Girl costar
4 Italian city on the Adriatic
5 Sultan's palace
6 Dinner for the shamed?
7 Senatorial staffers
8 Walked like a tosspot
9 Penta- doubled
10 Right-angle bend
11 Mogambo star
12 Crowbar, e.g.
13 In a tough spot
21 Gave comfort to
22 Royal jelly producer
26 It has its ups and downs
27 Physicist Niels
28 "Zip-___ Doo-Dah"
29 Ventilation of sorts
30 B&B
32 Fire-breather of myth
35 Six-pt. grid plays
37 French statesman Coty
38 2007 homer leader, for short
40 Patronize U-Haul
41 "___ Howdy Doody time!"
42 Cyclist's choice

47 Where Kiev is: Abbr.
48 Went through the cracks
50 Rare ___ (scandium, yttrium et al.)
51 ___ coffee (bar order)
52 Year-end temp
54 Country singer Crystal
57 Drops the curtain on
58 Ballet bend
59 Abstract composer Satie
60 Blow to kingdom come
61 Nettled, with "off"
63 Sturm ___ Drang

SWIT(C/H)EROO

Across

1 Greek consonants
7 Presidential turndown
11 Everyday article
14 Oxygen-dependent organism
15 Bring in
16 Neighbor of Ukr.
17 Tree surgeons' assistants?
19 Little rascal
20 Antarctic waters
21 Sitarist Shankar
22 The whole shebang
25 Mall bag
26 Political analyst Myers
28 "Told you so!"
29 La-la lead-in
30 Alternative to contacts
31 Lettuce unit
33 Plow maker John
34 Frugal trawler's motto?
40 Arctic or Indian
41 Impose, as taxes
43 Snake, e.g.
46 Ave. intersectors
49 Actress ___ Dawn Chong
50 Five Nations tribe
51 At the acme of
52 Toronto's prov.
53 Land in which Farsi is spoken
54 Collapsed
57 ___ Cruces, NM
58 Nag's chauffeur?
62 Psyche part
63 Get wind of
64 Mexican miss, e.g.
65 Cub Scout group
66 Lucci's elusive prize
67 Puts into office

Down

1 Profs' aides
2 Villain's chuckle syllable
3 Screw up
4 Sightseeing trip
5 Half of "Who's on First?" team
6 Electric eye, e.g.
7 Poem part
8 Lighten up
9 Operated a potter's wheel
10 Add-___ (extras)
11 Simple chords
12 Jeep's modern kin
13 Catches sight of
18 Ashe Stadium org.
21 Close up again
22 Blond shade
23 Wine sediment
24 Jacob's first wife
27 Donkeys have big ones
30 U.S. Grant or R.E. Lee
32 Pay a casual visit
33 Newsman Rather
35 Cooled down
36 Israel's Begin
37 Touch gently
38 ___ Beach, Fla.
39 Politico Bayh
42 "Is it soup ___?"
43 In need of laundering
44 Cause to see red

45 Use one's noodle
46 Hobo fare
47 Take baby steps
48 Spin like a well-tossed pigskin
51 Hi-fi pioneer Fisher
55 Composer Khachaturian
56 TV's Nick at ___
58 Any boat
59 Old ___ (London theater)
60 Med. specialty
61 ___ Tafari (Haile Selassie)

TO, BUT NOT FRO

Across

1 Chocolate substitute
6 Letters of immediacy
10 ___ instant (quickly)
14 Dwelling
15 "___ Only Just Begun"
16 Dumb cluck
17 In direct confrontation
19 Nobel Peace Prize city
20 Writer Buntline
21 Poke fun at
22 Not carrying a piece
23 Duking it out
26 "'Taint" comeback
27 Up to now
30 *Get Shorty* actress Rene
32 Nest eggs, for short
33 Brylcreem, for one
37 Peace accords
39 Blast furnace input
40 Coffee shop come-on
41 Preteens' party, maybe
43 Recipe amts.
44 Utter nonsense
45 V-formation honkers
46 Quid pro ___
48 Like some grins
52 Famine-stricken
54 Airline to Ben-Gurion
55 ___ kwon do
58 Slanted type: Abbr.
59 At close quarters
62 Popsicle taste
63 The life of Riley
64 ___ Hall University
65 Souvenir shirts
66 Newshawk's query
67 Serengeti scavenger

Down

1 "High Hopes" lyricist Sammy
2 ". . . sting like ___"
3 ___ rage (highway peril)
4 Like a single sock
5 $2 window patron
6 Not care ___
7 Take care of
8 Gardner of film
9 ___ XING
10 Teen fave
11 Arguing heatedly
12 Statesman Stevenson
13 High times
18 Be in the hole
22 Jai alai basket
23 Checker for poison, maybe
24 Judge or juror
25 ___ Gang
27 Enjoys brandy
28 Like some vaccines
29 In-person, as a discussion
31 Mailroom worker
33 Hang like a hummingbird
34 Lionel Richie's "You ___"
35 Little devils
36 Four six-packs
38 Gathered intelligence
42 ___-Locka, Florida
45 Foul-weather overshoe
46 It may be crazy

47 Set free, in a way
49 High-strung
50 From days of yore
51 Scarf down
53 Lodge members
55 Family of British art
   galleries
56 Bartlett's abbr.
57 Best or Ferber
59 Cut down
60 "What a relief!"
61 "You there!"

THAT AIN'T HEY!

Across

1 Bikini parts
5 Triangular sails
9 They beat tens
14 Wash up
15 Biblical garden
16 Depth charge target
17 State positively
18 Suffix with million
19 Dreadlocked one, for short
20 Helping after seconds?
23 Ryan of *You've Got Mail*
24 In one piece
25 Ankle bones
27 "Unhand me!"
30 Destroyer, slangily
33 Hardly tanned
36 Butter holders
38 Motown founder Berry ___ Jr.
39 Brewpub offering
40 Puts in more film
42 Mag. staffers
43 "___ fast, buster!"
45 Toy block maker
46 Apollo's instrument
47 Early German
49 River of Lyons
51 Kama ___
53 ___ oneself of (sell off)
57 A-Rod award of 2007
59 Imprisoned actress Susan?
62 Like a howl in the night
64 Apple throwaway
65 Iranian monetary unit
66 Holey utensil
67 Limburger emanation
68 Suffix with major or kitchen
69 More foxy
70 Shipping units
71 Hammer-wielding god

Down

1 World-weary
2 Poe's "nevermore" speaker
3 Fend off
4 Bootlicking
5 MacDonald of old musicals
6 Hippie's "Understood!"
7 Ernie's Muppet pal
8 Hägar the Horrible's dog
9 Assembles, in an improvised way
10 "___ Daba Honeymoon"
11 Outer-space actor Fernando?
12 Allie's sitcom pal
13 Dateless
21 Steamed feeling
22 "Mangia!"
26 ___-Caps (candy brand)
28 Beach scavenger
29 Double-reed instruments
31 Info on a mailing env.
32 Wall Street letters
33 Respire like a dog
34 Natural burn soother
35 Lions' supplication?
37 Heroic tale
40 Soda in a float
41 Makers of margin markings
44 Early Beatle Sutcliffe
46 Young hare

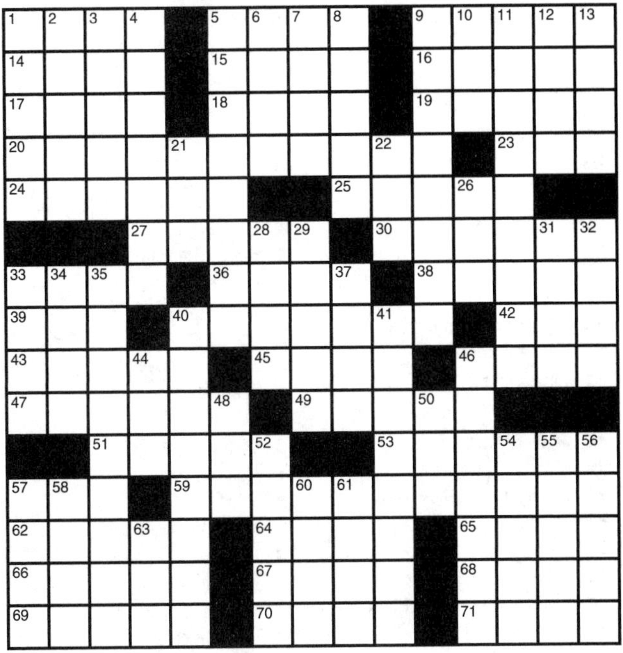

1
2
3
4
5
6
7
8
9
10
11
12
13
14
15
16
17
18
19
20
21
22
23
24
25
26
27
28
29
30
31
32
33
34
35
36
37
38
39
40
41
42
43
44
45
46
47
48
49
50
51
52
53
54
55
56
57
58
59
60
61
62
63
64
65
66
67
68
69
70
71

48 Gun rights org.
50 Nada
52 Fancy neckwear
54 Archie Bunker's wife
55 1954–77 defense gp.
56 Steven of Aerosmith
57 Boot camp fare
58 Part of a bride's attire
60 Well-___ (rich)
61 Mineral in spinach
63 "___ had it up to here!"

RACK 'EM UP!

Across

1 ___ Park, Colorado
6 Hunk of marble
10 ___-Pei (wrinkly dog)
14 Skillful deceit
15 Mrs. Nick Charles
16 An option for Hamlet
17 The devil
19 Regrets deeply
20 Summer pest, informally
21 Hurry-scurry
22 Teller's stack
24 Absolutely loathe
25 Be able to pay for
29 Assembled in advance
31 Like some losers
32 Go over the wall
33 Retina cell
36 Come before
39 Harass, as with questions
41 "I told you so!"
42 *Peanuts* character
44 ___ avis
45 Outings on the mound
47 *Working* author Studs
49 Longtime baseball manager Anderson
51 Laugh-track syllables
53 Like some checking accounts
54 Dispensed amounts
59 Brain wave
60 Storage area, of a sort
63 Brad of *Troy*
64 Walkie-talkie word

65 Put up with
66 Shows, as a watch
67 Cracker topping
68 Feel in one's bones

Down

1 Swelled heads
2 Have a long face
3 Bay of Fundy feature
4 Choice word
5 Combat zone
6 High-hat's neighbor
7 Sodom escapee
8 Pendulum's path
9 Cry to Cratchit
10 Levels of society
11 Train, in a way
12 Shills for
13 Revert to 12:00, say
18 Tear apart
21 Tests the weight of
23 Masseur's milieu
24 Take-out order?
25 Egyptian slitherers
26 Links warning
27 Backfield position
28 Set of Brit. tomes
30 ___ off (has an effect)
32 ___ one's spleen
34 Tyrannical sort
35 "Agreed!"
37 Much the same
38 Like Ho's bubbles
40 Like the vbs. "to see" and "to go"
43 Work the aisles, informally
46 Obedience school goodies

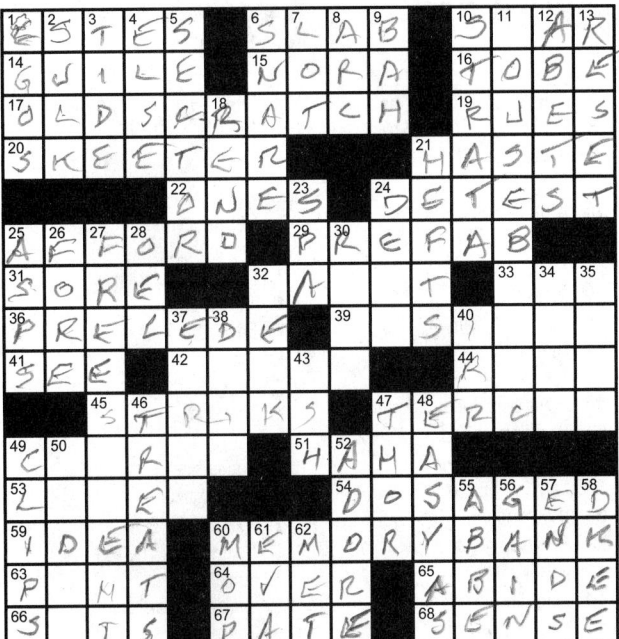

47 Hammer-wielding god
48 Words before "1-2-3" or "A-B-C"
49 Barbershop sounds
50 Lecturers' spots
52 Be crazy about
55 Cugat ex Lane
56 Yardage pickup
57 Wraps up
58 ___-Ball (arcade game)
60 Thick mane
61 Stowe heroine
62 Citi Field player

CLEAN IT UP!

Across

1 Mama __ Elliot
5 Gymnasts' protectors
9 Some petty officers, for short
14 Concerning
15 Inland Asian 20-Across
16 Set loose
17 Straggly evergreen
19 Ott was one
20 Neptune's domain
21 Like Methuselah
22 Fillets
24 Properly pitched
26 Hamilton's bill
27 Mike holder
28 Earl "__" Hines
31 Dove's sound
34 Gettysburg visitor, perhaps
37 Potter's buy
40 Singer K.T.
41 Liberals, with "the"
42 Like instantly
45 Bard's before
46 *Funny Girl* composer Jule
47 Wandered about
51 Prefix with bar or metric
52 Vintage Ford
53 Breakfast stack item
57 "Alley __!"
58 __ Quentin
59 Had a TV dinner, say
60 Expound, in a way
63 Former Senate Majority Leader Lott
64 "Rag Mop" brothers
65 Drummer Krupa
66 Noncom's nickname
67 Part of a Manhattan addr.
68 Baltic Sea feeder

Down

1 Currant cordial
2 Trip to the top
3 Levels of society
4 Trifling amount
5 Bowling pin wood
6 Bone-dry
7 Sunbather's goal
8 Tireless transport
9 Hobgoblin
10 Burger topper
11 Ollie's partner
12 Punch-in time, for many
13 Tennis units
18 Beulah of films
23 Simple hydrocarbon
25 Quitter's word
28 Suspicious
29 "It's __ a day's work"
30 Package securer
31 Give a line to
32 On vacation
33 Frequently, in verse
35 __ I (Yuri Gagarin's craft)
36 Leech's meal
37 Sault __ Marie
38 Sculler's need
39 1950s campaign name
43 Armand of *The Mambo Kings*
44 Prefix with sphere

48 Absolute, as a right
49 *Seinfeld* gal
50 One of Santa's reindeer
51 Cupcake topper
52 Beatrix Potter rabbit
53 Butter servings
54 Razor brand
55 __-do-well
56 Actor McGregor
57 Yoked beasts
61 One of the Little Women
62 Swelled head

HI-LO

Across

1 Croquet site
5 Trepidation
10 Tom Sawyer's half-brother
13 Fibula's neighbor
14 Dickens's Barnaby
15 Country club figure
16 Corn squeezin's
18 Actor Holm
19 Completely
20 Audit time, perhaps
22 1960 Wimbledon champ Fraser
24 Pie-chart lines
25 Like ozone-layer "holes"
28 Top invitees
31 '50s campaign name
32 Morale
35 Drainage pit
39 Conestoga wagon, informally
42 Yield, as interest
43 Do some cobbling
44 "___ pig's eye!"
45 "There ___ atheists . . ."
47 It's a fact
49 Ziti alternative
52 Cause of merchandise shrinkage
55 Turns informer
58 Girlie mags et al.
62 Razor-billed bird
63 "Gag me with a spoon" speakers
65 Wimpy's payback time: Abbr.
66 Football-shaped
67 Great Lakes Indians
68 Draft org.
69 Blubbers
70 Tom's respectful reply to Aunt Polly

Down

1 Friend of Androcles
2 Touch on
3 Actress Ryder
4 Idle talker
5 Attack a cavity
6 Kennel area
7 MacDonald's partner
8 Pulitzer writer James
9 Popular Scotch brand
10 Worked like Maxwell Smart
11 Tabriz native
12 Comics orphan
13 Pa. energy plant in the news in '79
17 Highly rated
21 ___ Rizzo ('69 Hoffman role)
23 Hearing range
25 Accessory for Frosty
26 Creole vegetable
27 Jet-set jet
29 Cooties
30 ___ Jury (Spillane novel)
33 Pup's pop
34 Hammer end
36 Textbook chapter
37 Beanery handout
38 Soho stroller
40 Nonsensical
41 Stodgy one
46 Assert again
48 Duds

49 Jrs.' exams
50 Horse genus
51 Blows to smithereens
53 Listens to
54 Ending with mock or crock
56 Wash up
57 ___-eyed
59 Showy bloom
60 Mr. Kadiddlehopper
61 Nincompoop
64 ChapStick target

TWIRL SERIES

Across

1 Tear to shreds
6 Alternative to check or credit
10 Eminem's genre
13 Tickle the fancy of
14 Marriage, for one
15 Big name in PCs
16 Baton user
18 Referee's guideline
19 Involves by necessity
20 Porky Pig's girl
22 Playbill listing
24 Make better
25 Far East boat
29 Sea lion's entourage
32 "___ a Grecian Urn"
33 Strauss of jeans
34 "___, poor Yorick"
38 Start a hand
39 One who doesn't think for himself
40 Month for many Geminis
41 Dissenting one
42 Wrinkle remover
43 ___ acid (B vitamin)
44 Gives up
46 A lot of summer TV
47 Flu symptoms
50 Fell, as interest rates
52 Bambi's rabbit pal
55 Retiree's title
60 Capital overlooking the Pacific
61 Baton user
63 In a bit, to bards

64 "No harm done"
65 Track meet component
66 Word before dance or bride
67 Like a yenta
68 Takes five

Down

1 *Streamers* playwright David
2 "___ Old Cow Hand"
3 Fourth-down play, often
4 27-Down-inspecting inits.
5 Big-billed bird
6 Far from refined
7 Red Cross effort
8 Aerobics move
9 "Take this!"
10 Get together, as grads
11 Tuckered out
12 Argue one's case
15 Baton user
17 Pizzazz
21 ___ Bo (exercise system)
23 Springsteen, to fans
25 Fountain offering
26 Arabian Sea port
27 Vegetarian's no-no
28 Baton user
30 Mary Kay rival
31 Slowing, in mus.
33 Oral tradition
35 "To Sir With Love" singer
36 Have ___ (be connected)
37 Parts of mins.
39 Clear
43 Tennis great Roger
45 Psychic's sense

46 Frost-covered
47 Attorney-___
48 Tea service items
49 Sitcom material
51 Not watertight
53 "The auld sod," in verse
54 The Riviera's San ___
56 Carry on
57 Cools down
58 Fair sight
59 Some are fine
62 LAPD part

STOCK SPLITS

Across

1 Spherical bacterium, for short
6 "Matter of Fact" columnist
11 Salary max
14 Calcutta's land
15 Give birth on the farm
16 Air force hero
17 Antlered animals
18 More arid
19 Place for pickles
20 New-car shopper's reaction
23 Letterman list items
26 Metal playing marble
27 On the road
28 Hook or Kirk: Abbr.
31 Starring role
32 Check endorser's need
33 Get pooped
34 Idiot light word
36 Sprinter's aid
41 Take a gander at
42 Do perfectly
43 The Chiffons' "__ So Fine"
45 Membership fee
48 Gunpowder holders
49 Prefix with space
50 Itemized bill
53 Cook in a wok, perhaps
55 "Time out!"
58 Genesis boat
59 Mideast's __ Peninsula
60 Job jar items
64 Feel sorry about
65 Signs of spoiled food

66 Dickens's Heep
67 Club __ (resort chain)
68 Nairobi's land
69 Beef serving

Down

1 Bro's sib
2 Blaster's need
3 Critic __ Louise Huxtable
4 Messy place
5 Waste maker, proverbially
6 Electrical letters
7 Carefree outing
8 Most guileful
9 In plain view
10 In itself
11 Coax with flattery
12 Tree that exudes gum arabic
13 Unlike instant coffee
21 Egg on
22 Name tag word
23 Listening device
24 Is in the hole
25 Huff and puff
29 *Exodus* hero
30 Tubular pasta
33 Take a whack
34 San Luis __, Calif.
35 Not in the pink
37 Man of many morals
38 Comedian's bit
39 40-Down, for one
40 "The Galloping Gourmet"
44 Salty sauce
45 Render harmless
46 "That's a lie!"

47 Brought out
48 Enthusiastic about
49 Turkey's capital
51 "Not to worry!"
52 Scold mildly
54 Go on the fritz
56 Filmdom's Grant
57 Actress Kudrow
61 Take a load off
62 Krazy ___ of old comics
63 Like a wallflower

IN THE PAPERS

Across

1 Like the Marx Brothers
7 Bandy words
11 Playground
14 Take wing
15 Money since 2002
16 "Bravo, torero!"
17 Backbone
20 Descartes's "therefore"
21 Steeple swinger
22 Not saying much
23 Comedian Louis
24 __ mode
25 Recommend publicly
27 Victorian novel, e.g.
32 Don't exist
36 Hide the gray, say
37 Walked upon
38 Long skirt
39 Journalists, collectively
41 Grebe or grackle
42 Nursery school, for short
43 "For __ a jolly . . ."
44 Full of dandelions
45 Ranch house's lack
49 Have stamina
50 Maiden-named
51 Rack item, briefly
54 Like cheering crowds
57 Interval on a scale
59 Sight in an OPEC land
60 "The," to a grammarian
63 Keebler baker, in ads
64 "__ Fire" (Springsteen hit)
65 Grease monkey's container
66 Rejections
67 iPhone programs
68 Spreads apart

Down

1 Master hand
2 New York's __ Fisher Hall
3 Mournful melody
4 Roman called "The Censor"
5 Gorged on
6 Bit of rock
7 Beach ball balancer
8 Playthings on strings
9 Parabolic path
10 Discover by digging
11 Guided vacation
12 Charitable gift
13 Word before splicing or therapy
18 Be a parent to
19 1970 Beatles chart-topper
24 To the point
26 Lofty lines
28 Words of clarification
29 One of five "Greats"
30 Clothesline, e.g.
31 MacDonald's partner in old movies
32 Current units
33 Like some stamps or steaks
34 One hired by a corp. board
35 Composer Rimsky-Korsakov
39 Advanced degs.
40 Weary motorist's oasis
44 Slingshot shape
46 C.S. Lewis's land

47 Fit to serve
48 Printers' proofs
51 Place of pilgrimage
52 Put to rest, as fears
53 Secluded valleys
54 Yemeni port
55 Move, informally
56 Does in, slangily
58 Some perfect scores
59 Shortz of *Wordplay*
61 Misbehaving tot
62 Word of advice

DISNEY AND DAT

Across

1 Go together, colorwise
6 The Crimson Tide, for short
10 Links standard
13 "Am not!" rejoinder
14 Flower part
15 DC's Pennsylvania, for one: Abbr.
16 *The Apprentice* star
18 WWE win
19 Te-___ (cigar brand)
20 Atkins or South Beach
21 Just got by
23 Jack Dempsey, "The ___ Mauler"
25 Ceremonial staff bearer
26 The Yankees' #7
30 Boston skater
33 TV's ___ & *Clark*
34 Motorists' org.
35 "Fan dancer" Sally
36 Olympic skiing champ Alberto
38 Barbecue rod
39 Egg: Prefix
40 Prefix with marketing
41 Holds a session
42 *Good Will Hunting* actress
46 Nemo creator Jules
47 To no extent
51 Worldwide relief org.
53 *American* ___ (Fox TV hit)
54 Post-ER place
55 ___ "King" Cole
56 Henry James heroine
59 Put into service

60 Track shapes
61 *Oliver Twist* villain
62 Alfred E. Neuman's magazine
63 Marshy areas
64 Idyllic settings

Down

1 *Call Me* ___ (Berlin musical)
2 Coffee allure
3 Mortise mate
4 Civil War initials
5 Doesn't release
6 Ernie's *Sesame Street* pal
7 *The Simpsons* storekeeper
8 Musical based on the songs of Abba
9 Andean wool sources
10 Data storage medium, on old computers
11 Gung-ho
12 Slots city
14 T-bone, e.g.
17 Frisbee or checker
22 Cozy room
24 In the center of
25 "Butt out!", initially
27 Fudd of cartoondom
28 Café au ___
29 Gobbles down
30 ___ Bones (Sleepy Hollow bully)
31 Sitarist Shankar
32 Like a party crasher
36 Britney Spears, once
37 "Ye" follower, on shoppe signs
38 Medical fluids
40 Bored by

41 Insurance company pitched by Snoopy

43 Japanese computer giant

44 Auto racer A.J. Foyt won four

45 "Va-va-__!"

48 Lower part of a hull

49 Strand in winter, maybe

50 Lefts and rights

51 E pluribus __

52 Apollo 13 org.

53 Archipelago units: Abbr.

57 Bond creator Fleming

58 Young fellow

ABDOMINABLE

Across

1 Gave false hope to
6 Tout's offering
9 Misbehave
14 Dean Martin song subject
15 "Bullet," in poker slang
16 Water park slide
17 Hack novel
19 Frost-covered
20 Had a corrosive effect on
21 Sound system components
23 Last letters, in London
24 Election winners
26 Set eyes on
27 Western alliance initials
29 Looking peaked
31 And others: Abbr.
34 NO U TURN et al.
37 Dew, e.g.
39 Buckeye's sch.
40 What the first parts of this puzzle's theme entries are synonyms for
43 Org. once headed by Bush 41
44 Off-season baseball news, slangily
46 Mr. Schindler
48 Storybook starter
49 Eagle plus two
50 Caught on to
51 Wagering sites, for short
53 Enjoy Vail
55 Sparkling wine city
59 Sack time

62 Film or sculpture, e.g.
64 *Cheers* waitress
65 Splashy dive
67 Jimmy of the *Daily Planet*
68 Hoppy brew
69 Chaucer pilgrim
70 Abandoned-lot growth
71 Zippo
72 Ford flop

Down

1 Capital at 12,000 feet
2 Overdo it onstage
3 Acted grandmotherly
4 "Pretty Woman" Singer Roy
5 Former Dodge model
6 Eagle's grabber
7 It may be sold in blocks
8 Guilty one, in cop-speak
9 Farm units
10 Gift that sprouts
11 Cosmetic abdominal surgery
12 Lone Star State sch.
13 Crosswalk users, for short
18 "How sweet ___!"
22 Museum artifact
25 Boils gently
28 Mgr.'s aide
30 Mauna ___
32 La Scala highlight
33 Father of Cordelia
34 Area of London or Manhattan
35 "Help ___ the way!"
36 Chance for an easy A
38 "Scat, cat!"
41 ___-turvy

42 Egg cells
45 Avoided a trial
47 Provided with workers
50 "You go, __!"
52 Pintos, e.g.
54 Superman's birth name
56 Golf club parts
57 Hoard of treasure
58 Urge forward
59 Garbage hauler
60 Revolutionary hero Nathan
61 Diplomat Abba

63 Radial for a Jaguar, e.g.
66 Inventor Whitney

HIT ME!

Across

1 Makes joints, as in metal
6 __ Jim (snack sausage)
10 Oz creator L. Frank __
14 Native Alaskan
15 Bat Masterson's weapon
16 Forearm bone
17 Replay feature
18 Has a bug
19 Radar image
20 Like the stereotypical umpire
23 Time to give up?
24 Toddler's glassful
25 *I Love Lucy* episodes, now
28 Blusterer
32 Newsman Sevareid
33 The color of honey
36 Environmentalist's prefix
37 Show with Annette, Cubby et al., with "The"
41 NATO member
42 Scolds, with "out"
43 Routine learning
44 Year-end temps
46 Embroidery yarn
48 "Take __ a compliment"
50 *American Gothic* painter Grant
51 Begin working
56 Tabloid fodder
57 "__ me in!"
58 Make amends
60 Like some vaccines
61 Dudley Do-Right's girl
62 Religious principle
63 Choice word
64 Vein yields
65 Beats by a hair

Down

1 Is no longer
2 Cinders of old comics
3 Most August babies
4 Accidental success
5 Like a fence's wares
6 Barely sufficient
7 __-back (easygoing)
8 Acquired relative
9 Voice mails, e-mails, et al.
10 Good ol' boys
11 __ breve (music marking)
12 Mil or mile
13 Tour book feature
21 Social connections
22 In the know
25 Storytelling uncle
26 IRA-establishing legislation
27 Costa __
29 "Look out __!"
30 Sharp as a tack
31 Lonesome George of early TV
33 Sawboneses' org.
34 Popular tattoo word
35 Urban transport
38 Poetry Muse
39 Ambiguous answer
40 Entered in black ink, perhaps
45 Football great Y.A.
46 Comedian Bill, briefly
47 Reposition, as tires

6/24/20 15 min

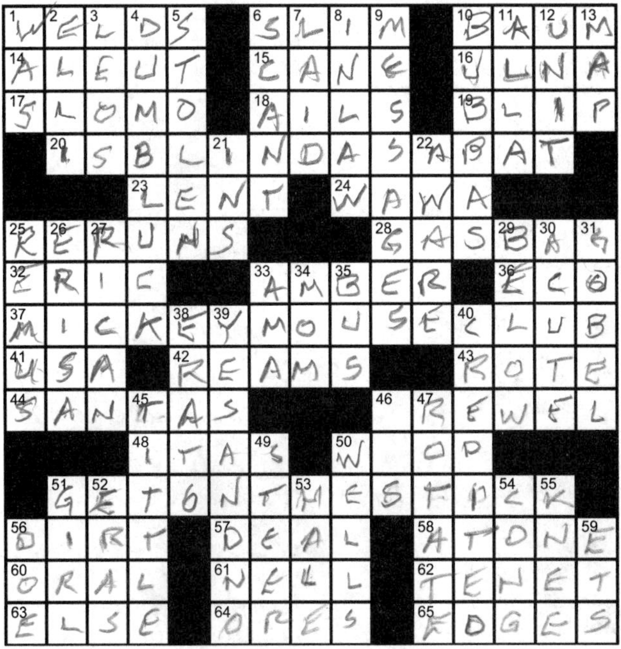

49 Beef on the hoof
50 Wishers' spots
51 Lassie
52 Bull pen stats
53 In the pink
54 Viet ___
55 Dummy's perch
56 Anonymous John
59 Sci-fi visitors

AFTER WORDS

Across

1 Sat for a shot
6 Flash of brilliance
10 Sign of Aries
13 Higher than
14 In the neighborhood
15 Mah-jongg piece
16 Candy in a roll
18 "We try harder" company
19 Caused to jump
20 Honshu port
21 Did laps
22 Cloaks
24 Where Bowie fell
28 "Rug"
30 Air travelers' annoyances
32 Colonial bug
33 Donkey pin-on
37 Try to slim down
38 *The Sopranos* restaurateur
40 Kid in *Blondie* comics
41 Beauty queen's wear
42 Brenda who sang "I'm Sorry"
43 Virginia suburb of DC
45 Romeo and Juliet, e.g.
48 Sling missile
49 Scattered, as seeds
52 Indy service area
54 Orange container
55 Custodial staff
60 Act the nomad
61 What violence or obscenity might have, in movies
63 Currier's partner
64 Dixie bread
65 Gladiator's workplace
66 Sword's superior, in a saying
67 Gung-ho
68 Theater sections

Down

1 They hang together
2 "In memoriam" item
3 Napper's spot
4 Partner of anon
5 Totally trash
6 Cook up
7 Owner's paper
8 Vulcan's pointy body part
9 "___ gratia artis"
10 One in a love triangle
11 Much the same
12 Flat formations
15 Coke vs. Pepsi event, e.g.
17 In the style of
20 Free throw's point value
22 City bond, informally
23 More suitable
24 Tacks on
25 *Star Wars* princess
26 Brewpub brews
27 High school problem-solving team
29 Shoot-'em-up
31 Soothing stuff
34 Choir member
35 "___ a roll!"
36 Lacking a partner
39 Marsh plant
44 Of summer

46 Have a tab

47 __ out (in a fog)

49 Rx, for short

50 Discovered treasure

51 Poe avian

53 Tattooist's supply

55 "Woodstock" songwriter Mitchell

56 Source of poi

57 Designer Cassini

58 Old Anglo-Saxon letter

59 Salty seven

61 Masseur's workplace

62 __ lane (carpoolers' convenience)

IN THE FICTION AISLE

Across

1 "Anywhere but here" acronym
6 À la mode
10 Part of a parachute
14 Like very much
15 Life-saving firefighter
16 Bridge maven Sharif
17 Spanish or Italian
20 The Hatfields or the McCoys
21 Cleopatra biter
22 Like many beach bums
23 Malicious gossip
25 Siege site
26 Heady order
29 Unidentifiable entrée
34 "That's it!"
36 Chow down
37 "By logic, then . . ."
38 Aleutian island
39 Euro fractions
41 Mujahedin land
42 Stadium replaced by Citi Field
43 Bullfight bravo
44 Govt. bill
45 Distressing experience
49 Business owner's dreaded ink color
50 Green Gables girl
51 Trite theatrics
53 Show signs of
56 __ standstill
57 FEMA recommendation, briefly
61 Omelet on bread
64 Cleveland's lake
65 Gray of *Buck Rogers in the 25th Century*
66 Hello from Honolulu
67 Stood up
68 Certain Scandinavian
69 Tippecanoe's mate

Down

1 Drug dealer's nemesis
2 The golden calf was one
3 Manhattan cultural ctr.
4 Cattle identifier
5 Japanese currency
6 Tool holders
7 "S.O.S.!"
8 Investor's option, for short
9 Twists out of shape
10 Eager joiner's comment
11 Land on the Arabian Sea
12 All the __ (wildly popular)
13 Scott who sued for his freedom
18 Grant of *Notorious*
19 City on Lake Michigan
24 "I think," succinctly
25 Remarkable achievement
26 Make ashamed
27 Art print, for short
28 Big PC key
30 Principle
31 Debugger's target
32 Banded stone
33 __ up (got in shape)
35 Written assurance
39 Trapped, in a way

40 "What __ is new?"

44 Norse war god

46 A Grimm beginning?

47 Gas pump number

48 Speckled horse

52 As of late

53 Water server

54 __ Beach, Fla.

55 Fertility goddess

56 X, __ "xylophone"

58 Old fiddle

59 Persistent pain

60 Blacken, as steak

62 Shooters' grp.

63 "Who __?" (New Orleans Saints fans' chant)

HOTEL AMENITIES

Across

1 Eva of *Green Acres*
6 Aspen gear
10 Salty spot
14 Kate's sitcom pal
15 Ox-drawn vehicle
16 Bus. school course
17 Minnesota Fats, e.g.
19 *Nautilus* skipper
20 Leave port
21 House style of New England
23 In order
25 In need
26 Office honchos
30 Brand for Fido
32 Fall back
35 Some iPhone messages
36 Martian or Venusian
37 "All the Things You ___"
38 Test the weight of
39 Really steamed
40 Related by blood
41 Get grayer
42 Escorted to one's seat
43 Dutch artist Jan
44 Slangy denial
45 Pindaric pieces
46 Like clear night skies
47 Molecule builder
49 Pueblo tribe
51 ___ status (questionnaire item)
54 Where nautical cable is wound
59 River of Hamburg
60 Classroom prankster's missile
62 Air Wick target
63 A sister of Bart Simpson
64 Vehicles for VIPs
65 Boer and Crimean
66 The Emerald Isle, to poets
67 Idyllic settings

Down

1 Breaks in continuity
2 Natural soother
3 Rorschach image
4 Some paintings
5 Spruce up the walls, maybe
6 La ___ (opera house)
7 Mary ___ cosmetics
8 Ticks off
9 Short on cash
10 Slowly, on a score
11 Party warmer-upper
12 Early TV crooner Perry
13 The "K" of James K. Polk
18 Fish tales
22 Bird on Canada's dollar
24 Around 6, say
26 *Borstal Boy* author Brendan
27 Last Greek letter
28 Place of refuge
29 Remain unused
31 Claim on property
33 Prickly plant
34 Jack, the tightwad
36 White House worker
39 Rhode Island's state tree
40 "Now ___ theater near you!"
42 Rioter's take
43 Paint with dots

46 Rigging support
48 Org. chart levels
50 Huge expanse
51 ___ Mix (cat food brand)
52 Pierce player
53 Beast's abode
55 Lost traction
56 Easy to manage
57 Unnamed auth.
58 Legendary loch
61 Air pump letters

SPREADING THE WORD

Across

1 Sea east of the Caspian
5 Stereotypical hobo fare
9 Perry's aide
14 Buster's bulldog
15 Basilica area
16 Inventor Howe
17 Urban thoroughfares: Abbr.
18 Electric co., for one
19 Architectural drawings
20 One way to spread the word
23 Chip giant
24 Eur. airline
25 Like white water
29 Sandy expanse
34 PC's "brain"
37 Cut at a 45-degree angle
39 Garfield's foil
40 One way to spread the word
44 Feverish chill
45 One-named New Ager
46 Place to surf
47 Charts anew
50 Simple kind of question
52 Shepherd's place
54 Napoleon, on Elba
58 One way to spread the word
64 Jazz keyboardist Chick
65 Like a church mouse
66 Arp's genre
67 Save up
68 *Bus Stop* dramatist
69 New Haven collegians
70 Al ___ (pasta order)
71 Genesis son
72 1/1 song ender

Down

1 Pong maker
2 Torn apart
3 Bond or Smart
4 Flatt of bluegrass
5 Give the brush-off to
6 Mr. Hulot's creator
7 Devil's doings
8 Wishers' places
9 Boot from office
10 Raines of old films
11 Fact fudger
12 Touch the tarmac
13 Dummkopf
21 Bowie's last stand
22 Good, in the 'hood
26 More, musically
27 ___-bitty
28 Commuter's headache
30 Impresario Hurok
31 Perfect place
32 Bar mitzvah, e.g.
33 Dry run
34 Burn a bit
35 Summon via beeper
36 Word on a dime
38 Lacoste of tennis
41 Bust-making org.
42 Ques. response
43 Of higher quality
48 Tot's "magic word"
49 Red or Dead

51 Rust and tarnish
53 Savory jelly
55 The Tiber's land
56 Ushered through the door
57 Prepare for reuse, perhaps
58 "___, James!"
59 '80s foe of Iraq
60 Take it easy
61 Hawaiian coffee center
62 Jellystone Park bear
63 Small songbird
64 No-goodnik

THREE VIRTUES

Across

1 Gild, say
6 Trombone part
11 Killer snake
14 Paul of *American Graffiti*
15 Gondola guide
16 News initials
17 One who professes to cure through ritual
19 Plating metal
20 Throw in a chip
21 Landers of advice
22 *Cheers* bartender Sam
24 Sentry's word
26 Did a new parent's task
27 Aim high
30 Ray of *The Rat Pack*
33 Amount bet
34 Hockey thug
35 Half a score
38 Never say die
42 Flock mother
43 Ship of 1492
44 Zellweger of *My One and Only*
45 Makes even shorter
48 Like many company cars
49 Urge forward
51 Potential juror
52 Of France
54 Took the trophy
55 University town in Iowa
59 "Heart of Dixie": Abbr.
60 Philanthropic event
63 U-Haul rental
64 Toys with tails
65 Kate's TV roommate
66 Gaze at
67 Public row
68 __ out (apportioned)

Down

1 __ Romeo (sporty auto)
2 Faculty head
3 Forget to include
4 Bad news for utilities customers
5 This word has no vowels
6 All tuckered out
7 Bank offering
8 "Well, __ be"
9 Judge to be
10 Off the mark
11 Mechanical men
12 Place for a title
13 Had a yen
18 In the pink
23 Long. crosser
25 Plane figure
27 Netman Arthur
28 Pack in the hold
29 Classroom missile, perhaps
30 Pork or beef cuts
31 Island near Mull
32 Switch positions
34 Horse's pace
36 Olympics blade
37 Scholarship factor
39 Bearded antelope
40 Shoe shaper
41 Within earshot
46 Electric swimmer

47 PC mouse actions
48 Fronted, in a way
49 "__ at the office"
50 Language of Kuala Lumpur
51 Model's forte
53 All the rage
54 St. Paul's architect
56 Soda shop treat
57 Writer Wiesel
58 Vehicle on runners
61 Absorbed, as a loss
62 Thanksgiving vegetable

BENCHWARMERS

Across

1 "On the contrary!"
6 She, at sea
10 Out of room
14 At attention
15 Catherine, the last wife of Henry VIII
16 Big atlas section
17 Operating room aide
19 Mtge. adjustment
20 Follow closely
21 Sitcom planet
22 Less overcast
24 Abner's old radio partner
26 Sahara rarity
27 Baseball contract feature challenged by Curt Flood
33 Othello's people
35 Place for icicles
36 Vintage auto
37 Assns.
38 Frat members
39 Israeli diplomat Abba
40 Fannie __
41 Hoops player
42 Stockpile
43 It might be labeled "B"
46 Pirate Lafitte
47 Ugly as __
48 Extends, in a way
51 ". . . __ of thee"
53 Utah ski site
57 Co. bigwig
58 Post office branch, perhaps
61 Angry to-do
62 Fast-shrinking sea
63 Mail, as payment
64 Little 'uns
65 Sovereign address
66 Superstars, to fans

Down

1 Avian home
2 Shamu, e.g.
3 Garr or Polo
4 Some oarsmen
5 Gambling spot, in brief
6 Cowboy boot attachment
7 __ back (return to a previous point)
8 Destination for a W-2
9 Book introductions
10 Hot breakfast fare
11 Manual reader, say
12 "Get a __!"
13 Bandit's refuge
18 Iditarod's finish
23 Is indisposed
25 Enterprise letters
26 April 18, 1775 rider
27 Synonym compiler
28 Gipp portrayer
29 Catering hall parker
30 Densely packed, in a way
31 Salton and Sargasso
32 Years and years
33 NYC gallery
34 Nonwritten exam
38 Bull Run, to the South
39 Came forth

41 Shell team
42 *Kim* horse trader
44 Removes, as a CD
45 "Hey there!"
48 Mark on a score
49 Trade fair
50 Clean and orderly
51 Way up a mountain
52 Sunny vacation spot
54 Bride and groom's vehicle
55 Slave away

56 Bugs in a hill
59 Geller with a psychic act
60 *Exodus* hero

FIXING A HOLE

Across

1 Mattress innards
6 Pyramid bottom
10 Artsy Big Apple area
14 Bovine milk source
15 Opera highlight
16 Grace ender
17 It's found in a crust
19 YOU ARE ___
20 Politician's goal
21 Moth-eaten
22 South American plains
24 Baylor University city
26 Seal in, as a steak's juices
27 Aid for one kicking a smoking habit
32 Golfer's set
34 Word after dog or salad
35 Reporter's question
36 Tennis great Björn
37 Sub part
39 Flag down
40 An end to alcohol?
41 Pepper dispenser
42 Vito Corleone's eldest
43 Bit of unabashed self-promotion
47 City near Provo, Utah
48 Produces cackleberries
49 Like a wasteland
52 Did a 10K
53 Prima donnas' problems
57 Where to get off
58 Largest of Ireland's 32

61 Cinders of old funnies
62 Cut and paste
63 Rumba or samba
64 "Cold one"
65 Declare untrue
66 Ending with home or bed

Down

1 Recipe measures
2 *Garfield* pooch
3 Light bulb, in comics
4 Liberal faction
5 ___ Lanka
6 Something to cast
7 Like Death Valley
8 Thing to confess
9 Keen observer
10 Much of North Africa
11 Straw in the wind
12 Ticker-tape parade honoree, perhaps
13 White Monopoly bills
18 Plumb crazy
23 Miler's quartet, often
25 Rm. coolers
26 Go bananas
27 ___ Jean (Marilyn, originally)
28 Worshiped ones
29 Country music tone
30 Goatee's spot
31 Like Toledo?
32 Hieroglyphics bird
33 ___ Hashanah
37 Hushed up
38 Skelton's Kadiddlehopper
39 Indoor kitty

41 "A __ formality!"
42 Like a fox
44 Pestle's partner
45 Like italic type
46 Breathe hard
49 English TV channel, with "The"
50 Wheel shaft
51 Stir up
52 Totally destroy
54 Sold, to an auctioneer
55 Black and white predator
56 Depot posting, informally

59 Poem of Sappho
60 Gridiron divs.

HAIR'S HOW

Across

1. *The Sound of Music* setting
5. April 1 victim
9. Cloak or boa
13. 20–0 baseball score, e.g.
14. Language of Delhi
15. Take on
16. "Hottest spot north of Havana," in song
17. *My Fair Lady* horse race
18. Chief Norse god
19. Moses was commanded to do this
22. "Watch it!"
23. Agile deer
24. Self-sacrificing type
28. Chowder morsel
30. "I __ Rock"
33. Bailiwick
34. Drop a line
35. Word after gender or generation
36. Do a detective's work
40. "Just __ am . . ."
41. Like a tough guy's voice
42. Give the evil eye
43. Opposing prohibition
44. Alias of Romain de Tirtoff
45. Proper to a fault
47. In the dumps
48. Additionally
49. Perform up to snuff
56. *SNL* alum Carvey
57. Roomy skirt
58. Was clad in
60. Bad to the bone
61. Idaho, e.g., informally
62. Bakery need
63. Big bash
64. *Citizen Kane*'s Rosebud, e.g.
65. Like a dirty old man

Down

1. Slo-pitch path
2. Aerial maneuver
3. Stage after larva
4. Sheriff's symbol
5. Arousing suspicion
6. "Just this __ . . ."
7. "P.U.!" elicitor
8. Well-read folks
9. TV's __ *Line Is It Anyway?*
10. Tilt-A-Whirl, e.g.
11. "Caro nome," e.g.
12. Check endorser's need
14. Bigoted one
20. Biblical possessive
21. Like the Taj Mahal
24. Brightly plumed parrot
25. Came up
26. "Please __" (invoice request)
27. "Running" amount
28. Brunch offering
29. *History of Rome* author
30. Moorehead of *Bewitched*
31. Fends off with a spray
32. Playful copying
34. All-star game team, maybe
37. Be generous, at a bar
38. Construction crew
39. "Boola Boola" collegian
45. Perplexing problem

46 "Hogwash!"
47 Days-old
48 Like pianos and engines, ideally
49 Place to hibernate
50 Joule or ampere
51 Airline founded in 1948
52 Teeny arachnid
53 Mil. no-show
54 Gad about
55 Took from the deck
56 Slangy "excellent"
59 Cut funding to

RING JOB

Across

1 Artist Chagall
5 Dogie snaggers
11 Compadre of Fidel
14 Kitchen tubful
15 Just about
16 You can take it or beat it
17 Place for a napkin ring
19 Hoppy brew
20 Signs over
21 Sage one
23 Cop's stunner
26 Fraternity P
28 Blows to smithereens
29 Haight-Ashbury crowd of yore
31 Slow down
33 Scenery chewer
34 Steno's group
35 $200 Monopoly squares: Abbr.
38 Suffix with go or two
39 Hightailed it
41 Bastille Day's mo.
42 Vietnamese holiday
43 Celebration suffix
44 Go over the wall
47 Noted Big Apple restaurateur
49 Strong-armed
50 Wolfgang Puck's eatery
52 Poker champ Ungar
54 Movie shots
55 PTA part
57 Most Al Jazeera viewers
59 St. crosser
60 Place for the Tweed Ring

65 Thieves' hideout
66 Cosby's "fat" guy
67 Buffalo's lake
68 Period to remember
69 Some car deals
70 Shoulder muscle, briefly

Down

1 Snappy dresser, in the '60s
2 2001 Will Smith biopic
3 Toon Chihuahua
4 Ad campaign start
5 Kitchen fat
6 Takes in or lets out
7 Broadway success
8 Cry hard
9 Capital on a fjord
10 Of the breastbone
11 Place for a decoder ring
12 Berry of *Monster's Ball*
13 Olympics blades
18 Like Stephen King novels
22 Diving bird
23 Grand ___ auto
24 Anouk of film
25 Place for a boxing ring
27 Bassoon's cousin
30 Pulled a boner
32 Glitzy Beverly Hills Drive
34 Int. rate
36 Delhi bread
37 Flexible Flyers, e.g.
40 Without guarantees
43 ___ lobe (brain part)
45 Save for future use
46 Attended without invitation

48 The big 4-0, for example
49 Arrow poison
50 Sleuth Sam
51 One of a road crew
53 Breaks at the ranch
56 Suspicious story
58 Colonial bugs
61 Wharton deg.
62 "___ you nuts?"
63 Al Capp diminutive
64 Tennis do-over

WATCH WHERE YOU'RE GOING

Across

1 Newspaper opinion pages
6 Deluxe sheet material
11 Perp prosecutors, briefly
14 Admiral's force
15 Word with grand or soap
16 Mine treasure
17 Quarterback option (follow directions!)
19 Take the gold
20 Classic cars
21 Vocal qualities
23 Wrestling duo
27 What 23-Acrosses do
29 Ventura County city
30 South-of-the-border nap
31 Does not mention
32 Clear the stubble
33 Since 1/1, to a CPA
36 Hardly racy
37 Goatees' locales
38 Barbra's *Funny Girl* costar
39 ___-Cat (winter vehicle)
40 Nursery purchase
41 Ones nearby
42 Reef formers
44 Fake-outs
45 Of the past
47 Stands for
48 Puerto Rican port city
49 Caldwell's *Tobacco* ___
50 Simile words
51 Side roads (follow directions!)

58 Sales pro
59 Family emblem
60 Prefix with -hedron
61 Play about Capote
62 Clinton-era cat
63 Get-go

Down

1 Out of sync
2 Mideast gp.
3 Always, poetically
4 Morning drops
5 Long lookers
6 City destroyed by fire and brimstone
7 iPhone downloads
8 Oolong, e.g.
9 4/15 inits.
10 Tennis great Ilie
11 Partial outlay (follow directions!)
12 Disney mermaid
13 Have a gut feeling
18 Go for a part
22 Make a choice
23 Whistle blasts
24 Lumberjack
25 On the rise (follow directions!)
26 ___ St. Ives (English museum)
27 Jack's fairy-tale foe
28 Guns, as an engine
30 They may get splints
32 Source of oil
34 Nibble on
35 Muumuu, e.g.
37 Non-chatty sort
38 Buckeye State

40 Rectory figures
41 Looks after
43 Like non-Rx drugs
44 Heroic deed
45 Eyeball-bending work
46 Luckless one
47 College digs
49 Smell something fierce
52 As well
53 List-shortening abbr.
54 Barbie's doll
55 Small change: Abbr.

56 "What ___ the odds?"
57 Face the hurler

GETTING IN YOUR HAIR

Across

1 Burns flick of 1977
6 Privateer's potation
10 Appliance letters
14 Handy's ___ *Street Blues*
15 *All in the Family* producer Norman
16 Completely botch
17 Ecdysiast's act
19 Florence's river
20 Delectable dish
21 Corn morsel
23 Bring up from the minors
26 Ungentlemanly sort
27 Lode load
28 Billy Joel's "___ to Extremes"
29 Instrument popular in zydeco music
33 Pizza perimeter
35 Met melody
36 Poetic dusks
39 Skating legend Sonja
40 PX frequenters
41 Like fresh concrete
42 Sundance's girlfriend
43 FedExed, say
44 Like Peary's expeditions
45 Prohibited, in a way
48 "Give ___ whirl!"
49 Mean mutt
51 Response to a ques.
52 Surveyor's support
54 Tack on
56 Battery type
58 Used the cuspidor
59 Minor crises
64 Forked-tailed flier
65 Having the know-how
66 Start of an Irish refrain
67 Madrid Ms.
68 Steam up
69 Tough to climb

Down

1 Out-of-date: Abbr.
2 ___ up (angry)
3 Long-snouted fish
4 Three-time batting champ Tony
5 Remove hair from
6 Watkins ___, NY
7 Pore over
8 Western treaty gp.
9 Windward Islands nation
10 Omani or Qatari
11 Sneer
12 Roadside eatery
13 100 smackers
18 Soft end of the Mohs scale
22 Infamous Amin
23 Nouveau ___
24 Plumed wader
25 Opposite number
26 Monte ___ sandwich
30 B-ball players
31 Kind of gasket
32 Vintner's prefix
34 *The King and I* land
37 "Peachy-keen!"
38 Fine fiddle, for short

41 Gliders' boosters
43 Seafarer's obstacle
46 Roll-on name
47 Inscribe with acid
49 Playbill listings
50 Less desirable berth
53 Blitherer
55 Sicilian spouter
56 Amounting to nothing
57 Therapist's response
60 Sacrifice-fly stat
61 Name in a 1973 decision

62 Prior to, in old times
63 Syrup source

SUITS ME FINE

Across

Across

1 Dallas hoopsters, for short
5 Crick in the neck, e.g.
10 Some flies or bunts, for short
14 *Village Voice* award
15 Pantyhose color
16 Obstinate sort
17 Book protection
19 "Zip-___-Doo-Dah"
20 Attendance fig., often
21 Source of iron
22 Samurai, for one
24 Fits out with biker's garb, perhaps
27 Ashe Stadium do-over
28 Power holders
29 Fox hunters' calls
34 Whimpers
37 ___-mutuel
38 Quince or pear
39 Kaffiyeh wearer
40 Stand-up kind of guy
41 Sutherland song
42 Socks complement
43 Did a takeoff on
44 Airborne annoyances
45 City legislators
47 Like much Cajun cuisine
48 Forum greeting
49 Scoring attempt, of sorts
54 President with a Kitchen Cabinet
58 Sheet music abbreviation
59 Reveal, in poetry
60 Zoning measure
61 Very small
64 Hart, for one
65 Conjure up
66 Prefix with nautical
67 Sidewalk stand libations
68 Take the plunge again
69 Cannon of *Ally McBeal*

Down

1 Runway strutter
2 Treat like dirt
3 Panoramic view
4 Several reps, in the weight room
5 Pre-fight psych jobs
6 Rug wearer-outer
7 Razor-billed bird
8 Gush out
9 Like the rare-earth elements
10 Wisenheimer
11 Automaker that made the Quattro
12 *Pinocchio* goldfish
13 Carson's Carnac, for one
18 Artist Jasper
23 Fam. member
25 Overtime periods
26 Pollen-bearing organs
30 Bone-dry
31 Circle dance
32 Pass over
33 Ross and Bering
34 One of a bear trio
35 River to the Caspian
36 Placed down
37 Castel Gandolfo resident

40 Visited

44 Sign with a major league team, say

46 Mobile vacation homes, for short

47 Performed like a Marx

50 Deli pancake

51 Obviously contrived

52 *The Magic Flute*, e.g.

53 Grand ___ (Wyoming peak)

54 Actress Pinkett of *The Nutty Professor*

55 Sailed through

56 Native Canadian

57 Campbell of *Scream*

62 Boar's mate

63 No-goodnik

HUNKS O'CHEESE

Across

1. Eligible for Mensa
6. Cook in a wok
9. Landscaper's tool
14. Half a 45
15. Philosopher ___-tse
16. Three-time AL batting champ Tony
17. Highway barricade
19. Quietly understood
20. ___ Paulo, Brazil
21. ___ Sabe
23. Krazy ___ of comics
24. Make available
28. Thief's crime
30. Aches and pains
32. Uncool sort
33. Bridge expert Culbertson
34. Low-budget pads, for short
36. Brake components
39. Smooth-talking
41. Cast-of-thousands films
43. Voting coalition
44. Good ___ (fixed)
46. Zero-star fare
47. Lyricist Gershwin
48. Glitzy, like some rock music
50. Came to the top
53. Wealthy widow
56. Boat steerers
57. Smelter input
58. Cut and paste
60. End of Ripley's slogan
61. Down source
63. Gymnastic feat
68. Elephant gone amok
69. Outer: Prefix
70. Went for congers
71. Dummy Mortimer
72. Barbecue morsel
73. Croupiers' tools

Down

1. Ukraine, once: Abbr.
2. "O Sole ___"
3. Letters on a toothpaste tube
4. Moses parted it
5. Chaucer's ___ Inn
6. Mr. Ziegfeld
7. Lamb cut
8. Li'l Abner, e.g.
9. Went for a drive
10. Suffix with scram
11. Characteristic of a duffer's drive, often
12. Bottled water name
13. Moth-eaten
18. One of TV's *Jeffersons*
22. Checker, e.g.
24. Ohm's symbol
25. Goes sprawling
26. Crowd-penetrating police formation
27. Cops collar them
29. Nursery item
31. Makes filthy
35. Jamboree attendee
37. Apple gadget
38. A whole bunch
40. Lugosi of film

42 100-meter race, e.g.
45 Played a quinella, say
49 Rx item
51 "___ power" (hippie's slogan)
52 Tennis great Gibson
53 Active sorts
54 Celestial hunter
55 Kitchen extruder
59 Fare carrier
62 Where Lux. is
64 Knock over, in a way
65 Bugling beast

66 Shoebox marking
67 Mormons, initially

ZIPPING ALONG

Across

1 Zip along
4 Copperfield's field
9 D-Day beachhead
13 Wally of cookie fame
15 Playground retort
16 Prefix with phone or bucks
17 Air show stunt
19 Loser to Braddock
20 Arrange by type
21 Old-timer
23 "The Waste Land" monogram
24 Crack the books
27 Bird's buoyancy aid
30 Nighttime reading lights
32 Ben-___
33 Showed partisanship
36 Warner ___
37 Nintendo competitor
38 Saudi Arabia neighbor
39 Anglican topper
40 Hawaiian necklaces
41 Act the mother hen
42 Little Sheba's creator
43 Low-calorie brews
44 "Sort of" suffix
45 Not allowed out
47 Optimally
49 Cheers barfly
50 Navigator's need
53 Nebraska's largest city
55 One-celled creature
57 Bangkok native
59 Pest control, of a sort
62 Witch's blemish
63 Run-of-the-mill
64 With "the" and 65-Across, pull an upset
65 See 64-Across
66 Gentle gallops
67 Rap's Run-___

Down

1 Morocco's capital
2 Minutemen's sch.
3 Like Vikings
4 Fountain treat
5 Sheet music abbr.
6 Metro automaker, once
7 Castaway's home
8 Come crashing down
9 Earthy shade
10 Ad buyer's proof of purchase
11 Cake candle count
12 Laugher's syllable
14 Full-house sign
18 Slipped up
22 Put down, on the street
25 White rat, e.g.
26 Tranquilizing weapon
28 Hanna-Barbera's ___ Doggie
29 Lacking couth
30 Uncle ___ (rice brand)
31 Rita of West Side Story
33 Capital of Bulgaria
34 "___ be dreaming!"
35 Odometer locale
37 Lost traction
39 Jolly
43 Helpful theorem

45 Fed. purchasing org.
46 Talks Dixie-style
48 Gives out
50 ___ out (allotted)
51 Crosswise, on a ship
52 Third section, perhaps
54 In addition
56 Pony players' locale, in brief
57 Tandem's capacity
58 Made a fool of
60 "Uh-huh"
61 Oil can letters

EASY GOING

Across

1 Steeple topper
6 Public relations skill
10 Baglike structure
13 Mike with a punch
14 Wahine's dance
15 Triumphant cry
16 Desilu co-founder
17 River to the Baltic
18 Olfactory stimulant
19 "Understand?"
21 Oozy ground
22 Queen or rook
23 Trip up a mountain
25 Burrowing pest
29 Underwater detector
31 1952 Winter Olympics site
32 Wrathful foe of Captain Kirk
34 They're taken to the cleaners
38 Atheist Madalyn Murray __
40 Justice Fortas
41 Bandleader's command
42 Approval power
43 Not as much
45 Equine parent
46 Fields persona
48 Microwave button
50 Cascades peak
53 Valuable rock
54 RC, for one
55 Country on the Gulf of Guinea, as it's commonly known
62 Sparkling wine locale
63 Kelly of TV talk
64 Mrs. Perón
65 Stage after a sunburn
66 '50s British PM Anthony
67 Station wagon alternative
68 Be human
69 Quiz show sound
70 Lewis Carroll critter

Down

1 Just for men
2 Pile to be burned
3 "Winning __ everything"
4 Wander about
5 Digestive aid
6 Point on a prickly plant
7 Autobahn auto
8 Staff symbol
9 Highlander's textile pattern
10 __ Hawkins Day
11 Doll up
12 Sign of insertion
15 *Top Gun* star
20 Thanksgiving meat request
24 Beauty pageant attire part
25 Icky substances
26 Workers' protection agcy.
27 DVD button
28 Start a voyage
29 Cavalry sword
30 Till compartment
33 Fit as a fiddle
35 Medical suffix
36 Tucker out
37 Editing order
39 Etymological basis
44 Light on one's feet

47 Like DNA strands

49 Play time

50 Suffix with land or sea

51 Lout, north of the border

52 Rehem, perhaps

53 Red ape

56 "Veni, __, vici"

57 Not buttoned

58 Place for a roaster

59 Opera set in ancient Egypt

60 Castor or Pollux

61 Fail miserably

ICK!

Across

1 Biblical measure
6 Fail to mention
10 Cooking direction
14 Sports venue
15 Mrs. Dithers of *Blondie*
16 ___-mutuel betting
17 Clean up broken glass, say
20 "Shame!" syllable
21 Tot's "piggies"
22 Battleship in 1898 news
23 Sideshow setting
24 Corporation's constitution
26 Leave high and dry
29 Limerick, e.g.
30 March 17 slogan word
31 Bit of punctuation
32 Greek T
35 Follow up a fried chicken dinner, maybe
39 Adversary
40 Comic Professor Irwin ___
41 *Bus Stop* playwright
42 A great deal
43 Large Andean flier
45 Diacritical marks above vowels
49 Extinct bird of Mauritius
50 Containing gold
51 Tibia or fibula
52 Hyundai competitor
55 Stand firm
59 Baseball's "Slammin' Sammy"
60 Bell-ringing cosmetics company
61 Noted Big Apple restaurateur

62 *Baseball Tonight* network
63 "I win," in chess
64 Some saxes

Down

1 Hook or Kirk: Abbr.
2 *Exodus* author
3 At one's ___ and call
4 Squid's defense
5 Stretch tight
6 Group of eight
7 Mineral hardness scale
8 Wrath
9 Beer source
10 Asparagus unit
11 Quietly understood
12 Castle or Cara
13 Choir's platform
18 Walden, for one
19 1967 Spencer Davis Group hit
23 Propane holder
24 Warm and snug
25 Half: Prefix
26 Egotist's love
27 The Kingston ___
28 Red beans go-with
29 Stands for a sculptor
31 Mint brand
32 Watch over
33 Jason's ship
34 Exploitative type
36 Basie's "One ___ Jump"
37 Lunch time, often
38 NFL Hall of Famer Marchetti
43 Scoop holder
44 Ukrainian port

45 Tricky pool shot
46 Mercury and Saturn, for two
47 Like fresh lettuce
48 Puerto ___
49 "Death Be Not Proud" poet John
51 Italy's shape
52 Russell of *Backdraft*
53 ___-European languages
54 Yard sale proviso
56 Scot's topper
57 Eggs, biologically
58 Guy's sweetie

FOR MEN ONLY

Across

1 Ersatz-fat brand name
6 "__ there, done that"
10 Wild guess
14 Esther of *Good Times*
15 Jai __
16 Huge volume
17 Liar
19 Austen heroine
20 Addison's literary partner
21 Musket attachment?
22 Way off
23 Lee or Grant: Abbr.
25 Shortstop's milieu
27 Breyer's garb
30 The Boy King
32 Jazz singer Laine
33 Former leader of Burma
34 Discharge
36 Politico Specter
39 Religious offshoot
41 Old-fashioned, in a fashionable way
43 Flu fighters
44 No longer available
46 Holier-__-thou
47 Pants problem
48 Ark grouping
50 Language suffix
51 Newcastle's river
52 Pimpernel color
55 Ritz lookalike, once
57 Leading lady Virna
58 "__ Hear a Waltz?"

60 Union issue
64 Last word of an ultimatum
65 Nonsensical
67 Slapstick ammo
68 Carpet cutter's calculation
69 Make amends
70 Like a sourball
71 Time traveler's destination
72 __ out (barely beat)

Down

1 Eyeballs
2 Barbarian
3 Model Macpherson
4 Make a claim
5 1960 Wimbledon champ Fraser
6 Take one's cuts
7 Writer Wiesel
8 Moved carefully
9 Corrosive acid
10 Seafood restaurant bucketful
11 Horseplay
12 Jordan's capital
13 Smith Brother attribute
18 Tuxedo shop customer, often
24 *Network* director Sidney
26 Cookbook phrase
27 Reddish brown
28 Ripe for drafting
29 Blame shifter
31 Church's 10%
35 Totally destroy
37 Leprechaun's home
38 Back of the neck
40 Most misty-eyed
42 Iroquoian language

45 Zilch

49 Bag man?

51 One of the eight in V8

52 Got some rack

53 Eyelashes

54 Start of an Irish refrain

56 No 97-pound weakling

59 Frozen treats

61 Andy's pal

62 Mudville complement

63 Monopoly card

66 Kit ___ (candy brand)

ROMAN AROUND

Across

1 Carson's predecessor
5 Belfry critters
9 Bawdyhouse figure
14 Malta's monetary unit, until 1/1/08
15 Field of expertise
16 "Time is money," e.g.
17 Mideast's Gulf of ___
18 Carrier to Ben-Gurion
19 Four-time Wimbledon champ Rod
20 Carriers of female characteristics?
23 Port of old Rome
24 "Smoking or ___?"
25 Spot for a stopper
29 Muscle-bone connector
34 Toothpaste tube abbr.
37 Finger or toe
39 Jason's craft
40 *Dianetics* author?
44 Prefix meaning "height"
45 Act the coquette
46 Start of a giggle
47 Go back into business
50 It might be broken at the gym
52 As well
54 Score marks
58 Channel for political coverage?
64 Appliance name
65 Agronomist's sample
66 Spanish appetizer
67 Busted, as a perp
68 Desirous deity
69 Estrada or Satie
70 Give this for that
71 "G'bye!"
72 Russo of *Tin Cup*

Down

1 Student of Socrates
2 Hospital helpers
3 "You ___ serious!"
4 Like spoiled butter
5 Heavyweight champ Max
6 He sang about Alice
7 "Twenty-Mule ___ Borax"
8 Where dos are done
9 Hoopster Karl or Moses
10 Economist Smith
11 Garroway of early TV
12 A long time
13 Debussy's "La ___"
21 "Another fine mess" victim
22 W.C. Fields persona
26 Football filler
27 Gershwin's "___ Rhythm"
28 Golf course halves
30 Slap the cuffs on
31 "Phooey!"
32 Mean dude
33 Junction point
34 A long way off
35 Chuck-a-luck need
36 Curly coif
38 Easing of tensions
41 Go one better than
42 "___ it or lose it"
43 Rutherford B. Hayes attribute

48 Simple hydrocarbon
49 ___ TURN (road sign)
51 Lab worker, perhaps
53 Kickoff
55 /, to a kegler
56 One-inch putt, say
57 Charmer's critter
58 Barbra's *Funny Girl* costar
59 Granny
60 Novelist Bagnold
61 *David Copperfield* wife
62 Situation for water cannons

63 Designer Schiaparelli
64 Gallery display

ALLOY OOP

Across

1 Made a choice
6 Salt's "Halt!"
11 1,000 G's
14 *Touched by an Angel* costar
15 Jamaican cultist, for short
16 Duffer's dream
17 Rum/vodka cocktail
19 Actress Vardalos
20 Drives, putts, etc.
21 Smoothing tools
23 A majority of August births
26 For all to see
27 Basketball statistic
32 Comparatively close
34 Pat or Daniel
35 Forearm bone
36 Words before and after "rose"
39 Some third-place finishers
43 Any pass from a QB: Abbr.
44 Get-well spots
45 Oscar winner Marisa
46 Snake sounds
49 They're sometimes blind
50 Computer command after "cut"
52 Sample CD
54 Uses rubber on
56 Final stage, in chess
62 Marina del ___
63 Twangy instrument usually played while seated
66 *A Chorus Line* number
67 Recorded, in a way
68 Leaning slightly, as a ship
69 Cigarette stat
70 Some college finals
71 Café order

Down

1 Planets and such
2 Hair product from Procter & Gamble
3 Symbol of wistfulness
4 "Happy Motoring" gas brand
5 Place for an inkwell
6 Hopped out of bed
7 Mover's rental
8 "Go ahead, shoot!"
9 Notable first for a baby
10 Polk's successor
11 Quirks, say
12 Less welcoming
13 Rock-bottom
18 Tuna ___
22 NYC's Park, e.g.
24 Being rented
25 Impels
27 "Waterloo" pop group
28 Do a laundry chore
29 One who warned Caesar
30 Wayfarer's stop
31 Utters, in Br'er Fox jargon
33 Rte. recommenders
35 Called balls and strikes
37 Let it be, editorially
38 Sale condition
40 Feminine suffix
41 It's put in an env.
42 Letters on a chit

47 The "I" in TGIF
48 Takes care of
49 Pick up, as ice
50 1992 and 1996 also-ran
51 Boxing locale
53 Pinochle plays
55 Marquee name
57 Twofold
58 __ monster
59 Going __ (fighting)
60 Crow's-nest site
61 Alias of Romain de Tirtoff

64 Smog-battling org.
65 Slithery fish

C'S THE DAY

Across

1 KP's peeler
6 Impact sound
10 "Away with you!"
14 Humble home
15 Dance performed in a grass skirt
16 *Anything Goes* composer Porter
17 Volume of a 64-Across of water
19 Where Marco Polo explored
20 One on the losing side in Super Bowl XLV
21 Wide-brimmed hat
23 Texas sch.
25 Like a hedgehog
26 Point the finger at
30 Rated X
33 Form of urban pollution
34 *The Lord of the Rings* hero
35 "I am such a dope!"
38 Fish in bagels
39 Storage battery type
40 Building manager, briefly
41 Inventor Whitney
42 Overcome by ennui
43 Dreads wearer, perhaps
44 Chicken-hearted
46 Exacta player, e.g.
47 Excited, slangily
49 Tobacco residues
51 Bring under control
54 Pal, slangily
59 Send off
60 *Blondie*, for one
62 White House worker
63 *Topaz* novelist
64 1000 kilograms
65 Do-gooder's doing
66 Fit snugly
67 Dish's companion in flight

Down

1 Big donors to office seekers
2 Touch on
3 Boxer's wear
4 Actress Sedgwick
5 Solitary sort
6 Info on an invitation
7 Pizza __
8 Pub round
9 Report card entry
10 Shrimp dish
11 Nebula particles
12 Venusian, e.g.
13 Visibly upset
18 __ out (apportion)
22 "That's all there __ it!"
24 Decimal fraction
26 One of the Brontës
27 Hard to fluster
28 Community leader's attribute
29 NAFTA ratifier
31 Fork's place
32 Lacking a match
34 Send packing
36 "It's __ you!"
37 Learn via the grapevine
39 All Saints' Day mo.
40 Took a load off
42 Offered, as a farewell
43 Won't cooperate

45 Patronized U-Haul
46 Bric-a-___
47 In the future
48 Ike's mate
50 Given to imitation
52 Soap residue
53 Needing kneading
55 Pull the plug on
56 Florence's river
57 El ___ (Pacific current)
58 Double-click, perhaps
61 Prefix meaning "wrong"

GUYS WE'VE MET

Across

1 Etching fluid
5 Prefix with comic
10 "Whoa!"
14 Ready for serving
15 Out of dreamland
16 Crosby's *Road* partner
17 He was a Met in 1963
19 "Yeah, sure!"
20 Bard of boxing
21 "Who ___ Turn To?"
22 Hacienda drudge
23 ___ Park (Edison lab site)
25 He was a Met in 1962 and 1963
29 Passover meals
31 Lend a hand to
32 Miracle-___ (garden brand)
33 November 11 marcher
34 Fuse word
35 Splint alternative
36 He was a Met in 1965
39 Something to wish upon
41 Wrigley Field greenery
42 Smelter input
43 *High* ___ (Anderson play)
44 Hail, to Caesar
45 Little rascals
49 He was a Met in 1965
53 "And thereby hangs ___"
54 Young 'uns
55 Like fine wine
57 PC linkup
58 Showed up
59 He was a Met in 1972 and 1973

62 Beehive State Indians
63 Freud contemporary Alfred
64 Pulitzer winner James
65 Royal pain
66 MacArthur victory site of '44
67 Cowpoke's pal

Down

1 Gomez or Morticia
2 Grand ___ Dam
3 How one may be repaid
4 It's barely passing
5 Yemen's capital
6 *Dallas* family name
7 Bicycle spokes, e.g.
8 '50s campaign button name
9 Neath's opposite
10 Drew back, with "away"
11 Winter coaster
12 Jacks or better, e.g.
13 Kennel visitor
18 Basket maker
22 Peas' place
24 *Roots* star Burton
26 Hasty escapes
27 Aquatic pachyderms
28 D.T.'s sufferer
30 Make a big effort
34 "___ day now . . ."
35 Deal from the bottom, e.g.
36 Stratego and Risk, for two
37 Perpetually
38 Skee-Ball site
39 Porker's place
40 Past the deadline
44 Tummy muscles

46 Sweet wine

47 ___ piano

48 Had a hunch

50 That is to say

51 Come-from-behind attempt

52 Shoelace tip

56 De Valera's land

58 Putter's target

59 ___-Mart (retail chain, as it was once known)

60 Suffix with ox- or sulf-

61 Orienteering reference

GOING GREAT GUNS

Across

1 Tierra del Fuego co-owner
6 Cast-of-thousands film
10 Rule, for short
13 Of the blood
14 Fuji flow
15 Boot bottom
16 Dungeon device
18 Use a word processor
19 Sarge, e.g.
20 Cable network
21 Wine town
22 *All My Children* vixen
24 Worm-eaten
26 Indy 500 letters
29 Earth-friendly prefix
30 Brick home
31 Lobster serving
33 Checked out
35 Not so many
38 Neck of the woods
39 Sin city
41 Hang in the hammock
42 Court game
44 Wrapper weight
45 Begin a fall
46 Wipe away
48 Bambi's aunt
50 As well
51 Kind of cat or goat
53 Family of early American painters
55 Outback leapers
56 Amigo of Fidel
58 Greasy spoon freebie
62 Famous cookie man
63 Engine attachment
65 Offered, as a farewell
66 The life of Riley
67 Cheap so-and-so
68 Decade divs.
69 December purchase
70 __ up (gather)

Down

1 Cleft locale
2 Hefty sandwich
3 Springsteen's "__ Fire"
4 Jouster's need
5 *Glitz* author Leonard
6 Lilly of pharmaceuticals
7 City west of Venice
8 Currier's partner
9 Baseless rumor
10 "Hot Legs" singer
11 Upper crust
12 Gain acceptance
15 Shoulder harness adjunct
17 Priest's closetful
23 Wile E., for one
25 Sock-in-the-gut sound
26 Sharp pain
27 South Seas staple
28 Fabrics sold to dressmakers
30 Renée of silents
32 Sport in which "attack" is a position
34 Author LeShan
36 Operatic Pinza
37 Seized auto
40 Hank Ketcham's Dennis, e.g.

43 Musical ability
47 Scented packet
49 Clock radio features
51 Sheikdom of song
52 Baseball's Garciaparra
53 "__ porridge hot . . ."
54 System of values
57 Try, as a case
59 "Slammin' Sammy"
60 AOL patron
61 Balzac's *Le __ Goriot*
64 Kicker's aid

CEREAL NUMBERS

Across

1 Go splitsville
5 *The Lion King* meanie
9 Champs-Élysées sights
14 Numbered piece
15 Gelato holder
16 *Hägar the Horrible's* wife
17 Raised flatland
18 Prefix meaning "height"
19 Chocolaty cookies
20 Post-touchdown cereal?
23 Ring of fragrant blossoms
24 Didn't hang in
25 Fastball, slangily
28 Witty Wilde
30 Fly high
33 "___ is real! . . .": Longfellow
34 Round Table title
36 Pope from 1939 to 1958
38 Nth degree
39 Cereal for the road?
43 Aussie jumper
44 Biblical beginning
45 It's definite
46 And more
48 Singing Mama
50 Florida keys, e.g.
54 Early Ford
56 Good times
58 Something to grind, in a saying
59 Cereal for Letterman?
63 Does not mention
65 Common Seattle forecast

66 Anchorman Lester
67 Officer-to-be
68 Money maker
69 Phrase of understanding
70 Wedding cake levels
71 Where pirates go
72 Magazine publisher Condé ___

Down

1 Big citrus fruit
2 High points
3 Backwoodsy
4 Nicholas II was the last
5 Scotland's ___ Flow
6 Analogies' punctuation
7 Pro's rival
8 Jockey's handful
9 Collapse in the clutch
10 Like some Google Maps views
11 Means of avoiding rush-hour traffic
12 Swellhead's problem
13 Carrier to Copenhagen
21 Get there
22 Rocket propulsion
26 Page sent by computer
27 Stout of whodunits
29 Solid ___ rock
31 Begins the bidding
32 Garage freebie, sometimes
35 Baggage handler
37 Flaky rock
39 Dog in Oz
40 Fire hydrant locale
41 Bossy's milieu
42 "For ___ a jolly . . ."

43 Sleep phase, for short
47 Varsity member's award
49 On one's back
51 Singer Julius, who was fired on live TV
52 Banished dictators, e.g.
53 Medium-sized jazz band
55 Strong cravings
57 Prefix with gram or meter
60 ___ *La Douce*
61 Honoree's place
62 Like a dime

63 UN Day mo.
64 ___ tai cocktail

THE HERMITAGE

37 Place for a charm
38 Flexible Flyer, e.g.
40 Thieves' hangouts
41 Tall drum
43 Calcutta cash
44 More expensive
46 Greta Garbo was one
47 ___ grinder
48 Diabolical sort
49 Do without
50 Cheese from Holland
51 Turner or Cantrell

52 Welcome forecast for schoolchildren
56 "___ y Plata" (Montana's motto)
57 TV's "Science Guy" Bill

ROUND THINGS WITH HOLES

Across

1 Neither fem. nor neut.
5 Jeffersonian belief
10 Jeanne ___ (French saint)
14 Part of a Welk intro
15 How an actor may enter
16 Landfill problem
17 Documentary film about basketball
19 Protuberance
20 Make ___ of (jot down)
21 Fraternity letters
22 *Trinity* novelist
23 Photograph ruiner, perhaps
26 It's pitched before it's even used
28 Middle Eastern sultanate
30 Faux ___
31 Cinder block material
35 Moppet
39 Grad student's hurdle
40 Saint Kitts and ___ (Caribbean nation)
43 Nabisco classic
44 Word before code or colony
46 Caper
48 Give in to gravity
50 Iranian currency
51 Behan's ___ *Boy*
55 Put up with
60 Controversial apple spray
61 Water closet
63 Anne of *Wag the Dog*
64 Ventura County's ___ Valley
65 Partner of a nut and bolt
68 Roulette play
69 Milo of movies
70 ___ off (sore)
71 Hong Kong's Hang ___ Index
72 Indiana's state flower
73 Venomous varmints

Down

1 Taj ___
2 Make amends
3 Sinatra made his fans do it
4 Egyptian Christians
5 *Le Coq* ___ (Rimsky-Korsakov work)
6 Ending with ethyl
7 Words of confidence
8 Give a recap
9 Make untidy
10 Stereotypical 31-Down's hangout
11 Be nuts over
12 *The Thinker* sculptor
13 Kingfisher's topper
18 *Better Homes and Gardens* concern
24 "Right on!"
25 Cracker topper
27 Source of funds in DC
29 "In a pig's eye!"
31 He's got the beat
32 Assayer's specimen
33 A Bobbsey twin
34 Senior's purchase
36 Roth ___ (investment choice)
37 Blazed the trail

38 Anonymous litigant
41 Egyptian fertility goddess
42 "Amscray!"
45 Long. crosser
47 Hawaii hi
49 It's faster than a canter
51 They're occasionally loaded
52 Bar garnish
53 Japanese soup
54 On the lam
56 Socialite Perle
57 Needs ibuprofen

58 Chick's call
59 Groups in roundups
62 ___ Rios, Jamaica
66 Lay of the Enron scandal
67 "___ cool!"

OVERSIZED

Across

1 List-ending abbr.
5 First letter
10 Hook with a handle
14 Storm in Hollywood
15 Mark down, maybe
16 River to the Caspian Sea
17 Steinway product
19 Hack's customer
20 Noted Big Apple restaurateur
21 Place for smokeless tobacco
23 Creator of Perry and Della
26 Absorbed, as a cost
27 Broadway's theater district
33 When doubled, a dance
35 Rolling in dough
36 Cropped up
37 Hauled on board
39 Bobby Fischer's game
42 Got taller
43 5-Across's opposite
45 Geraint's lady
47 Line to Stockholm
48 Salad morsel, maybe
52 "My mama done ___ me . . ."
53 Something to pick
54 Indonesian capital: Var.
59 Subterranean dwarf
63 Broccoli ___
64 Orwellian omnipresence
67 50-50
68 Novelist Zola
69 Prefix meaning "within"
70 Coiner of the term "horsepower"
71 Too much, musically
72 Diana or Betsy

Down

1 Bacon partner
2 Skater Lipinski
3 Controversial apple reddener
4 Shylock, for one
5 Dada pioneer
6 Ring around the collar?
7 Education gps.
8 ___ Montana (Miley Cyrus character)
9 Guinea pig cousin
10 Back talk
11 Qatari, for one
12 Casino game
13 Show off one's bod
18 More calamitous
22 Salty cheese
24 Of the flock
25 Design with acid
27 Chairman's hammer
28 Revolutionary invention
29 Joule part
30 More severe
31 Between ports
32 Evergreens that don't bear true cones
33 Partner of van. and straw.
34 ___ erectus
38 Swellhead's problem
40 Nose-in-the-air sort
41 Cylindrical structure
44 Nick and Nora's pet
46 Dog down under

49 Cold dessert
50 Nissan model
51 One letting off steam
54 Took a gunslinger's dare
55 54-Across's island
56 Help in wrongdoing
57 Strongest man on The Planet?
58 Opposed to, in dialect
60 "Not that!"
61 Subway Series team
62 Libidinous god
65 Crunchy sandwich

66 Pierce Arrow contemporary

OH, DEER!

Across

1 Some murder mystery suspects
6 Perfumery bit
11 __-relief
14 Places in the heart
15 Supersized
16 Place for ashes
17 Worrisome economic period
19 Secretive org.
20 Flies off the handle
21 Selfish one
23 Board area in Clue
25 Hit the sauce
26 Incites
30 Showy shrub
32 Sing like Bing
33 Staff symbols
34 Harden
37 "Don't take another step!"
38 Sacred composition
39 Capital on a fjord
40 Like some jobs
41 Cuts back
42 Popular workout program
43 Walking on air
45 Low-flying seabird
46 Discussion groups
48 Hook's underling
50 "God bless" elicitor
51 Laces into
56 Hindu honorific
57 1941 Gary Cooper movie
61 Pewter component
62 Even if, familiarly

63 Not at full power
64 Throw in
65 A choir may stand on one
66 Coming-of-age period

Down

1 Leftovers dish
2 Singer James or Jones
3 Some portfolio holdings, briefly
4 Baltic capital
5 Paella ingredient
6 Aristotle's teacher
7 Break bread
8 Prefix with state or gram
9 "Long __ and far away . . ."
10 Soup legumes
11 Blame shifter
12 *The Tempest* sprite
13 Marching band drum
18 Symbol of courage
22 Big goon
24 Soda shop treats
25 Last mustachioed president
26 Lover of Narcissus
27 Alum
28 Sir Francis Drake's ship
29 Boozer
31 Zorro's marks
33 Part of an apple or the earth
35 River of Hamburg
36 Chisel, e.g.
38 Car floor items
39 Quaker morsel
41 California observatory
42 Start of a hole
44 Summer sign

45 Mexican moolah
46 Ziti or vermicelli
47 Bitter-tasting
49 Captain's superior
52 *Green Gables* girl
53 Run in neutral
54 Wacko
55 ___ up (clinches)
58 Whitney of gin fame
59 SAT-administering co.
60 Not just "a"

END GAMES

45 Reinforcements

46 Far from flustered

47 Roguish sort

48 Bill who led the Comets

49 Like Santa's helpers

50 Visibly upset

52 Italian beach resort

53 Seaport of Yemen

54 Greenish-blue

55 Have ___ good authority

56 Wearing pumps, e.g.

57 *Citizen* ___

61 Aussie outlaw ___ Kelly

GET LOST!

Across

1 "___ number one!"
5 Conjure up
10 Down in the dumps
14 Cake finisher
15 Wisconsin college
16 Sub ___ (in secret)
17 Western flicks
19 ". . . ___ of thieves" (Matt. 21:13)
20 Outlaw-chasing group
21 Battle of Britain flier
23 Give it ___ (try)
26 Lilly of pharmaceuticals
27 Common morning fare
34 Equipment
36 ___ *Blas*
37 *Dallas* matriarch Miss ___
38 River through Pisa
39 ___ und Drang
42 ___ bonding
43 Gyro holders
45 TV's Charlotte
46 "I need it yesterday!" letters
47 Ding-a-lings
51 Suffix with pay
52 Trinidad/Tobago bridge
53 Grown-up aphid lion
58 Flood barrier
63 Grueling exam
64 Motoring, in a way
67 Singer Simone
68 Broom ___ (comics witch)
69 Ray of film

Down

1 Skinny one
2 Canyon phenomenon
3 Collectors' cars
4 Cupid, to the Greeks
5 Poetic preposition
6 Razzmatazz
7 *Outland* penguin
8 Former *Nightline* newsman
9 Preserve, as fodder
10 Seles rival
11 Garden State city
12 ___-friendly
13 Leonine locks
18 Run like heck
22 Bay of Fundy feature
24 Stand-up's arsenal
25 Forget about
27 Yuletide temp
28 Zagreb resident
29 Publicist's piece
30 Violinist Mischa
31 ___ jaw (pug's liability)
32 ___ monster (large lizard)
33 Slip through the cracks
34 Spark plug settings
35 Leif's father
40 ___ avis
41 Miserly
44 Put in a hold
48 Otis, the elevator man
49 Like spoiled butter

50 In mothballs
53 Word on a jacket label
54 What the fat lady sings?
55 Bat Masterson's weapon
56 Mideast airline
57 Aqua regia dissolves it
59 Chapters of history
60 TV handyman Bob
61 Pulls the plug on
62 They can be bruised or inflated
65 Lofty verse
66 Wee bit

SALAD DAYS

1 Pie-in-the-face sound
6 Smelter waste
10 One of the Smurfs
14 Mount the soapbox
15 Sighter of pink elephants
16 Base no-show
17 Russian art treasure
19 Timer filler
20 Pro-___ (some tourneys)
21 Séance sounds
22 Try to take in
24 Playbill listing
25 Pitcher in the rotation
26 Kiss
29 Tetched in the head
30 Lash of old oaters
31 Donut feature
32 Rugged rock
36 Guinness or Waugh
37 Sound engineer's control
38 One of a Triceratops's three
39 Go well together
40 Hunchbacked lab assistant
41 1965 march setting
42 Barrens trees
44 Overrun, as with pests
45 Finish with Crayolas
48 Tuneful Tori
49 Tapers off
50 "___ me five!"
51 Elk's place
54 Pro ___ (in proportion)
55 Cheer for Julius

58 Leave unsaid
59 *Legally Blonde* girl
60 Kevin of *Dave*
61 iPod model
62 Belmonts' frontman
63 Auto produced until 1932

Down

1 Place for a 24-Down
2 Brit's buggy
3 Black or chocolate dogs
4 Broke bread
5 Apartment balcony
6 Used a broom
7 Bunches of bull
8 *Hulk* director Lee
9 Enterprising one
10 Napoleon experts?
11 Hang out for
12 Explorer ___ de León
13 Tree with catkins
18 Nasty cut
23 DC ballplayer
24 Tube addict
25 Cobbler, at times
26 Shut hard
27 Bull, cob, or tom
28 Assayed materials
29 Birds clubbed to extinction
31 Uta of stage and screen
33 Gipp, to Reagan
34 Locales of ulnae and humeri
35 Pesky swarmer
37 Consumed totally
41 Correction fluid brand
43 Ill temper

44 Apple debut of 1998
45 Star of *Gigi* and *Lili*
46 Bo's master
47 Word after pig or vulgar
48 __ wrench (L-shaped tool)
50 Fodder's place
51 "No guarantees"
52 Greenhouse square
53 Bipedal dino
56 Baron Cohen's *Da __ G Show*
57 Some urban rails

STEADY IMPROVEMENT

Across

1 Show some backbone, slangily
6 Supersecure airline
10 Did some groundbreaking
14 Without an escort
15 Niels Bohr, for one
16 160 square rods
17 Rarity for a new parent
20 Not so dilute
21 Work in tandem
22 Aurora's Greek counterpart
23 Day-__ colors
25 Highest degree
26 Joan of Arc, e.g.
30 Visible
31 Algerian port
32 Bit of slapstick
33 NFL nail-biters
36 Inventor's goal, proverbially
40 KLM competitor
41 Like a tack
42 __ Lee cakes
43 Cede the pigskin
44 Put to use
46 Run-D.M.C.'s music
49 "__ Loser" (Beatles song)
50 Day before a big event
51 Clear, as a tape
53 Painter's wear, perhaps
58 Item on a *New York Times* list
61 "For __ us a child . . ."
62 Subway rider's wish
63 Beethoven wrote for her
64 Oxtail __
65 Rick's __ Américain
66 Like a dim bulb

Down

1 *Mad* and *Elle*, briefly
2 Jillions
3 Koh-i- __ diamond
4 Disassemble
5 Retailer J.C. __ Company, Inc.
6 Does some lawn work
7 Cowardly Lion portrayer
8 Hard-working insect
9 Moonves of CBS
10 Saintly topper
11 Liner's milieu
12 Not slouching
13 Pool measurement
18 Stereotypical lab assistant
19 Candle bracket
23 Start a new day
24 Floral garlands
26 Sale scenes
27 Square footage
28 Hamelin's problem
29 Blaster's need
30 Show derision
32 Radarange maker
33 Like much lore
34 Poi source
35 Fix, as a pet
37 Catches sight of
38 Baba au __
39 Cough medicine amt.
44 All caught up
45 Joined forces

46 Picture puzzle
47 ___ We All? (1923 play)
48 Fake jewels
50 Online party notice
52 Stash overhead
53 Norway's patron saint
54 Fully qualified
55 Butcher's cut
56 Result of a sack
57 ___-Ball (arcade game)
59 Upper-left PC key
60 Place to graze

HUMONGOUS

Across

1 "__ Whoopee"
6 The terrible __
10 Swabbies' implements
14 Coeur d'__, Idaho
15 Lend a hand
16 Aid in a scam
17 Black and white zoo critter
19 "__ Lisa"
20 Lavatory sign
21 Have a yen for
22 Model maker's adhesive
24 Sea __ (marine polyp)
26 Prefix with dynamic
27 Bonanza stuff
28 Founds, as a business
32 Really smelled
35 Walk through mud
36 Luau dance
37 Rowboat propellers
38 "Mule Train" singer
39 Highlands family
40 Tear carrier
41 Kitty starter
42 Speak boastfully of
43 Nonbelievers in God
45 AL East, e.g.
46 __-Rooter
47 "Close, but no cigar!"
51 Pita dip
54 Ushers do it
55 Workout unit
56 Fit for active duty

57 Prehistoric plant-eating behemoth
60 Beehive State natives
61 Track shape
62 Bonn's river
63 __ IRA
64 '60s talk show host Joe
65 *Bullitt* director Peter

Down

1 Molten rock
2 Sci-fi visitor
3 *The Family Circus* cartoonist Bil
4 Wayfarer's stop
5 ABC or CBS
6 Macbeth, for one
7 Took one's turn
8 Like Mother Hubbard
9 Period beginning with *Sputnik* I's launch
10 Kentucky tourist attraction
11 Double reed
12 Rival of Cornell or Brown, briefly
13 Doc's "At once!"
18 Glazier's unit
23 Pull a boner
25 Pop tune played around Halloween
26 Do penance
28 Gill openings
29 *Star Trek* helmsman
30 __ Bator, Mongolia
31 Huff and puff
32 Scotch's partner
33 Strung tightly

34 St. Louis landmark

35 ___ Domingo (Caribbean capital)

38 "End of the line!"

42 What a two-finger "V" might stand for

44 Debtor's note

45 Primatologist Fossey

47 1960 Wimbledon champ Fraser

48 Genetic attribute

49 See the old gang

50 Belgian city mispronounced "Wipers"

51 Billing unit, for some

52 "Do ___ others . . ."

53 Track competition

54 Lee of comics

58 Campus greenery

59 ___ Na Na

WOOD YOU?

Across

1 Policy position
6 Estate home
11 Fall back
14 Not so inept
15 Out of the way
16 Capote nickname
17 *Star Trek* journal
19 Towel stitching
20 Abrasive stuff
21 Deep gully
23 Bubble-gum brand
27 Spiked, as punch
28 Decks out
29 Turnstile inputs, once
32 Radius, ulna, etc.
33 Unlike a dirt road
34 TV's Magnum et al.
37 Dwarf planet discovered in 2005
38 Obviously contrived
39 Item on a to-do list
40 Football's Dawson
41 Warning wail
42 Showy violet
43 Quiet aircraft
45 Fabricated
46 Nautical quarters
48 Cake brand "nobody doesn't like"
49 Right this minute
51 Disputed strip
52 Women's wear item
53 Auto component containing cylinders
59 Scuba tank filler
60 18 holes, typically
61 Wood shaper
62 Young 'un
63 Op-ed piece
64 Clampett portrayer

Down

1 Cul-de-___
2 Awaiting scheduling, initially
3 Jungfrau or Eiger
4 Court barrier
5 Chinese New Year beasts
6 Suffix with ego
7 Man Friday: Abbr.
8 Having no value
9 Dump emanation
10 Wined and dined
11 Group investigating misconduct
12 Pickling liquid
13 Went by Greyhound
18 Ticks off
22 Delivery vehicle
23 Cacophonous tower locale
24 Be wild about
25 Variance-authorizing group
26 Tram loads
29 Greedy one
30 Place to use Easy-Off
31 A major, maybe
33 Dermal opening
35 Debate topic
36 Video chatting medium
38 Kept under wraps
39 Triumphant cry
41 Heartfelt
42 Story from the pulpit

44 Chinese author ___ Yutang
45 Puzzle on a place mat, perhaps
46 Overthrow plotters
47 Skylit courtyards
48 Like a beach
50 1961 space chimp
51 Actress Lollobrigida
54 Gloomy ___ (grump)
55 Chem room
56 Extra play periods, for short
57 Guerrilla Guevara
58 Author Kesey

HOUSEHOLD WORDS

Across

1 Sweetie
6 Pianist Dame Myra
10 Purchases for a shindig
14 Action spot
15 Song for Lily Pons
16 Terrible man?
17 Demo CD maker, perhaps
19 Screen pooch of 1939
20 Freddy Krueger's street
21 Speech setting
22 Easy mark
24 What you pay
25 Most reckless
26 In need of air freshener
29 Suitable place
30 Yule tune
31 What a debtor might be in
32 Takes a siesta
36 Garage-sale words
37 Fills to the gills
38 Meter opening
39 Pronoun in "America"
40 Rifles and such
41 Princess topper
42 Hose shade
44 A couple of fins
45 Dormant state
48 Soak up rays
49 Product-pitching price
50 Fresh-mouthed
51 Slip behind
54 Two-thirds of DIY
55 Charades, e.g.

58 Art Deco designer
59 Genesis shepherd
60 Bargainer at strike talks
61 At no time, to poets
62 Kitten-lifting spot
63 Clara Barton, notably

Down

1 Herb for stuffing
2 Russia's __ Mountains
3 Seed of an idea
4 Santa __ Winds
5 Ann or Andy, e.g.
6 Equestrian's garb
7 Time line divisions
8 Envy or sloth
9 Pathetic sorts
10 Dirty dishes site
11 Conjure up
12 Microsoft's Bill
13 Angry bull's sound
18 "Careful, now!"
23 Work the aisles, slangily
24 Clandestine diet-breaker
25 Puts through a food press
26 Style of jazz singing
27 Moonshiner's mixture
28 Niagara River source
29 Denier's cry
31 Bird-woman of myth
33 Actor Alda
34 Sweat source
35 Lower-left phone button
37 Chef's utensil
41 Debugging procedure
43 Kitchen pest

44 Pacific starch source
45 Heavily burdened
46 Love to death
47 Clichéd
48 Ball girl
50 Get-ready work
51 Cozy hideaway
52 Tori of pop music
53 Chromosome unit
56 Attorneys' org.
57 Bearded grazer

OOH!

Across

1 "Dumb" girl of old comics
5 FDR's pooch
9 Disney's ___ Theme Park
14 Each
15 Woeful word
16 Burn soother
17 Chicken's time-share?
19 Sets straight
20 Hexa- halved
21 Citi Field player
22 Tight-fitting necklaces
24 *Messiah* composer
26 "With parsley," on fancy menus
27 Nitrous ___ (laughing gas)
29 Sewing machine brand
33 Winter forecast
36 1959 Cadillac prominences
38 Shooting marble
39 Long, long times
40 Halloween goodie
42 Texas, the ___ Star State
43 Be useful to
45 Toledo's lake
46 Norwegian saint
47 1970s Cambodian leader
49 San Antonio mission
51 *Taras Bulba* author Nikolai
53 Wicker material
57 One with a self-satisfied smile
60 Dubbed one
61 Pindaric work
62 Paddler's boat
63 Playboy Mansion basketball court sight?
66 One in a cast
67 "What's ___ for me?"
68 Razor brand
69 Pinochle plays
70 ___ Gigio (old TV mouse)
71 Author Silverstein

Down

1 ___ Vader of *Star Wars*
2 *Carmen* or *Aïda*
3 1998 De Niro thriller
4 Well-put
5 Wrinkle-removing surgery
6 Frequently
7 Philosopher ___-tse
8 Pet protection org.
9 A Baltic State
10 Revenue from summonses?
11 Whodunit board game
12 Walkie-talkie word
13 Tracy's Trueheart
18 NYSE counterpart
23 Four-baggers: Abbr.
25 Cross used in searching for water?
26 Wesley Clark was one
28 In ___ straits
30 London lockup
31 Sicilian erupter
32 Coral mass
33 Circus barker
34 De ___ (from the start)
35 ___ even keel
37 Jib or lateen

41 Verbally assault
44 ___-on (spectators)
48 Size abbr.
50 Partner of Peter and Paul
52 Planetary path
54 Cuspid or canine
55 Be wild about
56 Katmandu's land
57 Confidence game
58 Mugger subduer
59 Like JFK Airport: Abbr.
60 Scissors sound

64 Popular card game
65 Suffers from

TEAM COLORS

Across

1 Dollar, slangily
5 80-day circumnavigator
9 ___ metabolism
14 Go nuts
15 Abu Dhabi honcho
16 Sunshine State city
17 Not sunny-side up
18 Sitar selection
19 Dickens's Heep
20 Pete Rose played for them
23 Welcoming word
24 Original sinner
25 *First Blood* character
29 Reprimand loudly
34 Hibachi residue
37 Sylvester's frequent costar
39 Top-flight
40 Jim Brown played for them
44 Weight deduction
45 Do figure eights
46 Rode the bench
47 Word with metric or merit
50 Grain parasites
52 "Cara ___"
54 It comes from the heart
58 Satchel Paige played for them
64 Forged-check passer
65 Word often following "Ye"
66 Short swims
67 Circular gasket
68 Bank holding
69 "Understood!"
70 *Siddhartha* author
71 Songstress k.d.
72 Five-time Socialist candidate

Down

1 "Bad, Bad Leroy Brown" singer
2 Linda of *Alice*
3 Ten-percenter
4 "Moon River" lyricist Johnny
5 Frond-bearing plant
6 OPEC sultanate
7 Billion: Prefix
8 Fireplace item
9 Bach composition covered by Jethro Tull
10 Cornfield measure
11 Port ___, Egypt
12 Shakespearean "Bummer!"
13 "Well, ___-di-dah!"
21 Plenty sore
22 Wrigley Field flora
26 Start to function?
27 *Gil ___* (Le Sage novel)
28 Porkers' patter
30 Thai's neighbor
31 Weather map regions
32 Visitor to Siam
33 Microphone word
34 Gets off the fence
35 Send rolling in the aisles
36 One of a matched set
38 Ponderosa boy
41 November marcher
42 A/C unit
43 Mark down, maybe
48 Exit one's cocoon
49 Relative of 26-Down

51 Morally degraded
53 Wake Island, e.g.
55 Poker ploy
56 Laid-back sort
57 Obstinate ones
58 Bring on board
59 Mayberry tosspot
60 Department store department
61 Essayist's alias
62 Mideast gulf
63 ___ Xiaoping
64 The ___-i-noor diamond

JACKIE

Across

1 Pollutant banned by the EPA
4 Wanders aimlessly
8 More custard-like
14 "Bingo!"
15 *On the Waterfront* director Kazan
16 Brunch cocktail
17 Jackie, who broke baseball's color line
19 With 58-Across, baseball executive who brought Jackie to the majors
20 ___ Set (construction toy)
21 Have in mind
22 Old Ford flop
23 Feudal slave
24 Company with a dog in its logo
27 Stadium where Jackie starred
31 Places to unwind
35 Eliciting a "So what?"
36 1961 Charlton Heston title role
37 Grow limp
38 Desi Arnaz, by birth
40 Nathan of stage and screen
41 Pentium maker
43 Gambling town
44 Hightailed it
45 Dodgers' great famously pictured with his arm around Jackie
48 Do wrong
49 Pub round
50 Fernando or Lorenzo
55 French biplane of WWI
56 Kind of onion or omelet
58 See 19-Across
61 Jackie's number
62 Trainee or detainee
63 Botanical balm
64 Microwave, slangily
65 Lombardy province or its capital
66 Conks on the head
67 Election winners

Down

1 "Gay" city
2 Combination of notes
3 ___ in Toyland
4 Having a soft touch
5 In addition
6 Designer Christian
7 ___ Diego
8 Smoldering remains
9 Tall quadruped
10 FBI operative
11 Accelerator bit
12 PC bailout key
13 When repeated, gung-ho
18 Diamonds, slangily
21 Marsh hydrocarbon
23 Navy building crew
24 Brief news report
25 "Crazy" singer Patsy
26 Threw in
28 Inits. on a telly
29 Fuzzy, as vision
30 Sorry situations
31 Filch
32 Heartsick one
33 Rehem, say
34 One-pot meal

39 Rejections
42 Axel or lutz performers
46 Comic Boosler
47 Tickles pink
51 At least one
52 Actress Gaynor
53 Dam site in Egypt
54 Hits the mall
55 __-Ball (arcade game)
56 Sans help
57 Stage item
58 *6 Rms __ Vu*

59 __ huff
60 NFL line pos.
61 "Groovy!"

SANDWICH SHOP

Across

1 Drum accompanying a sitar
6 Bundle of papers
11 "Rumor ___ it . . ."
14 Best possible
15 Puccini opera
16 Genesis boat
17 Ersatz spaghetti go-with?
19 Hosp. scan
20 Highly regard
21 Trillion: Prefix
22 Toddler's "piggy"
23 Home of twigs
25 Reduces in width
27 Fish tales
30 Moderator Russert
32 Tea leaves reader
33 Director Lee
34 Red-coated cheese
36 Brown tone
39 Letterhead symbol
41 Nigeria's largest city
43 Watch readouts, briefly
44 Go for fish
46 Old Italian coin
47 ___ Moines, Iowa
48 Copier paper quantity
50 Baseball's Ripken Jr.
51 Petty officer, for short
52 Political asylum seekers
55 Plumb crazy
57 U-Haul rental
58 *The Thin Man* dog
60 May honoree

64 Unaffiliated pol: Abbr.
65 Coward cited for valor?
67 Get on in years
68 Painter Matisse
69 Scriptwriter Ephron
70 Hide-hair link
71 Fragrant compound
72 Court call

Down

1 It's money, proverbially
2 Fruity quaffs
3 Ready to collapse
4 Grows dark
5 *The Zoo Story* playwright
6 Cardinal's monogram
7 Textbook publishers ___, Rinehart and Winston
8 Ruhr valley city
9 MDX and TL of autodom
10 Shelly of *The Donna Reed Show*
11 Anti-overemoting-actor weapon?
12 Directional sign shape
13 Heavens above
18 Light beer brand
24 Word before wave or basin
26 Virginia dance
27 In ___ land (spaced out)
28 Barge ___ (interrupt)
29 Machine in the Fabergé plant?
31 Mandrake's field
35 Aesop story ender
37 Bad time for Caesar
38 Org.
40 Cassini of fashion
42 Biblical dancer

45 Otic malady
49 Fits together
51 Pester
52 Perrier competitor
53 Juicy tropical fruit
54 Time on the job
56 Co-op alternative
59 Field measure
61 Had in hand
62 Toledo's lake
63 Crowd noise
66 Cassis-flavored aperitif

LETTERWOMEN

Across

1 Hollywood statuette
6 Ziti or penne
11 Guy's partner
14 Zeus turned her to stone
15 Some saxes
16 Prefix with bar or therm
17 Comics "Cinderella" of 1925–61
19 Well put
20 Fixed part of a dynamo
21 Initial stake
22 Op. __ (footnote abbr.)
23 Slaughter of Cooperstown
25 Apartment balcony
27 Plays the ponies, say
30 DC baseballer, in headlines
32 Movie rating unit
33 *Exodus* hero
34 Nest eggs, for short
36 Cabinet department
39 Neeson of *Kinsey*
41 Explorer John or Sebastian
43 Winter fall
44 Mr. T movie of 1983
46 Vincent Lopez's theme song
47 Icky stuff
48 Oodles
50 Anthem contraction
51 Defraud
52 Places to buy ice cream
55 __ Lee cakes
57 Discount tag abbr.
58 New Jersey university
60 Get underhandedly
64 Before, to bards
65 "Give me your tired, your poor . . ." poet
67 __ and feathers (old punishment)
68 Oater "necktie"
69 Make into law
70 Nautical assent
71 Mild oaths
72 Titled women

Down

1 Till stack
2 River sediment
3 Soft drink choice
4 Slackens off
5 Scout's mission, for short
6 Give two thumbs down to
7 Alan of *M*A*S*H*
8 Surgeon's blockage reliever
9 Rich pastries
10 States positively
11 Supermodel played by Angelina Jolie
12 Jellied garnish
13 Singer Lenya
18 Like an O. Henry story
24 Clear kitchen wrap
26 Ghetto scurriers
27 Like Kojak's pate
28 Director Rohmer
29 Cassandra Wong player in *Wayne's World*
31 Forbidden
35 Cobbler's supply
37 Hammer or sickle

38 Furry *Star Wars* creature
40 Shopaholic's mecca
42 Pacific battle site of 1943
45 One of a library pair
49 Earthquake preceder, perhaps
51 Fruit in a split
52 Michelangelo masterpiece
53 Orderly formation
54 Pago Pago's island group
56 Tore to the ground
59 Tweed caricaturist Thomas
61 Unit of fat

62 Writer Clare Boothe ___
63 Repair shop figs.
66 Guitarist ___ Paul

TOPSY-TURVY

Across

1 Wooden shoe
6 *The* ___ (amorphous sci-fi being)
10 Classic cleanser
14 Site of a big event
15 One with forked tongue
16 Plenty mad
17 Change 2/3 to 3/2, say
20 Moviedom's Myrna
21 Atomizer's release
22 The ___-Finnish War
23 Margarita glass coating
24 Render pancake-shaped
26 Edit, as tape
29 Speechify
30 Homecoming guest
31 "Mack the ___"
32 "___ whiz!"
35 End a relationship, say
39 Clairvoyant's claim
40 Locker room handout
41 Online journal
42 Prim and proper
43 Prim and proper
45 Sonnet endings
48 Parrot's meal
49 Turns white
50 Essay page, for short
51 Ring outcome, briefly
54 Reverse a lower-court decision
58 Patched together
59 Like Aesop's grapes
60 Object trivially
61 "Happy Motoring" brand
62 Durante's protrusion
63 Overdo it onstage

Down

1 Jib or spinnaker
2 River of Florence
3 Group of quails
4 Sacagawea denomination
5 Takeoff or landing site
6 Good time, in slang
7 Essex elevator
8 Regatta implement
9 Bikini top
10 Quick-witted
11 Ceiling supporter
12 Sprang up
13 Arc lamp gas
18 Mah-jongg piece
19 Volcano feature
23 Dim bulb
24 Brand-X lack
25 Joke response, informally
26 "Smooth Operator" singer
27 Good thing
28 Gravy problem
29 NO RIGHT ___
31 Fuzzy fruits
32 Toothpaste types
33 Slaughter in Cooperstown
34 All wound up
36 Affirm to be true
37 Bearded farm animal
38 Footnote abbr.
42 Buffet table heater
43 Social equal
44 Shed pounds

45 Slangy "What if . . ."
46 Icicle sites
47 Zillions
48 Fifth wheel
50 Cross to bear
51 TV show digitizer
52 Make cardigans
53 Eye amorously
55 Mil. branch
56 Pal of Pooh
57 Leave in a hurry

BAGGING FOWL

Across

1 Undomesticated, like an alley cat
6 Timetable, for short
10 Herring variety
14 ___ acid (protein component)
15 Right-hand man
16 Hard to hold on to
17 Phone message to an easy target?
20 Arboreal amphibian
21 Skylit courts
22 Long, long time
23 Kids' card game
25 Relaxation room
26 Place for a brewski
30 Football's Crimson Tide, for short
31 Lena of *Chocolat*
32 Shop lingo
33 Butter serving
36 Super-expensive desk lamp?
40 Chowed down
41 An inert gas
42 Pacific salmon
43 Lift one's blindfold
44 Steakhouse orders
46 Docs' org.
49 Mag. staffers
50 "___ 'nuff!"
51 Like some eclipses
53 Shop VIPs
58 Alaskan marksmanship contest?
61 Nabisco cookie since 1912
62 Poet ___ Angelou
63 Novelist Zola
64 Bills picturing Hamilton
65 Banana throwaway
66 Find a new tenant for

Down

1 Go on a hunger strike
2 Mideast ruler
3 Baptism or bar mitzvah
4 Chip in
5 Hang out without purpose
6 *Cosmos* host Carl
7 Captain ___ (legendary pirate)
8 School's URL suffix
9 Boxing Day mo.
10 Sunni or Shia
11 Got wind of
12 Kate's TV pal
13 "Blowin' in the Wind" composer
18 Hands-up time
19 Dojo discipline
23 Conestoga, for one
24 Cookiedom's Famous ___
26 Frat party garb
27 Oodles
28 Awful-tasting
29 Wind up
30 Trout's home
32 De Mille of dance
33 Lowly laborer
34 Need ibuprofen
35 Stats for pugs
37 Dab hand

38 Have to have
39 Sgt. or cpl.
44 "__ went thataway!"
45 Dog, slangily
46 Broad necktie
47 Bond portrayer Roger
48 Burns partner
50 Walk off with
52 Hubbubs
53 Terrier type
54 "Alas"
55 Muddy up

56 Pineapple name
57 Editor's mark
59 Diamond figure
60 Actress __ Dawn Chong

ALL-NEW

Across

1 __ of (lacking)
6 Restorative sites
10 TV rooms
14 On the perimeter
15 "Bye-bye"
16 *Chocolat* actress Lena
17 Asimov offering
19 Film composer Rota
20 Gives the thumbs-up
21 Expose to view
22 Walk with a cane, say
24 Gal's dream date
25 Office worker of comics
26 A Little Rascal
29 Charity recipient
30 Candidate's concern
31 Reliever's success
32 Gift tag word
36 Labor leader Walesa
37 Trig ratios
38 Shankar tune
39 Biz boss
40 Chest muscles, for short
41 Obey an RSVP
42 Grammarian's concern
44 Hindu social groups
45 Generally
48 Wool eater
49 Scratched up
50 Reaction to a pinch
51 Not a lot
54 Act the crybaby
55 "You snooze, you lose"

58 Unspoiled area
59 Type of blue or green
60 Clunker of a car
61 By __ of (due to)
62 Mailing ctrs.
63 Campaign stop, e.g.

Down

1 Middling
2 Literary pal of Tom
3 Porter's regretful Miss
4 Make some calls
5 Former New York newspaper
6 Baby deliverer
7 Do roadwork
8 Grazed, say
9 Freebies with soup
10 "Mind your manners!"
11 Powers that be
12 San Francisco NFLer, for short
13 Show derision
18 Zola classic
23 __ Miss
24 Potential cause of circuit damage
25 Peaceniks
26 FBI info
27 Wall St. board
28 200-meter, e.g.
29 Highland fling, e.g.
31 Assault on Troy, for one
33 Deeply absorbed
34 Eye with desire
35 Willie of the Polo Grounds
37 Big name in rubber balls
41 Squalid digs

43 Trial lawyer's advice
44 Chanel's nickname
45 Psyched up
46 Riyadh resident
47 "Stormy Weather" composer
48 Tones down
50 Nobel Peace Prize city
51 Starlet's aspiration
52 School founded by Henry VI
53 Took one's turn
56 Broker's offering
57 *My Name Is Asher ___*

JOINT SESSION

Across

1 Playing marble
6 Green "pets"
11 Hole starter
14 Like repopularized fashions
15 Sunday songs
16 X, as in Xenophon
17 Hilarious joke
19 President pro __
20 Roth et al.
21 Mr. T and pals, with "The"
22 Motorist's attention-getter
23 Trojan War counselor
25 Netanyahu's party
27 Pasta choice
32 Cow of ads
33 Lined up perfectly
34 Work wk. ender, for many
37 Make void
40 Earl Grey, e.g.
41 Ancient letters
44 Sam of the links
47 Going-steady symbol, maybe
51 Trumpet noise
52 Bowling alley buttons
55 Smoke-filled room folk
57 Birdbath gunk
60 Letters at Calvary
61 Swellhead's trouble
62 Zoot suit feature
64 Tate collection
65 Build up
66 Spread sand or salt on
67 Electric-guitar pioneer Paul

68 __ Domingo
69 Jobs for body shops

Down

1 *Catch-22* star Alan
2 Romance or sci-fi, e.g.
3 Opposite of "Ten-hut!"
4 Highway overpass
5 Aurora's counterpart
6 Cyberspace conversation
7 Promotional hoopla
8 Chevy model
9 Lacking vitality
10 Belarus, once: Abbr.
11 Role-played
12 Coaster rider's cry
13 Like a wet noodle
18 Godfrey regular Julius
22 Duelist of 1804
24 Neither par. nor perp.
26 Kit __ (candy brand)
28 Take all the marbles
29 Brain gang
30 Bridal bio word
31 *Rhoda* mom
34 __ Diavolo
35 Camden Yards score
36 Rorschach test patterns
38 Never used, in coin-collecting shorthand
39 Looked lustfully
42 Pipe bends
43 Coral or Sargasso
45 Hoppy quaff
46 1954 Brando film
48 The Creator, in Hinduism

49 Grant another mortgage
50 Tough spare for many bowlers
53 Plot of land
54 Beef units
55 Bell sound
56 Folklore meanie
58 Rush of wind
59 "Not to mention . . ."
62 Airline to Stockholm
63 Hall, formerly of *The Tonight Show*

NOT!

47 Like Limburger
48 Analyze, as a sentence
50 You might RSVP online to this
51 City near Dayton
52 *The ___ Sanction* (Eastwood film)
53 Shock-jock Howard
54 Stack-serving eatery
55 Gefilte fish fish
56 Rum-soaked cake
57 Rarely, if ___
58 Clayey soil
59 Moo ___ pork

QUARTERBACK OPTIONS

Across

1 Place for a mower
5 Suffer from a charley horse
9 Paparazzo's target, for short
14 Puzzle with a start and an end
15 Schedule position
16 Laughing gas is one
17 Not "fer"
18 Organize alphabetically, say
19 Nonviolent protest
20 Subject oneself to physical punishment, in a way
23 Football support
24 Cricket sides
25 Rocks at the bar
26 Hill builder
27 Facetiousness
32 Prim and proper
35 Field of engineering: Abbr.
36 ___-wolf
37 Give way, in a relay race
41 *Foucault's Pendulum* author
42 Liberal pursuits
43 They can be split or charged
44 Big draw at the Louvre
47 *The Office* character ___ Halpert
48 Ham, to Noah
49 ___ out (missed)
50 Not yet scheduled: Abbr.
53 Request at a weenie roast
58 Rich organic soil
59 Shakespeare's town
60 In the thick of
61 Dean Martin song subject
62 "Java" trumpeter Al
63 October gem
64 Neon, argon and xenon
65 Pub pints
66 With it, mentally

Down

1 Sharp as a tack
2 World Court site, with "The"
3 Some cyber-reading
4 Subject of an insurance appraisal
5 Nod, e.g.
6 Jobs for plumbers' snakes
7 Dance to "Hava Nagila"
8 Words to Brutus
9 Sam's Club competitor
10 Banishes to Siberia
11 Beer variety
12 Abridge, perhaps
13 Gridder Roethlisberger
21 1953 John Wayne oater
22 Suitable place
26 Lend a hand to
27 Volkswagen model
28 Phil who sang "Draft Dodger Rag"
29 Relationship words
30 McAn of shoes
31 Deep desires
32 Brother of Ham
33 Tijuana treat
34 Shortly, in verse
35 Producers: Abbr.
38 Barely visible

39 Teases maliciously
40 Sign at a convenience store
45 Make certain
46 The second number in a record
47 Sunday drives
49 Camper's dessert item
50 Florida's ___ Bay
51 Jones, once of the Stones
52 Discombobulate
53 Fast feline
54 Football's ___ Alonzo Stagg

55 "That's funny!"
56 Dr. ___ (Mike Myers character)
57 New Mexico resort town
58 Witch

YOUNG 'UNS

Across

1 Soccer segment
5 Wavelike pattern
10 Used to own
13 Violinist Stern
15 Bean or Welles
16 New England sch.
17 Ernie Banks's teammates
19 Command to Fido
20 Completely out of it
21 AOL "conversation"
22 Nuke, perhaps
25 Kerouac's *Big __*
26 Lhasa __
27 Actress __ Alicia
28 __ Plaines, Ill.
30 Vegetarian's staple
32 "Mazel __!"
33 Subscription unit
36 Copy, for short
39 Kristen of *Ryan's Hope*
41 "The Waste Land" monogram
42 Savory jelly
43 Like a bucket of song
44 Clip joint?
46 Bank acct. earnings
47 __ facto
49 Decline in value
50 Linguist's suffix
51 Facts and figures
53 Net holder
56 Afternoon service
58 Like some airports: Abbr.
59 Common word in proclamations

61 Candles' significance
62 Leo Gorcey, Huntz Hall et al.
66 __ Tin Tin
67 Object of frequent "sightings"
68 Spine-tingling
69 "You betcha!"
70 Goatish comment?
71 Bohr or Borge

Down

1 Sot's sound
2 Louisville Slugger wood
3 My __, Vietnam
4 Prima __ evidence
5 State of mind
6 Willy and Shamu, for two
7 Subaru competitor
8 Led Zeppelin's Plant
9 USNA grad
10 Deep-fried cornmeal cakes
11 Coloraturas' tunes
12 "Same here!"
14 Canucks' rivals
18 Microsoft honcho
21 Latte purveyors
22 Cosine or secant
23 __ Gay (famous B-29)
24 Get furious, slangily
29 Sleek jets of old
31 Sugary drink
34 The Beach Boys' "Surfin' __"
35 Bioelectric critters
37 Dentist's request
38 Good-sized combo
40 Tibet neighbor
45 Like Cheerios

48 *Animal Farm* author
51 Frank work
52 1973 Rolling Stones hit
54 "__ a dream": King
55 TV, radio, etc.
57 Responded, on *Jeopardy!*
60 Take a load off
62 Society rookie
63 Author Levin
64 Cacophony
65 Match, as a raise

LOWER AND LOWER

Across

1 Sticks up
5 Big bash
9 Scissors sounds
14 Continental coin
15 Author Bagnold
16 Fortuneteller's card
17 Be particular about formalities
20 Apt. feature
21 Cleveland's lake
22 Halloween color
23 Like much of MTV's viewership
25 Fourth down option
26 Grand __ Opry
27 Dipstick wiper
28 Pint, to a quart
32 __ acid (protein component)
35 Cut off
37 Lav, in London
38 Don't play for a full year
41 Lyricist Gershwin
42 Gogol's __ Bulba
43 Palm leaf
44 Put up on eBay
46 Black or chocolate pooch
47 Relative of ante-
48 Hard to grasp
50 Ballerina Moira
54 __-Matic (classic tabletop baseball game maker)
57 Neighbor of Cambodia
58 "The odds __ . . ."
59 Be a slacker
62 Burns partner

63 Division word
64 Weigh down
65 Hacienda drudges
66 Like excellent corned beef
67 Author Silverstein

Down

1 Bowling alley button
2 Protruding navel
3 "I __ for animals"
4 Business partner, perhaps
5 Babe Ruth's given first name
6 Sandy's owner
7 Mature nits
8 Suffix with cannon
9 Howard of Sirius radio
10 Football's "Broadway Joe"
11 Spinach is rich in it
12 Beer __ (bar game)
13 Eyelid woe
18 Distribute, as cards
19 Red cosmetics
24 __, Nanette
25 Blacktops, say
27 "Drying out" program
29 To boot
30 Bird on a Canadian dollar
31 Warmly affectionate
32 Buyer's caveat
33 Mucky stuff
34 Slanted: Abbr.
35 Like an alley cat
36 Update, as a computer screen
39 Soap maker's need
40 Surface figure
45 Like a sinker

47 Particle with zero mass
49 Some jackets or collars
50 Year-end temp
51 Big Indian
52 Chip away at
53 James Dean persona
54 Assault from Moe
55 Mah-jongg piece
56 Move, in Realtor lingo
57 Without company
60 Zilch
61 Ernie of the PGA

ATHLETIC WOES

Across

1 Secret store
6 Iron-gloved god
10 Rod Stewart hairdo
14 Skater-turned-actress Sonja
15 Novelist Jaffe
16 Small, at Starbucks
17 Actor in a crowd scene
18 Cast-of-thousands
19 Essayist's alias
20 Hurt athlete's least favorite vegetable?
23 Apt. extras
26 Tennis do-over
27 Bottomless pit
28 Not of the cloth
30 Yes-man
33 ___ salts
34 Klutz's comment
35 ___-mo replay
38 Hurt athlete's least favorite accommodations?
42 Yodeler's perch
43 WWII-era pope
44 Former Three Stooges associate Ted
45 Bonn's river
47 Nurses, at a bar
48 Claro residue
51 One in a six-pack
52 Suffix with acetyl
53 Hurt athlete's least favorite system of reasoning?
58 Cookie holders
59 Male porker
60 French fries source, slangily
64 *Bus Stop* playwright
65 "Arrivederci, ___"
66 *The Gift of the Magi* literary device
67 Middling grades
68 Taken by mouth
69 Name in fine china

Down

1 "That's all ___ wrote"
2 Cowpoke's moniker
3 Aardvark's morsel
4 Impersonal letter opener
5 It may keep fast food warm
6 Doggie bonus
7 Kachina doll–making tribe
8 "Come ___, the water's fine!"
9 Talladega 500, e.g.
10 Words after "slowly I turned . . ." in a comic routine
11 *Roots* author Alex
12 Name after "aka."
13 ___ jaw (pug's liability)
21 Fam. member
22 Pop
23 A Baldwin brother
24 *It's a Wonderful Life* director Frank
25 Rope fiber
29 Makes more compact
30 Knitted cap
31 Important work
32 Naked ___ jaybird
34 Father of 6-Across

36 Car dealer's offering
37 Fabric created by DuPont
39 Prefix with center or dermis
40 Nasal woe
41 1/1 song title word
46 FDR's successor
47 Mattress problem
48 Storage place
49 59-Across, e.g.
50 Piece of hardware on a 55-Down
51 Reef makeup

54 River of Spain
55 Way in or out
56 Tibetan monk
57 Fish used in gefilte fish
61 Excessively
62 Put a stop to
63 Nursery rhyme pocketful

AT THE BAGEL SHOP

Across

1 Separates with a sieve
6 "__ Mia"
10 Salami haven
14 Marina's place
15 Track shape
16 March 17 slogan word
17 Love like mad
18 Balderdash
20 Saskatchewan city
22 Mitigates
23 Manuscript mark
24 Fan dancer Rand
27 Dosages similar to pills
30 Encyclopedia unit: Abbr.
31 Photo __ (media events)
34 Comrade in arms
35 Short digression
37 Princess tormentor
38 Ode title opener
39 Seaside aroma
41 NYC hours
42 T'ai __ ch'uan
43 Online mortgage broker
44 Empire builder of old Peru
45 Solo in *Star Wars*
46 __ Z (everything)
47 Inks the attendance sheet
50 Producer of sweat or tears, but not blood
52 Zap, in a way
53 Indian metropolis
56 Hardly laughing
60 Russian church topper
63 Raise the spirits of
64 Lightning catchers
65 Geological periods
66 Pago Pago's locale
67 Secy., e.g.
68 Pioneer's heading
69 What's hot

Down

1 Famous twins' home
2 Prefix with Chinese
3 Land adjacent to a river, often
4 With no words wasted
5 Addison's literary partner
6 Lola's club of song
7 Is frank about
8 Gangsta __
9 Tour de France peak
10 Tooth problem
11 Cupid, to the Greeks
12 Wingless parasites
13 Well fluids
19 Disney's *Old* __
21 Boeing 737, e.g.
25 Audubon subjects
26 Napoleonic victory site of 1796
27 Work behind the plate
28 Hawaii hi
29 Brawl site in a western
31 Magic words for Ali Baba
32 *My Cousin Vinny* star Joe
33 Underworld figure
36 Penn, e.g.: Abbr.
39 Protect, as freshness
40 Utah ski spot
44 Isolated, as a people

48 Call __ day
49 Most courageous
50 Scrooge's visitor
51 *Three Musketeers*' chronicler
53 "Dumb" girl of comics
54 NASA chimp of 1961
55 Pots' tops
57 Homes of twigs
58 Princes' school
59 Like Latin, today
61 Morning drops
62 "-ite" compound, often

HISS MAJESTY

Across

1 Meat stamp inits.
5 One of AA's twelve
9 Shrimp or tuna dish
14 Work-order detail, for short
15 Be a snitch
16 Choreographer Tharp
17 "___ quote you on that?"
18 Rights org.
19 Stared lustfully at
20 Observation after a genetic engineering mishap?
23 Feels regret over
24 Risk a perjury charge
25 Sounds from a flock
28 Sound from a stockyard
30 Letter after epsilon
34 Wing it
35 Iranian's tongue
37 "___cool!"
38 A family member's duck costume?
41 Clean air org.
42 Horizontal line on a graph
43 "Inferiority complex" coiner Alfred
44 Thumbs-down votes
46 Loc. of the UN and MSG
47 Clown's props
48 Top-left PC key
50 Go ___ (tussle)
51 Pugilists' post-fight embrace?
58 Astrological Scales
59 Word after "Ye"
60 Baseball's "Sultan of Swat"
62 Place to moor
63 Trot or canter
64 The Bionic Woman's California hometown
65 Calvin with 12 PGA Tour wins
66 Princess born 8/15/1950
67 Dimwit

Down

1 Trojans' school, for short
2 E-junk
3 ". . . which nobody can ___"
4 Polluted precipitation
5 Puts on, as a play
6 Some NASDAQ stocks
7 ___ Enchanted (Anne Hathaway movie)
8 "In addition . . ."
9 Popular vodka, for short
10 Archie Bunker expletive
11 Grammy winner Lovett
12 One of the Baldwins
13 Florida's Miami-___ County
21 Beat in the ring
22 Heed the dentist's advice
25 When doubled, a German spa area
26 Parkinson's treatment
27 Broncos legend John
28 Wild-eyed and crazy
29 They lack refinement
31 Tom of The Seven-Year Itch
32 "Be silent," musically
33 Weather Underground cofounder Bill

35 Super-attractive
36 Headed for overtime
39 1933-41 veep John ___ Garner
40 Willow-to-Nome sled race
45 Not publicly known
47 Tampa neighbor, familiarly
49 Participate in *Disney on Ice*
50 Introduce to the mix
51 Radar image
52 One of a limerick's five
53 Up to the task
54 Lotus position activity

55 Pizazz
56 Stephen King's scary St. Bernard
57 List-ending abbr.
61 Chart-topper

JUST DUCKY

41 Ceramist's oven
42 HS experiment site
44 Muddied up
46 Take the helm
47 Mark in "mañana"
48 "For goodness __!"
49 Paper towel feature
51 Secluded valley
52 Batting avgs., e.g.
55 Sport __ (versatile vehicle)
56 Nuptials response
57 Yuletide quaff

58 Joanne of *Red River*
59 "__, Virginia . . ."

ONE FOR ALL, ALL FOR ONE

Across

1 A Musketeer
6 Titles for knights
10 List-ending abbr.
14 Bandleader Basie
15 Stage accessory
16 Hang on to
17 World-renowned razor sharpener?
19 Inter ___ (among others)
20 Lacking nothing
21 Seaside scavengers
23 Big name in PCs
25 Assayer's sample
26 Friskies eater
27 Sets of beads
31 1974 Peace Nobelist
33 Make a pick
34 Within earshot
36 Early Gleason role
39 "Just the facts, ___!"
41 Barely defeats
43 Mrs. Dithers
44 Give permission to
46 Bagel topper
47 Headstone inscription
48 X-ray vision stopper
50 Drug-induced stupors
53 Got a load of
55 ___ Altos, Cal.
57 Orbit period
58 Really perturbed
61 Most senior

65 Place for cash
66 Percussionist in the caveman orchestra?
68 Scandinavian capital
69 Mandolin kin
70 Peace goddess
71 Hatchling's home
72 School on the Thames
73 Mt. Rushmore mate of Abe, Tom, and George

Down

1 Need a rubdown
2 Any of the Simpsons
3 Go for game
4 Iroquois tribe
5 Warehouse user
6 Tanning lotion abbr.
7 Tax-deferred plans, for short
8 Shakespearean role for Leonardo
9 Federline's ex
10 Biblical twin
11 Flag on a 100-foot pole?
12 Walled city of Spain
13 Part of LCD
18 Lion or tiger
22 Cyclist's choice
24 City on the Aire
27 "Arrivederci, ___"
28 October birthstone
29 Places for graffiti?
30 Carl of *Cosmos*
32 Quirky behavior
35 Baton-passing race
37 View from Toledo
38 Big, fat mouths

40 Cohort of Curly
42 *Silkwood* star
45 *Pogo* cartoonist Kelly
49 In the realm of possibility
51 Coin flipper's phrase
52 Madonna's *Truth* ___
53 Suppress, as a story
54 Ouzo flavoring
56 Dark brew
59 Place for a token
60 Inner: Prefix
62 Got a load of

63 E-mail command
64 Deuce topper
67 Poet's dusk

MEAT MARKET

Across

1 Native-born Israeli
6 Containing gold
11 Get hard
14 John, who played Gomez
15 Site of many Goyas
16 Part of TNT
17 Sound-barrier breaker of 1947
19 CD-___
20 New Haven collegian
21 Rural tracts
22 Knot-tying phrase
23 Bruce Springsteen and the ___ Band
27 Mule, for example
29 Applies lightly
30 Like an illegal boxing blow
32 Bunny's tail
33 Icky stuff
34 Faucet problem
36 Bailiwicks
39 Soprano Moffo
41 Theme of this puzzle
43 Dalai ___
44 Oboe's pair
46 Raines or Cinders
47 Erie Canal mule
48 At ___ end (flummoxed)
50 Costa ___ Sol
51 "Miracle" team of '69
52 Ditsiness
55 Stereotypical place of exile
57 Alice's sitcom boss
58 Lab charges

60 ___ de plume
61 Country music's ___ Ridge Boys
62 Certain pass catcher, in old football lingo
67 Beehive State Indian
68 Corporate cow
69 Salami selection
70 The Blue Jays, on scoreboards
71 Smartly dressed
72 Dadaist Max

Down

1 Certain bunt, on a scorecard
2 Cheroot residue
3 A/C measure
4 Kitchen extruders
5 Spot for a bracelet
6 Big galoot
7 River to the Caspian Sea
8 Goes ballistic
9 Standards of excellence
10 Island of France
11 Demi Moore played one in 1996
12 Eat away at
13 East ___ (sovereign state since 2002)
18 Rates of return
23 ___ Rice Burroughs
24 River to the Rhone
25 Big name in the blues
26 Pastry from Linz
28 "Knit one, ___ two"
31 Handle with skill
35 Loses color
37 Fine fiddle
38 Zesty dip

40 Score after deuce
42 Tiger Hall of Famer Al
45 Get hard
49 "___ by Starlight"
51 Dues payer
52 Folder's phrase
53 "Peachy!"
54 Brewer's need
56 Victor of piano antics
59 Fit of pique
63 B flat or C sharp
64 Raggedy doll

65 Trig function
66 Herriman's "Krazy" one

THE STARTING GUN

Across

1 Purse part
6 Harshly criticize
10 Diplomat's asset
14 Tara family name
15 Cartoon skunk ___ Le Pew
16 Queens, NY, tennis venue
17 Signaled "hello"
18 State to be true
19 *South Park* boy
20 Construction worker's bagful
23 Gene Kelly's ___ *Girls*
24 Halloween witch features
25 Takes down a peg
29 Watergate hearings chairman Sam
32 One and only
33 Classic theater name
34 ___ up (absorb)
37 Make big plans, in a way
41 Mined rock
42 Leave stranded during winter
43 Sax type
44 Be gaga over
45 Any Swiss state
47 ___ acid (protein component)
50 Hoover, for one
51 Fail, slangily
58 "___ Lang Syne"
59 "Um, pardon me . . ."
60 ___ as a rock
62 Sloth's home
63 Whodunit hero Wolfe
64 Fill with glee
65 Means justifiers
66 "Absolutely!"
67 ___ out (distributes)

Down

1 Piglet's mother
2 "___ she blows!"
3 Great review
4 Geographical datum
5 Implement of pain, on hell night
6 Bombards with bogus offers, say
7 Strauss of jeans
8 Pyramid's point
9 Chicago exchange, for short
10 Abel, discoverer of New Zealand
11 Fall bloom
12 Gregorian music style
13 Portable shelters
21 Thumbs-up response
22 *Dallas* family name
25 To boot
26 A Capetown citizen
27 Pot builder
28 Pirate's realm
29 Dog on *Frasier*
30 Bit attachment
31 Rocket scientist Wernher ___ Braun
33 River to the Baltic
34 Bonneville ___ Flats
35 Dog at Camp Swampy
36 Lowly laborer
38 Lehár's *The Merry* ___
39 Green prefix
40 Rock's Steely ___
44 Battery parts
45 Black Halloween animal

46 Tickled pink
47 Rock with bands
48 Express grief
49 Wasted time
50 Exorcism target
52 The Darlings' dog
53 Not us
54 Roll call response
55 Western necktie
56 Line to Israel
57 Web spot
61 ___ Moines, Iowa

OX TAILS

Across

1 Burst of energy
6 Assist crookedly
10 Cathedral recess
14 Turkish bigwig of old
15 Wise old head
16 Churchillian gestures
17 Surrender site of 1865
19 Added stipulations
20 Beat the dickens out of
21 *M*A*S*H* procedure
23 Friend, in slang
24 *Candid Camera* creator Funt
25 Ground-rule ___
29 Discriminatory, in a way
32 Banks or Bilko
33 Tool with a bubble
34 Hirsute Himalayan beast
37 ___ *Flux* (Charlize Theron movie)
38 Talked wildly
39 "S.O.S." pop group
40 FYI part
41 Fan club reading, briefly
42 Grand jury's activity
43 "The buck stops here" president
45 Philadelphia university
46 Lucy and Ricky's landlady
48 Philosopher ___-tzu
49 Emerald Isle accent
51 Italian noblewoman
56 One of the Pentagon's five
57 Malady most common among children
59 School attended by 007

Down

60 Rwandan ethnic group
61 Be crazy about
62 Call to the first in line
63 Pindaric works
64 Place with a "vacancy" sign

Down

1 Often-filtered mail
2 Bearded Smurf
3 Snail-mail co.
4 Greek P's
5 Like potential circus animals
6 Baseballer with a star insignia
7 Hold back, as breath
8 Diva's problem
9 Contact by cell phone, in a way
10 Is of value to
11 Common place for a hockey thug
12 Marsh plant
13 Krupp Works city
18 1/640 square mile
22 Commuter option
25 Refusing to listen
26 Cookie since 1912
27 Hardly conventional
28 Clearance sale container
29 Dwarfs count
30 Nights, in ads
31 Marked wrong, perhaps
33 Clark's Smallville crush
35 Cugat ex Lane
36 Movie critic Pauline
38 Lens holder
39 "___ you nuts?"
41 Bantu language
42 Mets, Jets, or Nets

44 University big shot
45 Like a damp cellar
46 Buddy who played Jed Clampett
47 Cornball
48 Center of activity
50 Recording studio effect
51 Mention as a reference
52 Inner: Prefix
53 Dick and Jane's dog
54 Really ticked off
55 Rink leap
58 1963 Paul Newman movie

WOOFERS

Across

1 Tinker-Evers-Chance team
5 Whittle down
9 About 39 inches
14 On a cruise
15 Dumbbell material
16 Popeye's sweetheart
17 1972 US Olympic swimmer
19 Dress to the ___
20 Marsh birds
21 Dermatologist's concern
23 Suffix with insist or persist
24 Auto dealer's offer
25 Unaccounted-for GI's
27 Rocky, at the beginning of *Rocky*
34 One in cuffs
38 Swedish money
39 Stir up
40 Accomplishments
43 Height: Prefix
44 "All kidding ___ . . ."
46 Cousin or niece
48 Mad scientist's milieu, perhaps
51 Taken-back car
52 Hearth heap
57 Beaver's handiwork
60 Insurance assessment
62 On dry land
63 Jimmy Dorsey's "Maria ___"
65 Devilish sort
67 Tasty mushroom
68 Designer Schiaparelli
69 Home to most Turks
70 Knight's mount
71 Created a web
72 Mall rat, most likely

Down

1 Caravan beast
2 Grammarian's concern
3 Yogi of notable quotes
4 Libations with sushi
5 Domino spots
6 Onassis nickname
7 Campus military gp.
8 Biochemical catalyst
9 ___ Point (Long Island's end)
10 Inventor Whitney
11 Antler point
12 Neck and neck
13 Take a catnap
18 One-pot meals
22 Comic Caesar
26 Jack of rhyme
28 Justice Dept. arm
29 "___ you later!"
30 One of the Four H's
31 ___ sci (coll. major)
32 Golden rule word
33 Put on weight
34 Kuwaiti, for one
35 Rights activist Parks
36 Reformer Jacob
37 Church officer
41 Business card abbr.
42 Hearst-kidnapping org.
45 Ireland's color
47 Bring embarrassment to
49 Prefix with glottis or gram

50 Has a bite
53 Young pig
54 Roulette player's opponent
55 Kovacs of early TV
56 Roomy vehicle
57 Obama's gp.
58 Heaps
59 Insignificant
61 Kind of seaweed
62 Chester ___ Arthur
64 Society column word
66 Baton Rouge sch.

NO 17's, 36's, OR 57's

Across

1 Picket line flouters
6 Hazel's TV occupation
10 Mess maker
14 Rathskeller order
15 Farmland unit
16 Vena __
17 Dr. Seuss title
20 Caterpillar's construction
21 Partook of
22 Prepares to be dubbed
23 Four-star review
25 Mudville baseballer
26 Sea or moon follower
28 Give a shellacking to
31 Hockey thugs
32 Go yachting
33 Oil can letters
36 Words after "Go away!"
40 Shirt size abbr.
41 Assault like a goat
42 "Crazy" singer Patsy
43 Abu __
45 Tanker filler
46 Copy, briefly
49 Quiz option
50 Filmdom's __ May
52 'Hood address?
53 __ one's time
57 Ending of Matthew 22:14
60 Blue-pencil
61 *The Blackboard Jungle* author Hunter
62 Lumberjacks' competition
63 Most August births
64 E-mail button
65 Timetables, informally

Down

1 Gill opening
2 Spot for a java
3 Not "fer"
4 Philosopher Russell
5 Mexicali Mrs.
6 Dull finish
7 Tylenol target
8 High dudgeon
9 Send to the canvas
10 Coaster rider's reaction
11 Football feature
12 Seed-to-be
13 Deep, musically
18 Basilica area
19 Machu Picchu builder
24 Lhasa __
26 Nickelodeon selection
27 Part of UPC
28 Prickly flora
29 Run amok
30 Hard wood
31 128 oz.
32 Concert memento
33 Uttered
34 Teenager's torment
35 __ out (just manage)
37 Org. for Wizards and Magic
38 Linen color
39 Exam proctor's handout
43 Stops paying attention
44 Fine-tune

45 Moat critter, for short
46 Nat Turner, for one
47 Sidestep
48 Barbecue site
49 Pollster's concern
51 Flock members
52 Food in flakes
54 Castaway's home
55 Scout's act
56 Slaughter on the ballfield
58 Forum greeting
59 Round-trippers: Abbr.

BARRIERS

Across

1 Almost out of
6 Attire for Dracula
10 Brother of Little Joe on '60s TV
14 Spanish tourist center
15 Soon, in verse
16 *Ulysses*, for one
17 U.S. money market
19 Anniversary, e.g.
20 Tough to trick
21 Stick of gum, informally
22 Sweater type
24 Heroic deed
25 Holm of *Still Breathing*
26 Preacher's admonition
29 Strongly opposed
30 Publicist's assignment
31 "Warmer" or "colder"
32 "You gotta be kidding!"
36 45 or 78
37 Cagney's TV partner
38 Hatchery sound
39 __-eyed
40 Discordant deity
41 Converted split, e.g.
42 *Ivanhoe* author
44 Trample underfoot
45 Branch out
48 Ill-mannered sort
49 "Can't resist!"
50 Lover's __
51 __ up (make sense)
54 Huff and puff
55 Engineer or conductor
58 __ *Reader* (eclectic magazine)
59 Like dishwater
60 Oddball
61 Compote fruit
62 Nordic runners
63 Well-known

Down

1 Things on books
2 Place to do laps
3 See 20-Across
4 Feeling rotten
5 Just emerging
6 Shift-6
7 One more time
8 "The Gold-Bug" writer
9 Plea
10 Crop-dusting plane
11 Iridescent gems
12 Occupy, as a table
13 Noisy public fight
18 "Take __!"
23 Supermodel Carol
24 Indecisive sort
25 Road construction markers
26 Pete Rose's longtime team
27 Devil's doings
28 Cuban currency
29 OK to do
31 Literary Bret
33 Disorderly stack
34 Pianist Peter
35 All-comers tournament
37 Aerobics attire
41 Brief visit along the way
43 Stimpy or Sylvester

44 Take to the sky
45 Make confetti of
46 Quartz variety
47 Karan of fashion
48 Partners of whistles
50 Stripper St. Cyr
51 Comic Sandler
52 Fake out at the rink
53 Scott in a noted court case
56 Cousin of a puffin
57 In the style of

WHAT'S NEW?

Across

1 Descend like an eagle
6 Food with chips
10 Gift from a genie
14 *Broom* ___ (comics witch)
15 Division word
16 St. ___'s fire
17 One to respect
18 Idyllic place
19 Sphinx, in part
20 "You missed it!"
23 Pop-up cyber-annoyances
26 Calendar unit
27 Praised highly
28 Morsel in a box of bran flakes
30 Drink noisily
32 Credits as a source
33 Stable babe
34 Actress Zadora
37 It's needed to run appliances
41 Bad: Prefix
42 Like a stained shirt pocket
43 Like ghost stories
44 Soft tennis shots
46 Loses one's cool
47 UFO crew
50 Scholarship money
51 The Beatles' "___ It Be"
52 "Keep your hands to yourself!"
56 Weekend rancher
57 Nonwritten
58 Change for a sawbuck
62 Cow-horned goddess
63 Larry of *The Three Stooges*

64 In plain view
65 Well-groomed
66 Confused states
67 Take another crack at

Down

1 "___ sells sea shells . . ."
2 Comic Shriner
3 Moth-eaten
4 Poems of praise
5 Writer of song takeoffs
6 Intensely hot
7 "500" race
8 "Keep it in"
9 Waikiki Beach's city
10 Form, as tears
11 Tale of Troy
12 Whacked, bible-style
13 Put an edge on
21 Did a 10K, say
22 Dinghy propeller
23 Rainbow-shaped
24 When many newspapers are published
25 Places to build
29 Dry, to a vintner
30 Haberdashery buy
31 Like a doily
33 Act the rat
34 Trouble for Pauline?
35 How fish may be packed
36 "This is only ___"
38 Remove the soap from
39 Tries to get, as an acting part
40 Stimpy's pal
44 Can't stomach

45 Gerund ending
46 Jack Horner's fare
47 Introduce to the mix
48 No-goodnik
49 Columbus's 1492 goal
50 Van Gogh painted here
53 Rock's Cream, e.g.
54 Vampire's tooth
55 Drones' home
59 November 11 marcher
60 Go amiss
61 Barnyard digs

LAUGHING IT UP

Across

1 Have brake problems
5 Plant firmly
10 Nightclub of song
14 Taylor of *Six Feet Under*
15 Rita Hayworth title role
16 A Baldwin
17 Cobblers' tools
18 Offerer of insincere greetings
20 Catchall abbreviation
21 Catch in the act
22 "Mule Train" singer Frankie
23 Waffle maker
25 Paris Hilton, for one
27 Without a care
31 Bonaparte's punishment
32 Court star Arthur
33 Fruit center
36 "Or __!"
37 Simply smashing
39 Show anger
40 "Black-eyed" veggie
41 Philandering sort
42 Visit unexpectedly
43 Carnival ride with organ music
46 Submits an amended return
49 Safire piece, once
50 Speedy train
51 "Hail!"
52 It's clenched
56 Flag for Captain Kidd
59 Mental invention
60 Skin care substance
61 Fictional Scarlett
62 High-five sound
63 Subtle flavor
64 Woes for toes
65 Call to Fido

Down

1 __-dunk
2 New Zealand bird
3 Causes of misery
4 Faithful follower
5 Seasonal quaff
6 Alyssa of *Who's the Boss?*
7 Talk too much
8 Former Leno announcer Hall
9 Morse T
10 One who sings to the cops
11 Nostalgic number
12 Hammer parts
13 The 40 of "the back 40"
19 Much the same
24 Ham holder
25 Corn covering
26 Tunnel effect
27 Dickens's hateful clerk
28 Trucker's toll unit
29 Galileo's home
30 Cagney's TV partner
33 __ platter (Chinese menu choice)
34 Remark while anteing
35 Take care of
37 Like poor losers
38 Yours and mine
39 Salmon and trout, for two
41 Pass-the-baton race
42 Lead-in for law or med
43 Forage grass

44 Wield authority
45 *Manon* and *Carmen*
46 Big Indian
47 Gastroenteritis cause, maybe
48 One facing life, maybe
51 Gelling substance
53 Not in use
54 Mark with a branding iron
55 Piece of Watergate evidence
57 Bird in *Arabian Nights*
58 Exclamation of discovery

YOUGSTERS

42 Suffix with ethyl or methyl
44 Oater watering holes
46 Incite, as trouble
47 Work at, as a trade
48 Cottontails' tails
49 ___ noir (wine)
50 Word before rubber or ink
51 Worth a ten
54 Two pounds, plus
55 ___ Angel (West classic)
56 "We're toast!"
57 The Lion King Queen

58 North African port
59 In the ___ (performing poorly)

SAY AH!

Across

1 Garbage hauler
5 Little white lies
9 Pie-in-the-face sound
14 Aesop's also-ran
15 New York stage award
16 Hurler Satchel
17 Make English, in form
19 Shop talk
20 Ms. Shore, hitchhiking?
22 Not exactly a brainiac
23 Bo Derek's score
24 Goblet part
27 Emissions watchdog org.
30 Court figures, briefly
32 "___ had it!"
33 Pres. Jefferson
37 Poet's planet
39 Some Muslims
41 Zookeeper's words to a cat in a mud puddle?
44 String player of old
45 *Tic Tac Dough* win
46 Cereal-pitching tiger
47 "___ Beso"
48 Get-up-and-go
50 Gen-___ (boomer's kid)
52 Ring officials, briefly
54 Pro-Second Amendment org.
56 ___ *Irish Rose*
61 Talking bird with a hit record?
65 Spread open
67 San Marino or Andorra
68 Mount the soapbox
69 "No guarantees"
70 Author Bagnold
71 "The Highwayman" poet
72 David Bowie's "___ Dance"
73 Becomes solid

Down

1 Pottery fragment
2 Tippy craft
3 Grinder's instrument
4 Joins with a torch
5 Convergence points
6 Footnote abbr.
7 *Carmen* composer
8 Sign on a new lawn
9 Reach across
10 Law firm aides, for short
11 Attack vigorously
12 Make ___ of (succeed in)
13 Vietnamese holiday
18 Words of understanding
21 Where the Old Woman lived
25 Perrier rival
26 Having an open weave
28 Ominous sign
29 Sculptures, oils, etc.
31 Drag to court
33 Liv of *Armageddon*
34 Monopoly buy
35 Like a foul ball into the stands
36 Reagan-era mil. program
38 Abbr. meaning "no liquor provided"
40 Clear after taxes
42 WWW access enabler
43 Courteney of *Friends*

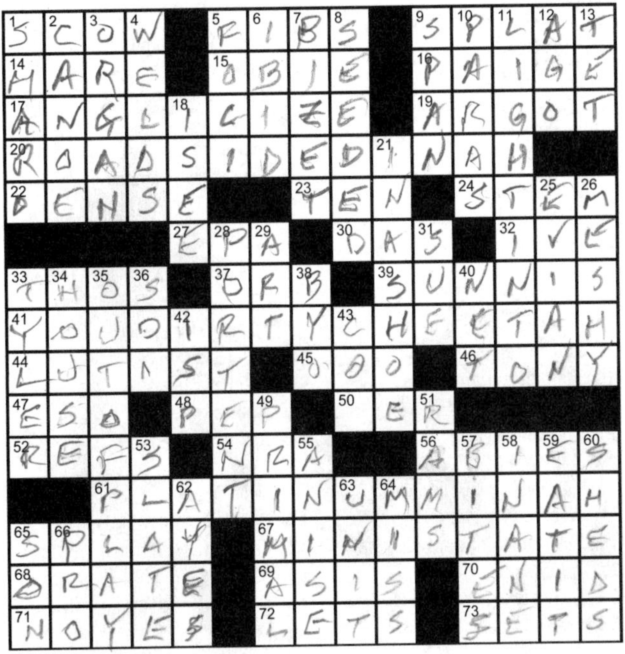

49 Word before scream or fear

51 Smashes into

53 Election Day list

55 Ouzo flavoring

57 Data storage units

58 Totally ridiculous

59 ". . . your cake and ___, too"

60 Loses one's fur

62 Salts' assents

63 Minute or mile

64 Be off the mark

65 Trinity figure

66 Country club teacher

UP THE POLITICAL LADDER

Across

1 Politico Alexander
6 Subtly suggest
11 Garfield, e.g.
14 Hockey venue
15 In abundance
16 Football's Cardinals, on scoreboards
17 Suave urbanite
19 Dream acronym
20 Matador's prize
21 Slap with a ticket
22 Left one's seat
24 440-yard path
26 Inexpensive, fuel-efficient wheels
29 Wildly lash out toward
32 ___ Domini
33 Distinctive glow
34 Livestock competition setting
39 Philosopher Lao-___
40 Single shot: Abbr.
41 Pro–Second Amendment org.
42 Presidential trip abroad
47 Sing like Ella
48 Impulse transmitter
49 Spheres of influence
51 First Lady, 1969–74
55 Seasonal song
56 Elite group
57 *Othello* role
59 Jet-setter's problem
62 ___-tickler (funny joke)

63 Big deal
67 Time of anticipation
68 Standing up
69 Patriots' Day month
70 Boob tube
71 Moves gently
72 Georgetown athletes

Down

1 Bodice feature
2 Lily Pons number
3 The city and beyond
4 "___ luck?"
5 Prank player
6 Walk or trot
7 Host a roast, say
8 Toll hwy.
9 Tap offering
10 Oppressive rulership
11 Chocolate substitute
12 Playground retort
13 Swatch competitor
18 Purple hue
23 Part of the mouth
25 By way of
27 Not posed
28 Toronto's prov.
29 Pool's Minnesota ___
30 Intense desire
31 The "T" in FIAT
35 Young ___ (tads)
36 Of lesser importance
37 Neighbor of Turkey
38 Charlie Brown's "Darn!"
43 Catches some rays
44 Investment sales charge

45 ___ populi
46 South Pacific kingdom
47 Manuscript encl.
50 Simoleons
51 Whittles down
52 Still in the game
53 Lhasa apso's land
54 Agnes de Mille, to Cecil B.
58 Cultural doings
60 Where the Gobi is
61 Hair goops
64 Memorable time

65 ___ Plaines, Ill.
66 ___ *Sharkey* (Rickles sitcom)

HOLDING WATER

Across

1 Major composition
5 Out of kilter
10 Some roll call votes
14 Goat cheese
15 Alfalfa's *Our Gang* heartthrob
16 Donuts, mathematically
17 Mellow brass
19 Bean grown for sprouts
20 Metallic quality
21 "Yer dern __!"
23 XXX part
26 LAX posting
27 Locales for sedges and reeds
28 Temptress's asset
30 The haves have it
31 Like an épée's point
32 Shrewd
33 Gave a thumbs-up to
36 Reply to "Shall we?"
37 Bulgaria's capital
38 On the briny
39 SASE, e.g.
40 Bird in a Poe classic
41 Bishop's topper
42 One with a cure
44 Instigate
45 Dry as a desert
47 Bert Bobbsey's twin
48 Guitar innovator __ Paul
49 Was gaga over
50 Burger unit
52 Rhett Butler's last word
53 Vacation spot on the shore
58 James, winner of a posthumous Pulitzer
59 Houston pro
60 Pipe problem
61 The Virgin Is., e.g.
62 Make even shorter, say
63 MacLachlan of *Twin Peaks*

Down

1 On vacation
2 __ capita income
3 Beehive State tribesman
4 __ serif
5 Stick like glue
6 Bill, host of *Real Time*
7 One of a set of clubs
8 Camera type, briefly
9 __ winds (California phenomenon)
10 Maximally
11 Lodging for young travelers
12 Banks in Cooperstown
13 Coaches give them
18 Visual aid in a presentation
22 Airport that serves Paris
23 Postpone, as a motion
24 Partner of Burns
25 Bobby Thomson's 1951 blast, notably
27 __ *Black* (1997 sci-fi spoof)
29 Young __ (tykes)
30 Piece of Necco candy
32 Witches' group
34 New Hampshire college town
35 Feathered missiles

37 Restaurant area with a sneeze guard
38 Align the cross hairs
40 Like proverbial hen's teeth
41 Billing period, often
43 One bringing home the bacon
44 Sailor's measure of depth
45 Nobelist with Begin
46 Pithy saying
47 Mollusk shell material
50 Garden walkway
51 The "sun" in "sunnyside up"

54 Language suffix
55 One-eighty
56 __ ammoniac
57 __ out (barely make)

IN THE 'HOOD

Across

1 Disney pup
6 Cleans the deck
10 Bite-size appetizer
14 Kukla and Fran's partner
15 Large part of an atlas
16 Beehive State natives
17 Myopia, familiarly
20 Hither's partner
21 NBC debut of 1/14/52
22 In reserve
23 Antifur org.
24 "Now I've ___ all!"
25 Eye covering
28 *Uncle Tom's Cabin* girl
30 Like a church mouse
31 Feared mosquito
32 Clark's costar in *Mogambo*
35 Where one's neighbor might live
39 Gingrich, e.g.: Abbr.
40 On the perimeter
41 Tabloid tidbit
42 By oneself
43 Mr. and Mr.
45 Ezra Pound pieces
48 1996 also-ran
49 Mellow woodwinds
50 Pan-fry
52 B-2's home: Abbr.
55 "Ju-u-ust missed!"
58 Bubble-gum cost, once
59 ___ pyrites (fool's gold)
60 Treasure store
61 Fateful day in the Roman senate
62 Free download, often
63 More astute

Down

1 PlayStation maker
2 Jazz singer Laine
3 Former Fed chairman Greenspan
4 Russian orbiter of old
5 Be a royal pain to
6 A Gabor
7 Worker-welfare watchdog: Abbr.
8 "So sad"
9 Manuscript encl.
10 Gene who dethroned Dempsey
11 Supped at home
12 *GoodFellas* Oscar winner
13 Black-ink item
18 Letter after theta
19 Childish rebuttal
23 Cuzco's country
24 Engineering detail, for short
25 Exchange verbal jabs
26 Nuke plant heart
27 Chicago business area
28 Giggly noise
29 River through Silesia
31 Env. abbreviation
32 Working colonists
33 Change course
34 Some black market goods
36 Riskless, as a bet
37 Burns and Allen et al.
38 Dough may do it
42 Bikini Atoll blasts

43 Marquand's Mr.
44 Sends to the Hill
45 Spherical bacteria
46 Differently ___ (challenged)
47 "___ will ever guess!"
48 "Beats me!"
50 Without a doubt
51 Splittable bit
52 Bug-eyed
53 Top choice, slangily
54 Term of address for
     Uncle Remus

56 Auction action
57 Nest egg, briefly

VOWEL MOVEMENT

Across

1 Java holder
4 1993 football movie
8 Hammerheads and makos
14 Pavarotti standard
16 Straight
17 Fenway or Wrigley
18 Missing links
19 Western treaty gp.
20 PRNDL pick
22 Doctors' org.
23 Doctrine
24 Salad veggie
27 "Very funny!"
29 Analogy words
30 British record label
31 Aproned ad animal
34 Got wind of
38 Jerusalem's land: Abbr.
39 TV's "Science Guy"
41 Toddler's "little piggy"
42 Helicopter part
44 Gridder-turned-actor Merlin
45 Howard Hughes's airline
46 Cry of pain
48 Author Eda
50 Cotton destroyer
55 ___ fruit (eggs)
56 "I've got it!"
57 Z ___ "zebra"
58 No-frills bed
59 City on the Loire
62 Matador's workplace
66 Understood by few
67 Highly regarded
68 Looked lustfully
69 Feudal drudge
70 Mag. staff

Down

1 Corn holder
2 "Surfin' ___" (Beach Boys hit)
3 Knitted pullover
4 Salesmen, for short
5 Actress Thurman
6 Solemn song
7 Rustic
8 Pitch raisers
9 Aware, slangily
10 Munched on
11 Chart anew
12 Krispy ___ doughnuts
13 Submarine detector
15 Andean wool source
21 Little green men
23 "You are not!" reply
24 Hope-Crosby film destination
25 Flammable hydrocarbon
26 "The Raven" author
27 One named in a will
28 Talmud language
32 Skiers' challenges
33 Feeling rotten
35 Back then
36 Martin's *Laugh-In* partner
37 Former Vermont governor Howard
40 School cheer
43 Olive ___
47 Rented out
49 Where to find driftwood

50 Hackneyed
51 Chicago airport
52 Jouster's weapon
53 Lionel Hampton's instrument
54 Rest room sign
58 Staff symbol
60 Road crew's supply
61 U-turn from WSW
63 PO box item
64 Sparks or Buntline
65 Mdse.

KICK ME!

Across

1 Usurer's offerings
6 Large earring
10 E-garbage
14 Facing the hurler
15 Jessica of TV's *Dark Angel*
16 "Would __ to you?"
17 Tuscany city
18 "New Look" designer
19 Bit of verbal fanfare
20 Return to square one
22 Baseball's Musial
23 Ancient alphabetic character
24 Set straight
26 Get a move on
30 Jellyfish attack
31 Trod the boards
32 __ away (drew back)
34 Chem room
37 Dr. Seuss's *If __ the Zoo*
38 18 holes, typically
39 Plexiglas sheet
40 Cariou of stage
41 Gets frothy
42 Dreadlocked one
43 Go limp
45 Knowledgeable
46 State with authority
48 Burn cause
50 After the buzzer
51 Bic product
56 "How sweet __!"
57 Inner: Prefix
58 1860s war side
60 Awful-tasting
61 Peacock tail features
62 Old TV sidekick
63 Fish caught in pots
64 Bloody, so to speak
65 Villainous look

Down

1 __ Palmas
2 Mayberry tippler
3 Assist in wrongdoing
4 Granny
5 Had the lead role
6 Sported
7 Place for a pimiento
8 Conical reed
9 Repeated unthinkingly
10 Joins the jam session
11 Window material
12 Quinn of *Benny & Joon*
13 Stood for
21 Winery vessel
25 Purge
26 It may be "golf ball–sized"
27 Plot unit
28 Negotiations hangup
29 Royal flush part
30 Confession recitals
32 Daytime TV offering
33 Play a kazoo
35 Initial stake
36 Wampum unit
38 Float ingredient
39 Hole goal
41 Part of FWIW
42 Astronauts' vision problems

44 Big name in candy
45 Bigwig, for short
46 Still in the game
47 Abstract composer Erik
48 Catkin-bearing tree
49 Unworthy of a cigar?
52 *Dragonwyck* author Seton
53 Privy to
54 Punching-in time, for many
55 Handy bag
59 "Neither fish __ fowl"

UL APPROVED

Across

1 Heed the alarm
6 __ mater
10 Bull baiter
14 Brief digression
15 Serengeti predator
16 Black cat, to some
17 Robert Herrick Christmas poem
19 Furnace output
20 Satellite launched 7/10/62
21 Rumsfeld headed it
23 Part of TGIF
25 Loan shark, e.g.
26 Bart Starr, notably
31 Chief exec, slangily
33 Kate's TV friend
34 Wide smile
35 Rebuke to Brutus
39 Words of revenge
42 Dele undoer
43 Blunted blade
44 Do penance
45 Zorro's marks
46 Not as friendly
47 Less meaty
51 Chinese "way"
53 Mosaic designs
55 Glacial debris
61 Common Seattle forecast
62 *The King and I* star
64 Singletons
65 Singer Sedaka
66 Make furious
67 Dixie bread
68 Nut source
69 Zeroes in on

Down

1 Bulb unit
2 Big Apple stadium
3 Germany's __ Canal
4 Häagen-Dazs rival
5 Not masc. or fem.
6 On one's toes
7 Dogpatch diminutive
8 It may swing
9 Certain Californian
10 Humorist Myron
11 Make changes to
12 "__ porridge hot . . ."
13 Butler's invitation
18 Thieves' hideout
22 Moroccan's topper
24 Most nimble
26 Is worthwhile
27 Zillions
28 Whodunit game
29 Bagpiper's wear
30 Sushi fish
32 In widespread use
34 Slack-jawed look
35 Kett of old comics
36 Suffix for a lengthy event
37 Antler point
38 Exploitative type
40 Henrik Ibsen play
41 __ Dawn Chong
45 Meditative sect
46 Secure in the harbor

47 Barbershop dangler
48 Schroeder's instrument
49 Tabloids abductor
50 Dentist's direction
52 Mosey along
54 Litigious sort
56 Whiff king Nolan
57 *Green Gables* girl
58 Actress Swenson
59 ___-do-well
60 Blows it
63 Break an oath

WHY 2K!

Across

1 With it, mentally
5 Cornfield array
9 Word before time or rights
14 Love personified
15 News item often written in advance
16 Sudden thrust
17 Highly adroit
18 RC or Jolt
19 Calf-length skirts
20 Piano's ivories
22 Desktop pictures
23 Remitted by mail
24 Old-time "Listen!"
26 Log some Z's
29 Chewed the fat
33 Smart remark
37 Trapper's ware
39 "Would __?"
40 Take the mound
41 Grandchild spoilers, maybe
42 Witty Bennett
43 Largest continent
44 Got a glimpse of
45 Trapshooter's target
46 Greg's sitcom wife
48 Poet Teasdale
50 The Keystone __
52 Refuse to budge
57 Spills the beans
60 Quirky joint
63 First astrological sign
64 Teased mercilessly
65 Like some chatter
66 Shavings-creating tool
67 "Back to you"
68 Festival showing
69 Puts in order
70 Carrots' mates
71 __ up (come clean)

Down

1 Swedish imports
2 Walk leisurely
3 Ryan in Cooperstown
4 Put up
5 Football legend Knute
6 Literally, "high wood"
7 Full of tricks
8 Squirrel away
9 Twain's New York resting place
10 Surprise play on the gridiron
11 Bring to ruin
12 Opposed to, in dialect
13 Discounted by
21 Spock's captain
25 Senate votes
27 One-horse carriage
28 Pitchfork prongs
30 *Fish Magic* painter Paul
31 Word on Irish stamps
32 Nimble-fingered
33 Punch card scrap
34 Seek a sorority
35 La Scala highlight
36 "Mild-mannered reporter" of TV
38 Word from the crib
41 Lowest high tide
45 Went under

47 Growths on tree trunks
49 Kitchen extruders
51 Barbershop sharpener
53 Flatbottom boat
54 The movie *Wordplay*, e.g.
55 Puts on eBay
56 Abounds
57 Bugle tune
58 He sang of Alice
59 Whopper creator
61 Go hither and yon
62 Invention starter

GOING UNDERGROUND

Across

1 Low voice
5 Hit a high
9 Morley of *60 Minutes*
14 Minstrel's instrument
15 Wheel holder
16 Give the slip to
17 Petri dish gel
18 Pro ___ (proportionately)
19 *Popeye* creator ___ Segar
20 Comstock Lode figure
23 Z, to a Brit
24 Fax precursor
25 Words on an expiration notice
27 Bacon unit
31 Mingo player on *Daniel Boone*
34 MDs' org.
37 Old, but new again
39 iPod model
40 MTA driver
44 Jessica of *Dark Angel*
45 Mr. ___ (Tati role)
46 FDR successor
47 Reese in Cooperstown
50 Units of force
52 Bosox rivals
54 Martini & ___ vermouth
58 Dept. head
60 Ed Norton, notably
64 Garlicky sauce
66 Geometry calculation
67 Go out together
68 Pioneer's path
69 Subcompact
70 "Tell it like ___!"
71 Discombobulate
72 Do a KP chore
73 Fender ding

Down

1 Use TNT
2 Hanna-Barbera's ___ *Doggie*
3 Play for time
4 Waits on
5 Henry VIII's sixth wife, Catherine ___
6 Proctored event
7 Height: Prefix
8 Reeves of *The Matrix*
9 Be furious
10 The whole shebang
11 Bush accused Gore of using this
12 Falco of *The Sopranos*
13 Sax player's buy
21 Newsboy's shout
22 Language suffix
26 Judge's seat
28 Marina del ___, Cal.
29 Result of a bug bite
30 Like a peacock?
32 Son of Seth
33 Do mailroom work
34 "Rush!" letters
35 Stubborn equine
36 Beatles album of 1969
38 Part of SRO
41 Baba ___ (Gilder Radner role)
42 Crime head
43 In ___ (not yet born)

48 Store, as fodder
49 ___ out (barely manage)
51 Morally degraded
53 Boggy area
55 Do figure eights
56 Take effect
57 "___ my case!"
58 Spy ___ Hari
59 ___ one's loins (prepare for action)
61 Toledo's lake
62 Artist Magritte

63 Cry like a banshee
65 Capp's ___ *Abner*

PICKLED

Across

1 Politico Thurmond
6 Out of harm's way
10 Fat unit
14 Tara surname
15 Nudge forward
16 Mortgage option, for short
17 Russian art treasure
19 "In memoriam" item
20 River crosser, perhaps
21 Churchill's V, for one
23 Marx instrument
25 Bewhiskered swimmer
26 Modern video gear
30 Printer's proof
33 Post-mark currency
34 Bother greatly
35 NYC sports venue
38 Hard to grasp
42 Kiltie's topper
43 ___ Irish Rose
44 1/640 square mile
45 Sign of a dying fire
46 Knitted blanket
48 "Forever" item first sold in 2007
51 Yemen's capital
53 Spa treatment
56 Metallic marble
61 Just sitting there
62 Misleading lead
64 Three-___ sloth
65 Sunburn spray additive
66 Alpha's opposite
67 Pulls a boner
68 Stoogian ammo
69 Went carefully

Down

1 Like talc, on the Mohs scale
2 "There's gold in them ___ hills"
3 Broccoli ___
4 Assayers assay them
5 George's first lady
6 Inside the Third Reich author
7 "___ we there yet?"
8 Verne's circumnavigator
9 Decorate the perimeter of
10 Blue ___ (Capri attraction)
11 Counter, in a debate
12 Full of zeal
13 Bishop's topper
18 ___ rock (Bowie genre)
22 Somewhat, slangily
24 Penance recital
26 Buffalo Bill's Wild ___ Show
27 Faulkner femme fatale ___ Varner
28 Fedora feature
29 Radar gun wielder
31 JFK postings
32 Faux ___ (boo-boo)
34 Ashtabula's lake
35 Branch of engineering: Abbr.
36 Blood fluids
37 Secluded valley
39 Argentine expanse
40 Slack off
41 Habitual complainer
45 War reporters, nowadays
46 Penny ___ poker
47 Denmark's ___ Islands

48 Clobber, Bible-style

49 House of Henry VIII

50 "Inferiority complex" coiner Alfred

52 Urn filler

54 Suffix with rat or rattle

55 Prefix with pad or port

57 Witty Bombeck

58 Word in some epitaphs

59 *Bus Stop* playwright

60 "Jeepers!"

63 Anonymous surname

NO!

Across

1 Conductor who studied under Bartók
6 Ste. Jeanne __
10 __ Benedict
14 Bird-related
15 Dealer's customer
16 Square footage
17 "No __!"
19 Take it easy
20 Slender instrument
21 Visit a bloodmobile, e.g.
23 Ball-shaped
27 __ out (apportioned)
28 Canadian dollar coin, familiarly
29 Manufacturers
32 Apportion
33 Poe bird
34 Noah's second son
37 Classic sneakers brand
38 Minolta competitor
39 Spelunker's spot
40 Hosp. locales
41 Element no. 5
42 Aral and Caspian Seas, really
43 Cashless exchange
45 Biological groups
46 Rude look, perhaps
48 Taos colonists
49 Dropped flies, e.g.
51 WWII foes
52 Pizarro's conquest
53 "No __!"
59 Folk singer Burl
60 Three monkeys' avoidance
61 Brief incursion
62 Senate helper
63 Gets hitched
64 Make, as bogus bills

Down

1 European carrier
2 Ab __ (from the start)
3 Imprisoned Peace Nobelist __ Xiaobo
4 Strike lightly
5 About to be punished
6 Large red hog
7 "__ sow, so . . ."
8 Vintage car
9 Icky stuff
10 One with an income
11 "No __!"
12 Beau __
13 Too full
18 Village Voice award
22 Black cat, to some
23 Relieve, as thirst
24 Raft propeller
25 "No __!"
26 '60s space chimp
29 Lord's home
30 Big name in cosmetics
31 Trivia whiz Jennings
33 Opposite of well done
35 Turn away
36 Western plateaus
38 Foldout bed

39 "Pretty please?"
41 Title in Uncle Remus tales
42 Doesn't punish
44 Stimulate, as curiosity
45 Indomitable spirit
46 Old photo color
47 Fountain locale
48 Skating jumps
50 Bouillabaisse, e.g.
51 In the heart of
54 "Well, __ had it!"
55 London facility

56 Boston Garden hero Bobby
57 Hang loosely
58 Mr. Potato Head part

SQUARE ONE

Across

1 Leak sound
5 Lion tamers' needs
10 Playoff breathers
14 Ur's land
15 Czech diacritical mark
16 Itty bit
17 China/Korea border river
18 Season starter
20 Piedmont wine center
21 Spring mo.
22 Pile up
23 Frosty coating
25 Teetotaler's order
27 Figure at which eBay bidding begins
32 Hall's singing partner
33 Lewd look
34 Spanish hero El ___
37 Kadett automaker
38 Sings the praises of
40 Okefenokee Swamp possum
41 Greek T
42 Buster Brown's dog
43 *Prizzi's* ___
44 Anonymously written bestseller
48 Very, in slang
49 "Cogito, ___ sum"
50 Show a good time to
53 Shaq's alma mater: Abbr.
54 Invoice stamp
58 Like much mail
61 Bassoon relative
62 *Thousand Days* queen
63 Bandleader's cry
64 Prime-time hour
65 What's left
66 Mimic's work
67 Reunion number

Down

1 "Howdy!"
2 S&L offerings
3 Old Navy man
4 Acorn-hoarding rodent
5 Amnesiac's question
6 Come to pass
7 Pastry chef's aide
8 Fenced-in area
9 Take part in a biathlon
10 Whopper alternative
11 *The Empire Strikes Back* mystic
12 Hellenic H's
13 Puts forth
19 Low point
24 "___ Not Unusual"
25 Hotfooted it
26 Sources of iron
27 Sweep's schmutz
28 Spanish finger food
29 Totally enjoyed
30 One using Elmer's
31 ___ Lodge (motel chain)
35 The Munsters' pet bat
36 "Blonde bombshell" Diana
38 Gimlet garnish
39 Seaweed extract
40 Sportsman's mount
42 Lama land
43 Big bike

45 Apple variety
46 Polite affirmation
47 Like a curmudgeon
50 Way, way off
51 Hoarder's word
52 Coffee dispensers
53 Like the White Rabbit
55 Irish Rose lover
56 New Rochelle, NY, college
57 Bambi, e.g.
59 When doubled, a dance
60 Back talk

WATCH IT!

48 Victorian or Big Band ___
50 Arrives at
51 Who's base
52 A Kwanzaa principle
53 Flower part
54 Humdinger
55 The "U" of UHF
58 Harvester's haul
59 Checklist part
60 Not a whit
61 Mail ctrs.
63 Gift-wrapping time, for some

FAD WEAR

Across

1 Myna bird, e.g.
6 Jack who ate no fat
11 Online chuckle
14 "__ plan, a canal . . ."
15 Popular fitness program
16 Bard's before
17 Fad wear of the '50s
19 Gilbert and Sullivan princess
20 Aid to the stumped
21 Clever ploys
23 Icy-road treatment
27 Full-length film
29 __ on (victimized)
30 Back-and-forth
31 Earth tone
32 Newswoman Roberts
33 Catchall abbr.
36 Deborah of *The King and I*
37 Slipped up
38 On the main
39 Web address ending
40 Remained firm
41 Soup-eater's faux pas
42 Strauss or Bach
44 Patio furniture item
45 Like Marilyn Monroe or Barbie
47 Diner table
48 Sulky puller
49 It's the truth
50 Benevolent fellow
51 '60s–'70s fad wear
58 Hail, to Caesar
59 Internet commerce
60 Writing pad support
61 No longer active: Abbr.
62 "Try this!"
63 Way out of practice

Down

1 __ 'n' cheese
2 "I think," online
3 Cultural Revolution leader
4 Bed-and-breakfast
5 Supermarket worker
6 Undercover operation
7 Huff and puff
8 Audio system button
9 "__ Daba Honeymoon"
10 Max for tax calculation
11 Fad wear of the '70s
12 "The usual," e.g.
13 Rental option
18 Warm-hearted
22 All-purpose vehicle, briefly
23 Did a dog trick
24 Rainbow-shaped
25 Fad wear of the '60s
26 Batik worker
27 Like UFO "sightings"
28 Chisholm Trail city
30 Element number 5
32 Political buddy
34 Not very chatty
35 Bank heist, e.g.
37 List-ending abbr.
38 An Arkin
40 Fruity dessert
41 Camera feature
43 Unlock, to a bard

44 Chanel's nickname
45 Asparagus unit
46 Share equally
47 Internet hookup, for many
49 Move like a moth
52 JFK posting
53 ___ Cruces, NM
54 Letter after sigma
55 Old spy org.
56 Big Apple attraction, with "the"
57 "You ___ dog, you!"

CODE RED

Across

1 Mother of Bristol, Willow, and Piper
6 Job seeker's success
11 Handheld computer, briefly
14 *I Pagliacci*, e.g.
15 Contest in the West
16 Seek a seat
17 Four-time Emmy-winning redhead
19 Gerund suffix
20 Softens, as leather
21 Tilter's weapon
23 Respectful tributes
27 Princess Diana's family name
29 Speedily, to bards
30 Blow up
32 High-speed-chase sounds
34 Paddock meal
35 Skeptical laugh
38 Tattooists' fluids
39 Tommyrot
41 Pack in the hold
42 President pro ___
43 Coral and Yellow
44 Nor'easters
46 Dreams up
49 Farmland divisions
50 ___ Gorilla (cartoon ape)
52 Syracuse, NY, college
54 Hand-wringer's words
55 Easily split mineral
56 Pa. nuke plant
57 Redhead who succeeded and preceded Jay Leno
64 Surfacing material
65 Halloween option
66 Shop slang
67 "___ to Joy"
68 Male and female
69 English Derby town

Down

1 Impresario Hurok
2 Homer Simpson's Indian friend
3 Camcorder button abbr.
4 Jackie's O
5 Lamp type
6 Threat ender
7 Watch chains
8 Drug-approving org.
9 Sushi order
10 Hair-curling aids
11 Redhead who's a royal
12 Nincompoop
13 Tick off
18 Tell a whopper
22 Director Lee
23 "Rumor ___ . . ."
24 State one's view
25 Redhead who topped Maris
26 Ideal serves
27 High-five sound
28 Party spreads
31 Library no-no
33 Great bargain
36 Commercial makers
37 *Siddhartha* novelist Hermann
40 Pro ___ (in proportion)

41 Plumb crazy
43 Picks out
45 Not too wild to be broken
47 Brazilian hot spot
48 Moves stealthily
50 "Semper fidelis," for one
51 Sportscaster Rashad
53 Green's prefix
55 Knight's club
58 Mine find
59 Give a thumbs-down to
60 Patch target

61 Helpful connections
62 Freudian topic
63 ___ de plume

GIFT RAP

Across

1 Jack of old oaters
5 Come-hither look
9 Words before car or cop
14 Rap group Salt-N-___
15 Caspian feeder
16 Pelted on October 31
17 Pastry prettifier
18 Make, as a putt
19 Wharton's Ethan
20 Place for Jack Horner's thumb
23 "Excuse me . . ."
24 *Wait ___ Dark*
27 Added zip to
30 Egypt's lifeline
32 Beat by a nose
34 Pal of Tigger
35 Big top headliner
36 It's served in spots
37 "Oh, how we danced" tune
41 It's opposite IX on clocks
42 Computer of 1946
43 Platte River tribe
44 Pince-___ glasses
45 Revered one
46 Have the means for
48 Left Bank river
50 Scads
51 Streaker's duds
57 No rocket scientist
60 ___ *Flux* (Charlize Theron movie)
61 Not duped by
62 Many an April baby
63 Pacific tuber
64 Ponderosa brother
65 He's on the fifty
66 Genesis setting
67 Barbershop fixture

Down

1 *Iliad*, e.g.
2 Poland's Walesa
3 Takeoff artist
4 Mexicali musician
5 Booted out
6 Fairy-tale brothers
7 Smallville's Lang
8 Fraternal fellows
9 Crude processor
10 Everglades wader
11 Vietnam's ___ Dinh Diem
12 President pro ___
13 Sidewalk-stand drink
21 Seashell seller
22 Whimperer
25 Altogether
26 One with a property claim
27 Most of Iberia
28 Racehorses, informally
29 Convert to charged particles
30 Like Willie Nelson's voice
31 Apple model
33 Summoned on the PA
35 Small combo
38 Most like a bodybuilder's biceps, perhaps
39 Rear-___ (road mishap)
40 Cajolery
46 AA-related org.

47 Vaudeville family name
49 *Peer Gynt*'s creator
50 Be nuts about
52 London art gallery
53 Beer topper
54 Bring to naught
55 Slanted type: Abbr.
56 "Sock it __!"
57 Nobelist Hammarskjöld
58 Pull a boner
59 Long or Peeples

TWO THUMBS DOWN

Across

1 Dukes it out, in practice
6 Picture holder
11 To's opposite
14 Actor Bean
15 Wino
16 Superman foe Luthor
17 Subject of Aristotle's contemplation
19 __ Miss
20 Having debt, figuratively
21 Fattened fowl
23 Cameo, e.g.
24 *Critique of Judgment* author Immanuel
26 Brother of Cain and Abel
27 Tex-__ cuisine
28 Secondary meaning
32 One in a cast
35 *Jurassic Park* dino
36 Wished undone
37 Aretha Franklin's genre
38 Moth-eaten
39 US Open's __ Stadium
40 Pop singer Amos
41 Stops after ORs, perhaps
42 Strand during winter
43 Requested
45 Demolitionist's need
46 __ Lackawanna Railway
47 December 24 and 31
49 Big wheel, for short
52 "The Highwayman" poet Alfred
54 Rogers's dancing partner
56 The works
57 Missile Crisis–era structure
61 Neckline shape
62 Love dearly
63 Upright, e.g.
64 __ drop soup
65 Unpaid-for autos, perhaps
66 Dutch painter Jan

Down

1 Edna Ferber novel
2 Wrinkled fruit
3 Silk-producing region
4 *Letting Go* novelist Philip
5 Type of billiards
6 Pale with fright
7 London lav
8 Bowery __
9 "__ as directed"
10 "Autumn Leaves" lyricist Johnny
11 Seedy lodging
12 Move, in Realtor lingo
13 Team in a yoke
18 Linseed oil source
22 Appeal to
25 Waterboarding, some claim
26 Like Victoria's Secret models
27 *The Misanthrope* playwright
29 Old pros
30 Classic soda brand
31 Idyllic spot
32 Nick and Nora's dog
33 Whispers sweet nothings
34 Thanksgiving serving
35 Soft or crunchy snack
38 In abundance

42 Shoe parts
44 Oust from practice
45 New Ager John
48 Posy holders
49 Curriculum ___ (career summary)
50 *Goodnight* girl
51 Argentina's Juan
52 Cathedral center
53 Cassini of fashion
55 Touched down
58 "To a ..." poem

59 Unruly mane
60 Sis's sib

AT THE HOSPITAL

Across

1 Teen love
6 Golf hazards
11 A Bobbsey twin
14 Haile Selassie follower, for short
15 Fire up
16 Game with a 108-card deck
17 Part of a fire drill
19 Corduroy feature
20 Gardener's sackful
21 Butter up?
23 "Spare tire," essentially
24 Eye impolitely
26 Nasal partition
30 Oregano and others
31 To no __
32 Zero-point Scrabble tile
33 Attila, e.g.
36 Yardage pickup
37 Treaty result
38 Whittle away
39 Charades "little word"
40 Sudden thrust
41 Blue-haired Simpson
42 Camera card contents
44 Did a valet's job
45 Most minute
47 Kobe currency
48 One in a cast
49 By necessity
54 West of Hollywood
55 One who takes boughs?
58 Mess up
59 Two under par
60 African antelope
61 Hobby room
62 Dalmatian features
63 Editorial strike-outs

Down

1 Field yield
2 Pink in the middle
3 Meat-grading org.
4 Editor's direction
5 Injurious
6 Lovers' liaison
7 Small, agile deer
8 *La Cage __ Folles*
9 "__ Love You" (Beatles hit)
10 Change for the worse
11 Bottom-dwelling kin of the great white
12 Singer O'Day
13 "Check," in poker
18 Good soil
22 "__ you for real?"
24 "The final frontier"
25 Fork feature
26 It's a long story
27 Politico Bayh
28 Certain summer job holder, maybe
29 Plating metal
30 Smelting byproducts
32 *The Devil and Daniel Webster* author
34 Spur on
35 "__ I say more?"
37 Snub-nosed dogs

38 The usual
40 Hamlet's slayer
41 __ Mann of '60s pop
43 "O Sole __"
44 Cuzco's country
45 No longer feral
46 Words of compassion
47 Affirmatives
49 Attack, as with eggs
50 Gawk at
51 Like McCoy?
52 Traffic marker

53 Means justifiers, for some
56 Kanye West specialty
57 Self-perception

THREE CHEERS

Across

1 Downhill racer
5 "Waterloo" pop group
9 In any way
14 Mah-jongg piece
15 Landlocked Asian country
16 "That's the truth!"
17 SIS
20 Left, after taxes
21 In a draw
22 Flared skirts
23 Part of a bedroom suite
25 One of the Mavericks
26 Cocks and bulls
27 "Yay, team!"
28 OK Corral lawman
32 *Taras Bulba* author
35 Sport with mallets
36 Route word
37 BOOM
41 Flower holder
42 City founded by Pizarro
43 Greets the judge
44 "O.K., why not?"
46 Has too much, for short
47 Just great
48 Still capable of exploding
50 Feast finale
54 Agreeing
57 ___ qua non
58 Alternative spelling: Abbr.
59 BAH
62 "Waste not, want not," e.g.
63 Purple shade
64 Big furniture retailer
65 Exodus commemoration
66 Some are inflated
67 For fear that

Down

1 Defensive effort
2 One with no hope of getting out
3 Make joyful
4 Rep. counterpart
5 Axis foes
6 Big name in aspirin
7 Investor's purchase
8 Faulkner's ___ *Lay Dying*
9 Bracelet site
10 This evening, on marquees
11 Author Paton
12 Lawn application
13 Fermentation dregs
18 An end in ___
19 Drive-in employee
24 "Scat, cat!"
25 Glider wood
27 Suite parts
29 Hertz rival
30 Altar happening
31 Shells out
32 Ancient land including present-day France
33 Fairy tale monster
34 Urbane fellow
35 Serengeti group
38 Short-billed shore bird
39 End of a #2
40 Barbecue fare
45 Icky stuff

47 Some property borders
49 Reason out
50 Hustle music
51 Conjure up
52 Goes ballistic
53 Pick up the tab for
54 "As __ saying . . ."
55 Junction point
56 Like much folk mus.
57 Overly self-assured
60 Expose, in verse
61 "Black gold"

PIGGIES

Across

1 Keystone lawmen
5 Fare behind a sneeze guard
10 Rigging support
14 Simple model train layout
15 Put up with
16 Kegger attire
17 *Apollo 13* actor
19 *Spamalot* creator Idle
20 Like some swimsuits
21 Wind chime sound
23 Prefix with athlete or cycle
24 Clad like Justice Roberts
25 Either of two First Families
29 Brunch libation
32 Undesirable berth
33 Safe place
34 Agent, in brief
37 Hang in there
38 Place with a "vacancy" sign
39 Novus __ Seclorum (dollar bill phrase)
40 Ice cream tycoon Carvel
41 Neon and xenon, for two
42 Faithful subject
43 Having spunk
45 Bit of ammo
46 Benny Goodman's "kingdom"
48 Taking after
49 "Uncle __" (Berle)
51 Personal magnetism
56 Height: Prefix
57 Britain's second-largest city
59 Grouchoesque look

60 Pumpernickel, e.g.
61 Move like *The Blob*
62 Harplike instrument of old
63 Burpee bagful
64 Some deer

Down

1 "Out of the inkwell" clown
2 Pizzeria fixture
3 Apply macadam to
4 Go sprawling
5 Cavalry swords
6 Early calculators
7 Cooties
8 Noisy commotion
9 Result of a fender bender
10 Dictation takers
11 Source of patronage jobs
12 Fast on one's feet
13 Did the Iditarod, e.g.
18 Compound in fertilizer
22 Anemic person's need
25 Utter failure
26 __ snuff (satisfactory)
27 Catcher of junk e-mail
28 "You, there!"
29 Brit's buddy
30 Currier's partner
31 Brooks or Blanc
33 Parasite supporter
35 Upper hand
36 Coffeehouse reciter
38 Some humanities degs.
39 Garage supply
41 Leslie Caron title role
42 Take lessons in

44 In one piece
45 Tartan patterns
46 Lower-case
47 Aviator Post
48 Sportscaster Rashad
50 Flows back
51 Canadian Indian
52 Frankenstein's assistant
53 "Scram, fly!"
54 Puzzle on a place mat
55 Iowa State's home
58 Ill temper

THE WHOLE SHEBANG

Across

1 Milk choice
5 Fuse units
9 Flowed back
14 "The Censor" of Rome
15 Gift doc.
16 Boring lecturer
17 Part of AKA
18 Ontario tribe
19 Place to shop in Tokyo
20 Sri Lanka export
21 Prevent entrance, in a way
23 Smelling a rat
25 Farm female
26 ___ up (fancily dressed)
28 Spiced 20-Across drink
30 Ad-___ (wing it)
33 Sudden hankering
34 Bar belts
35 "___ y plata" (Montana motto)
36 Prepare groceries for purchase
40 Bard's however
41 Rub out
42 Strong desires
43 Turf square
44 Signs of approval
45 *Grinch* portrayer Jim
47 Blowup: Abbr.
48 Baskin-Robbins stack
49 Drive quickly
54 Big galoot
57 Steer clear of
58 Dracula's tooth
59 Tropical tuber
60 Not well-kept
61 Ill-mannered
62 Workbook segment
63 Geometry findings
64 Evidence of rot
65 New Age pianist John

Down

1 "Get lost!"
2 Crinkly green
3 "Everything's cool"
4 ___ juice (milk)
5 Diplomatic success
6 One might beg for this
7 School for toddlers
8 Let it stand, editorially
9 Way to get a word in
10 Wedding cake figure
11 U2's frontman
12 Auto maker Ferrari
13 "___ diary . . ."
21 Appomattox signatory
22 Shrubby tract
24 TVA output: Abbr.
26 Uses a rag, maybe
27 Big name in lawn products
28 Kasparov's game
29 Nozzle site
30 Necking locale
31 Castle of the ballroom
32 Bovine nickname
34 Source of roe
37 Joe and Rose's clan
38 Under-bridge dweller of myth
39 Erato's instrument
45 Large eel

46 *Hulk* director Lee
47 IRA-establishing law
48 Co-op alternative
49 Bear Bryant's team, for short
50 State firmly
51 Abie's love
52 Early Michael Jackson 'do
53 Heap kudos on
55 *Exodus* author
56 One of a black-clad subculture
59 King discovered in 1922

PIE FIGHT

Across

1 Gastric woe
6 Mower stowage
10 WMD part
14 Eucalyptus muncher
15 Gondola propeller
16 Provo's state
17 Way of righting a capsized kayak
19 Bird clubbed to extinction
20 "Told ya!"
21 Said, "no contest," say
22 Local resident, to a collegian
24 __ bonding
25 Evening dos
26 Helen Hunt Jackson novel of 1884
29 Easter Island's owner
30 Untouchable Ness
31 Like many college dorms
32 "__ difference!"
36 Headstone word
37 Super reviews
38 HS math course
39 Coal layer
40 Rarely, if __
41 Stone propeller
42 Out-and-out
44 Alka-Seltzer pitchman
45 President after Zachary
48 Go like mad
49 Reformer Bloomer
50 Uncle Remus title
51 Blubber
54 Sitarist Shankar
55 Two-tone treat on a stick
58 Opposed to, in dialect
59 Revolting sort
60 Eat away at
61 Hardy heroine
62 Teed off
63 Less refined

Down

1 Hawaiian strings
2 Get whipped
3 Soap unit
4 Peyton's quarterback brother
5 Unchecked
6 Mall binge
7 Where the boyz are
8 Pipe bend
9 Shoulder muscles
10 Dirty fighter, of sorts
11 Make amends
12 Dogpatch's Hawkins
13 Alley rentals
18 __ podrida
23 Garage supply
24 Frank Willard strip
25 See-thru
26 Boys in gray
27 Natural emollient
28 Sorvino of *Mighty Aphrodite*
29 Nightclub charge
31 Yielded to pressure
33 Luyendyk of Indy
34 Pay heed
35 Like French toast
37 Takes back
41 Not so dense

43 ___ chi
44 Appear to be
45 Corday's victim
46 Publicist's concern
47 Some jeans
48 Piece of sports page news
50 Soldier Field player
51 Garbage hauler
52 Word after "ye" on signs
53 Stadium vendor's wares
56 Aussie bounder
57 Glass of public radio

DOOHICKEYS

45 Bo Diddley classic
46 Alabama march site
47 Popular theater name
48 Unlike a 61-Across, usually
49 Races in a chute
52 Agitated state
53 Red in the middle
56 Ruby or emerald
57 The "I" in FWIW
58 Unaffiliated: Abbr.
59 Enlistees, briefly

NUMBER, PLEASE

Across

1 Leaders' spots
6 Cake recipe verb
10 Lhasa ___ (dog)
14 Close to
15 30% of the world
16 Impact sound
17 Café's offering, perhaps
19 Mesa dweller
20 Church foyer
21 Public outbursts
23 ___- Magnon
24 Like neon or krypton
25 Soft drink selections
29 Cambridge student, informally
32 Fool's time
33 "Stompin' at the ___"
34 UK lexicon
37 Hawaiian necklaces
38 One of HOMES
39 Philippines native
40 Moon craft, for short
41 Cheney's successor
42 *Hi & Lois* child
43 Means of escape
45 Like an angry cat's back
46 Pago Pago's land
48 Jamaica, Barbados, etc.: Abbr.
49 Performers with big red noses
51 Some poor hoops shots
56 Tear apart
57 Bit of good fortune
59 Ensures, slangily
60 Dust Bowl refugee
61 Alternative to buy
62 Procter & Gamble shampoo brand
63 Ties the knot
64 Made less tense

Down

1 "That's a gas!"
2 Raven-colored, to bards
3 Crude dude
4 Erato or Clio
5 Sign painter's form
6 Battleship blast
7 "It makes sense"
8 Half a sawbuck
9 Small amounts
10 Greek goddess of wisdom
11 Superman's "dressing room"
12 "Excellent!"
13 Keats or Shelley
18 Happy hour stops
22 Half a gas mileage rating
25 Ominous cloud
26 Duel tool
27 Initial source of energy
28 "___ boom bah!"
29 Is interested
30 The Bard's river
31 ___ compos mentis
33 Brewski
35 Art Deco notable
36 "I ___ it!" (Skelton catchphrase)
38 Hotfoot it, old style
39 Boom box port
41 Cereal choice

42 Keep a ball bouncing
44 "___, young man" (Greeley's advice)
45 Not as planned
46 Company store money
47 Ralph's missus
48 Items in a rack
50 Not doing much business
51 Fatty ___
52 General vicinity
53 Grazing spots
54 Use a surgical beam

55 Agenda, for short
58 Hawaiian music maker

YES!

Across

1 Noggin tops
6 Dark lager
10 Game-broadcasting channel
14 Where the action is
15 "I'm __ you!"
16 Minstrel's instrument
17 "Yes!"
19 Some nest eggs: Abbr.
20 *Viva __ Vegas*
21 Hatcher of *Lois & Clark*
22 Fuel type, informally
24 Flamingo's perch, commonly
26 Further amend
28 Dutch dairy product
30 Not so trite
33 Big name in chips
36 __ riot (very funny skit)
38 *Goosebumps* creator
39 Pacific battle site, in brief
40 "Yes!"
42 "The Science Guy" on TV
43 Sans __ (carefree)
45 Bonheur or Parks
46 "Holy smokes!"
47 Nation of the Balkans
49 Humorous Bombeck
51 "Despite all that . . ."
53 Awakens rudely
57 State-of-the-art
59 Parodied
61 Chart-topper
62 Basic lessons
63 "Yes!"
66 Classic soda brand
67 Don't throw out
68 Epic or Arista
69 Distinctive flair
70 No effort at all
71 Eliminate, as a lead

Down

1 Spanish cellist Casals
2 Indo-__ languages
3 Make fun of
4 Blowup: Abbr.
5 Like tavern peanuts
6 Great Trek participant
7 Walking __ (elated)
8 UPS delivery: Abbr.
9 Like some Jewish delis
10 Snob of a sort
11 "Yes!"
12 Sch. groups
13 Treetop construction
18 Prefix with maniac
23 Thesis writer's "that is"
25 Brown with a Band of Renown
27 Ooze forth
29 Indian cotton fabric
31 New Ager who often sings in Gaelic
32 Clarinetist's need
33 Brainy Simpson
34 A wanted man, maybe
35 "Yes!"
37 Egg __ yung
40 Dressed to the __
41 Niagara Falls daredevil's craft
44 Collapses

46 ___ de toilette
48 Outflow's opposite
50 Lunar lander
52 Saharan springs
54 Biblical queendom
55 Scrabble pieces
56 Strunk and White subject
57 Swim meet division
58 First homicide victim
60 Castel Gandolfo resident
64 "C'mon, ___ sport"
65 Macadam ingredient

WAX AND WANE

42 Future fish
44 Maiden name indicator
45 Secluded valley
46 Ancient letters
47 *Ernani* or *Orfeo*
48 Airborne targets
50 Crucifix inscription
52 Scratch a dele
53 Pocket problem
54 Aardvark's meal
57 Swerve off course
58 ___ out (barely make)

ANT FARM

Across

1 Mustachioed surrealist
5 TAs' bosses
10 Do some telemarketing
14 Classic lab assistant
15 Moon valley
16 Twistable treat
17 Pre–Civil War
19 Word before bust or belly
20 Tennis official's call
21 On the briny
22 "___ Christian Soldiers"
24 Fainted dead away
26 Natural soother
27 Slip preventer
28 Features of some motel rooms
32 Rimes of Country
35 Sonny Corleone portrayer James
36 Off the sauce
37 Flak producer
41 "O Sole ___"
42 Scout's doing
43 Loyal subject
44 The Man Who Knew Too Much actress
47 Rolodex no.
48 Sawboneses
49 One of the Redgraves
53 Any of the Ivies
56 "Stupid me!"
57 Flat hat
58 In the ___ (informed)
59 1958 Rosalind Russell comedy
62 Oodles
63 Daytona entry
64 Bell-ringing company
65 ___ down (frisks)
66 Fancy jugs
67 Try for a role

Down

1 Uses a rotary phone
2 Vice president who resigned
3 Scratch-off ticket game
4 Angry feeling
5 Car radio button
6 All worked up
7 Stewpot, or its contents
8 Winter bug
9 Wheat for pasta
10 Halloween decoration
11 Field of study
12 Lecher's look
13 Man of the manor
18 One of a bunch
23 Alternative to smoking?
25 Prefix with potent
26 Oscar or Tony
28 "Be silent," in music
29 Add a fringe to
30 Knock out, in a way
31 1/1 song word
32 Poor, as excuses go
33 Geraint's woman
34 "This must weigh ___!"
35 Salad green
38 "My goodness!"
39 Defat, whaler-style
40 Shuttle-protecting piece
45 Takes as one's own

46 "You stink!"
47 Fleshy-snouted beasts
49 Lever puller, perhaps
50 Barrel part
51 Margaret Mead study site
52 Modify, as a law
53 Three Stooges assault
54 Fast-food drink
55 Show derision
56 Fable opener
60 Detroit org.
61 Put a scuff on

BURGER TOPPERS

Across

1. Ltr. addenda
4. One on the beat
7. Rug cleaner, for short
10. Unfilled, on a TV sched.
13. Well put
14. City near Oakland
16. Bard's nightfall
17. Dove's sound
18. Raw material for steel mills
19. Former Leno announcer Hall
20. Be an expert
23. Frozen waffle brand
24. One behind bars
26. Involve again
31. Folk's Pete
32. "___ Mio"
34. Duffel bag filler
35. Perform up to snuff
40. Barn topper
41. Harder to find
42. Holds tight
45. Margin jotting
50. TV's Geraldo
51. *Picnic* playwright
52. Find oneself in big trouble
58. Mangy mutt
59. Showy perennials
60. Hippie's home
61. *Treasure Island* monogram
62. Shade provider
63. Bullfight bravo
64. ___ kwon do
65. Easter egg colorer
66. Before, to bards
67. Wee bit

Down

1. Green Bay gridder
2. Spill picker-upper
3. Moe, for one
4. Mafia kingpin
5. Lena of *Chocolat*
6. DC gofer
7. ___ Beach, Fla.
8. Handsome fellow
9. Wolf or fox
10. New driver, usually
11. Mattress support
12. "Go on . . ."
15. Mal- relative
21. Took the prize
22. Greek alphabet ender
25. Drop an easy one
27. Understood
28. Volcanic spew
29. Attendee's suffix
30. Violinist Mischa
33. Lira's replacement
35. Roman emperor, 37–41
36. It's all there is
37. Basic principle
38. Get firm
39. La-la lead-in
40. Tape player
43. Bellyached
44. With a level head
46. Muscle spasm

47 Letter-writer's container of old
48 Crazy Horse, for one
49 Had to have
53 "Sock it __!"
54 Toronto's prov.
55 Suffix with concession
56 Use a spyglass
57 "Understood!"
58 PC monitor

WATERY CONCLUSIONS

Across

1 "Thou __ not "
6 Invader of old Rome
10 Cyberjunk
14 "Look out __!"
15 "Dancing Queen" pop group
16 *Beloved* writer Morrison
17 Turn-of-the-century décor
19 Safe havens
20 Zebras, to lions
21 Teensy
23 Part of a ship's rigging
27 Stove feature
28 Goofs
29 Seles of tennis
32 Star's rep
33 Fodder storers
34 Beatty of *Deliverance*
37 Talk back to
38 Bar fare
39 Lower-left phone button
40 Coast Guard officer below LTJG
41 Sweetie
42 Assault on Troy, e.g.
43 Puts up
45 Paintings on walls
46 Elks and Lions
48 Purse items
49 "Eh Cumpari" singer Julius
51 The middle-sized bear
52 Comics light bulb
53 French statesman nicknamed "Le Tigre"
59 Well-executed
60 Get jaded
61 Untagged?
62 Bearded beasts
63 Nostradamus, e.g.
64 On top of things

Down

1 Entrepreneur-aiding org.
2 Boating pronoun
3 Cockpit datum: Abbr.
4 Actor Chaney
5 Divided in halves
6 Judge's rapper
7 Do as directed
8 Pending, on a sched.
9 Fisherman's take
10 Sign of bad reception
11 Blend of two words
12 Common sprain site
13 *Silas Marner*, e.g.
18 *The Haj* author
22 Inflammatory suffix
23 Poke fun at
24 The Phantom's instrument
25 Media news source
26 Princes, e.g.
29 Marathon's 26+
30 Skin care brand
31 Nonverbal affirmation
33 Concrete ingredient
35 Sharp-eyed raptor
36 Vera Wang creation
38 Sun, personified

39 Knights' titles
41 Greet the villain
42 Stephen Foster title girl
44 Maritime hazards in WWII
45 Silent performer
46 Hold tight
47 Burdened
48 Whip-cracker
50 Does something
51 "A __ bagatelle!"
54 Fairway position
55 Moon jumper of rhyme

56 LAX posting
57 Tire filler
58 Beehive State native

BACK TO THE FRONT

Across

1 Marina features
6 Barry Manilow song locale
10 PDQ, in the ICU
14 *The Sopranos* restaurateur
15 State firmly
16 Cellar stock
17 Dull finish
18 Chicago exchange, for short
19 Utah ski center
20 McDonald's offering
23 Sushi bar order
24 Like an oboe's tone
25 Walked briskly
29 Sgt. Friday carried one
32 La Scala performance
33 One of the Osmonds
34 Took the bait
37 Lack of enthusiasm
41 Drano ingredient
42 April 1st baby, e.g.
43 Woody's musical son
44 Liver or pancreas
45 Fencers' moves
47 Name in kitchen foil
50 Onetime Saturn model
51 "Onward!"
58 Trampled
59 Intense exam
60 Caravan stopovers
62 Tear apart
63 Get pooped
64 Like Bo-Peep's flock
65 Mideast's Gulf of ___

66 Fax button
67 Obama's paternal homeland

Down

1 Anti-stick spray
2 '80s foe of Iran
3 Rebuke from Caesar
4 "Lovely" Beatles girl
5 Get really steamed
6 Former cigarette huckster Joe ___
7 [Continued on other side]
8 Criminal, in police lingo
9 With the bow
10 Al Jolson classic
11 The squiggle in "São Paulo"
12 Started the kitty
13 Like an onion peeler, perhaps
21 ___ time (course slot)
22 Pushed strongly
25 Satirical Mort
26 Highchair feature
27 Stir up
28 Bumbling sort
29 Made public
30 Cultural doings
31 Trivial Pursuit cube
33 Principal duct
34 Floating hazard
35 Home to Gilligan
36 General ___ chicken
38 George, football's "Papa Bear"
39 Mound stat
40 Tandoori-baked bread
44 Like fairy-tale goose eggs
45 Mauna ___

46 Release, in a way
47 Broadcast workers' org.
48 Like tabloid stories
49 Garlic hunk
50 Twiddled one's thumbs
52 Stud stakes
53 Pennsylvania port city
54 Yield as profit
55 Roof overhang
56 "It's ___ to tell . . ."
57 Declare untrue
61 ". . . two if by ___"

FROM BEGINNING TO END

Across

1 Palm off
6 "Hurry!"
10 Macadam construction
14 Scandal-ridden company with a tilted-E logo
15 Khartoum's river
16 Canyon effect
17 One of a baseball team's rotation
20 Muscle quality
21 *Collages* novelist
22 TV soldiers of fortune
23 Scouting outing
25 78s, 45s, etc.
27 Guarantee
30 University of Florida mascot
31 Shaq of the NBA
32 *The Mod Squad* role
33 HBO alternative
36 Neither liberal nor conservative
40 Sci-fi visitors
41 Chocolate factory vessels
42 *Atlantic City* director Louis
43 Houses for hoses
45 Fixes firmly
46 Auto mechanics' jobs
49 City on the Adriatic
50 Contents of Pandora's box
51 Find the total of
52 Soothing spots
56 Where social graces are taught
60 Prince Harry's alma mater

61 Racetrack shape
62 Tubular pasta
63 Descartes who thought "I think . . ."
64 Pound a Selectric
65 Found the total of

Down

1 Celebratory suffix
2 Aware of
3 1979 hostage site
4 Poor loser
5 Demolition need
6 Gal with a gun, on Broadway
7 Speak with one's hands
8 Sight from Lucerne
9 Javits Center architect
10 Church or college official
11 Autumn color
12 Having more gains than losses
13 Sites of some pillow fights
18 Deep black
19 Snack in a shell
24 "___ do for now"
25 Talks wildly
26 ___ A Sketch (drawing toy)
27 Not all
28 Part of BTU
29 Many lipstick shades
30 Magi's offerings
32 Wash units
33 ___ proprietor
34 Sentry's word
35 Horatian verses
37 Even once
38 Mideast VIP

39 Enraptured
43 IV solution
44 Greet the villain
45 Namath's last team
46 Send for consultation
47 You might RSVP online to this
48 Attach to a lapel, say
49 Horn on a base
51 Rice Krispies sound
53 Walden, for one
54 Top-quality
55 Musher's ride

57 All the rage
58 University wall covering
59 Reviewer of books, for short

Solutions

Page 2 — AT THE AIRPORT

```
B A L S A   D E A L   J I B
A R I E L   A C R E S   I D O
R U N W A Y M O D E L   L E A
A B E   T O I L E   A L T A R
  A R P E G E   N I N A
    L E A N I N G T O W E R
L E D O N   D E E S   O D E
A T I T   W A I S T   H O G G
U T E   S E R O   C A F E S
D U M B T E R M I N A L
    R O D E   C E N S E S
T A B O O   S L E E T   T W A
A X E   G A T E C R A S H E R
T E E   E L E N A   B E N E T
A L F   P R O P   S T O P S
```

Page 4 — HEAD STARTS

```
R I F T S   E M I T     A S S
A V I A N   N O S E   E L L E
T E A P O T D O M E   G L A D
A S T E R O I D   A G A T E
      T O V   S K I N N E R
P E A C E   E S C U D O
A S S E R T   T A D   O L L A
R A I L   A L A M O   D O O M
D U A L   P A R   S P L I C E
    B L A S T S   L E N O X
S T A L E S T   P R E
P Y L O N   T O E D A N C E
E P I C   S T R I N G B E A N
N E C K   A W O L   E L A N D
T S E   L O T S   D E L I S
```

Page 6 — INNER SELVES

```
E V E R S   M A R   S O F A R
V A L U E   A C E   O P I N E
A L I B I   I K E S   M A J O R
    I N N O T I M E   I D A
A T H E E L   A N A   L I E N
C R O S S E S T   D U E S
H O P   T E E N   S O L A R
E L I T I S T   A G E S A G O
S L I E R   S I R E   N R A
    N E A P   C Y L I N D E R
P A D S   O R E   A B A S E S
A N I   O P E R A T E D
S T A R K   M I D O R I   I T O
H E N N A   I N E   I R V I N
A S S A Y   X K E   A S S E T
```

Page 8 — PHONING IN

```
C E R T S   H I H O   S C U M
A V A I L   O D O R   P A T E
N A P K I N R I N G   A T I T
E N T I C I N G   S E T T L E
      E K E   B A L E R
G A L O R E   C A P O T E
A M A S S   M A V E N   C A L
G I T S   M I N O R   T A X I
A D E   B E N I N   M I L L S
    S A R D I S   B U L L E T
D I T S Y   S A D
R O B I N S   S T U D E N T S
O N U S   V O L U M E D I A L
L I Z A   E L A N   R I L L E
L A Z Y   N E W T   S T E E D
```

Page 10 — SO CLUMSY OF ME!

```
C O B B   G E T S   S L O P
O D E R   C O R E A   H A U L
P A R A T R O O P S   O T T O
A Y N   R O S S I   V O T E D
    S N O W E   D I E T E R S
M O T I V E   R E S
I R E N E   M A J A   H A L F
L A I C   Z E R O S   O N E A
A N N O   E X I T   N O T I N
    M I S   S E P I A S
W A R P A T H   W H I S K
I L I O N   A F O U L   N O I
L I L O   F R O O T L O O P S
D E E P   O P A L S   A C R E
E N D S   P O L Y   S K Y E
```

Page 12 — SMALL STUFF

```
B O M B   I B I S   S C O P E
E M I R   N O M E   H O P I N
N I N A   F E A T   E P E E S
  T I N Y A R C H I B A L D
      E M S   N A Y
P R I S S Y   S T L   S A N G
A E D E S   S P O O F   S E E
W E E W I L L I E W I N K I E
E V A   R O O T S   N O E L S
D E L T   C E E   F I D D L E
    U S A   P A S
  L I T T L E R I C H A R D
L I N T Y   T E N T   X E R S
A F O U L   O N T O   L E A P
D E N T E   N O O R   E D G Y
```

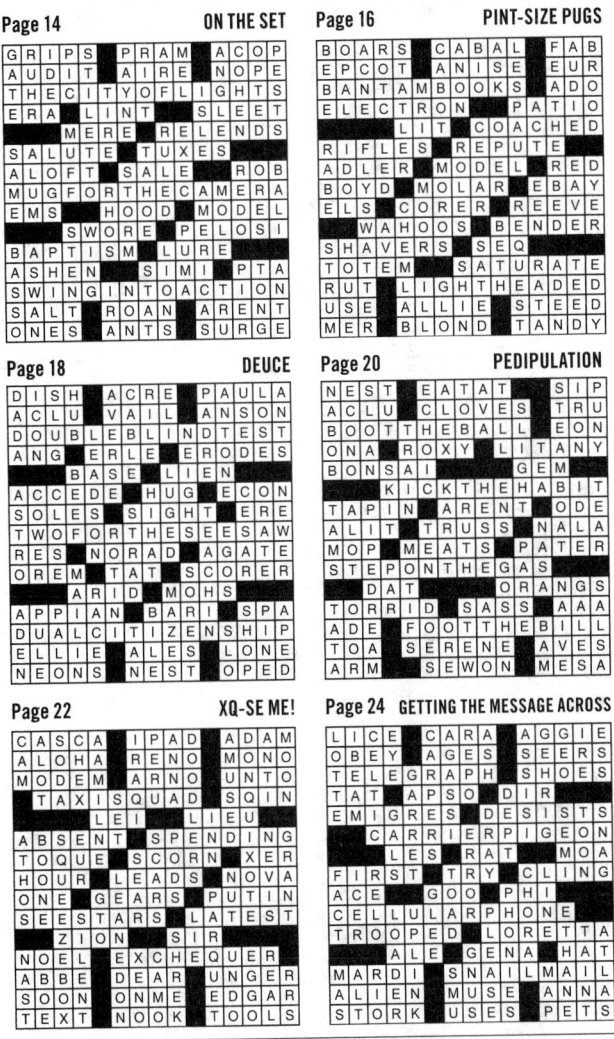

Page 14 — ON THE SET

G	R	I	P	S		P	R	A	M		A	C	O	P
A	U	D	I	T		A	I	R	E		N	O	P	E
T	H	E	C	I	T	Y	O	F	L	I	G	H	T	S
E	R	A		L	I	N	T			S	L	E	E	T
			M	E	R	E		R	E	L	E	N	D	S
S	A	L	U	T	E		T	U	X	E	S			
A	L	O	F	T		S	A	L	E			R	O	B
M	U	G	F	O	R	T	H	E	C	A	M	E	R	A
E	M	S			H	O	O	D		M	O	D	E	L
			S	W	O	R	E		P	E	L	O	S	I
B	A	P	T	I	S	M		L	U	R	E			
A	S	H	E	N			S	I	M	I		P	T	A
S	W	I	N	G	I	N	T	O	A	C	T	I	O	N
S	A	L	T		R	O	A	N		A	R	E	N	T
O	N	E	S		A	N	T	S		S	U	R	G	E

Page 16 — PINT-SIZE PUGS

B	O	A	R	S		C	A	B	A	L		F	A	B
E	P	C	O	T		A	N	I	S	E		E	U	R
B	A	N	T	A	M	B	O	O	K	S		A	D	O
E	L	E	C	T	R	O	N				P	A	T	I	O
				L	I	T		C	O	A	C	H	E	D
R	I	F	L	E	S		R	E	P	U	T	E		
A	D	L	E	R		M	O	D	E	L		R	E	D
B	O	Y	D		M	O	L	A	R		E	B	A	Y
E	L	S		C	O	R	E	R		R	E	E	V	E
			W	A	H	O	O	S		B	E	N	D	E	R
S	H	A	V	E	R	S		S	E	Q				
T	O	T	E	M			S	A	T	U	R	A	T	E
R	U	T		L	I	G	H	T	H	E	A	D	E	D
U	S	E		A	L	L	I	E		S	T	E	E	D
M	E	R		B	L	O	N	D		T	A	N	D	Y

Page 18 — DEUCE

D	I	S	H		A	C	R	E		P	A	U	L	A
A	C	L	U		V	A	I	L		A	N	S	O	N
D	O	U	B	L	E	B	L	I	N	D	T	E	S	T
A	N	G		E	R	L	E		E	R	O	D	E	S
			B	A	S	E		L	I	E	N			
A	C	C	E	D	E		H	U	G		E	C	O	N
S	O	L	E	S		S	I	G	H	T		E	R	E
T	W	O	F	O	R	T	H	E	S	E	E	S	A	W
R	E	S		N	O	R	A	D		A	G	A	T	E
O	R	E	M		T	A	T		S	C	O	R	E	R
			A	R	I	D		M	O	H	S			
A	P	P	I	A	N		B	A	R	I		S	P	A
D	U	A	L	C	I	T	I	Z	E	N	S	H	I	P
E	L	L	I	E		A	L	E	S		L	O	N	E
N	E	O	N	S		N	E	S	T		O	P	E	D

Page 20 — PEDIPULATION

N	E	S	T		E	A	T	A	T		S	I	P
A	C	L	U		C	L	O	V	E	S		T	R	U
B	O	O	T	T	H	E	B	A	L	L		E	O	N
O	N	A		R	O	X	Y		L	I	T	A	N	Y
B	O	N	S	A	I				G	E	M			
			K	I	C	K	T	H	E	H	A	B	I	T
T	A	P	I	N		A	R	E	N	T		O	D	E
A	L	I	T		T	R	U	S	S		N	A	L	A
M	O	P		M	E	A	T	S		P	A	T	E	R
S	T	E	P	O	N	T	H	E	G	A	S			
			D	A	T			O	R	A	N	G	S	
T	O	R	R	I	D		S	A	S	S		A	A	A
A	D	E		F	O	O	T	T	H	E	B	I	L	L
T	O	A		S	E	R	E	N	E		A	V	E	S
A	R	M		S	E	W	O	N		M	E	S	A

Page 22 — XQ-SE ME!

C	A	S	C	A		I	P	A	D		A	D	A	M
A	L	O	H	A		R	E	N	O		M	O	N	O
M	O	D	E	M		A	R	N	O		U	N	T	O
	T	A	X	I	S	Q	U	A	D		S	Q	I	N
			L	E	I				L	I	E	U		
A	B	S	E	N	T		S	P	E	N	D	I	N	G
T	O	Q	U	E		S	C	O	R	N		X	E	R
H	O	U	R		L	E	A	D	S		N	O	V	A
O	N	E		G	E	A	R	S		P	U	T	I	N
S	E	E	S	T	A	R	S		L	A	T	E	S	T
			Z	I	O	N		S	I	R				
N	O	E	L		E	X	C	H	E	Q	U	E	R	
A	B	B	E		D	E	A	R		U	N	G	E	R
S	O	O	N		O	N	M	E		E	D	G	A	R
T	E	X	T		N	O	O	K		T	O	O	L	S

Page 24 — GETTING THE MESSAGE ACROSS

L	I	C	E		C	A	R	A		A	G	G	I	E
O	B	E	Y		A	G	E	S		S	E	E	R	S
T	E	L	E	G	R	A	P	H		S	H	O	E	S
T	A	T		A	P	S	O		D	I	R			
E	M	I	G	R	E	S		D	E	S	I	S	T	S
			C	A	R	R	I	E	R	P	I	G	E	O	N
L	E	S		R	A	T		M	O	A				
F	I	R	S	T		T	R	Y		C	L	I	N	G
A	C	E		G	O	O			P	H	I			
C	E	L	L	U	L	A	R	P	H	O	N	E		
T	R	O	O	P	E	D		L	O	R	E	T	T	A
A	L	E			G	E	N	A			H	A	T	
M	A	R	D	I		S	N	A	I	L	M	A	I	L
A	L	I	E	N		M	U	S	E		A	N	N	A
S	T	O	R	K		U	S	E	S		P	E	T	S

```
B U R R O   D R I P     I S I T
O N I O N   E A S E     N O G O
B U M P E R C R O P     S L O P
S M E E   I R E     S T A R E
      B A N E   A S H E R
    B U R G E R F L I P P E R
S M A R T     H A I M   A R I
E A R N   S H O R T   G N A T
M I R   A C I D     P A E S E
I N A U G U R A L B A L L
      C N O T E   A E R O
B R U I N     E S T   S P E C
R E D O   T I L T A W H I R L
I N A N   O V A L   P E N T A
T O S S   E E L Y   A S K E D
```

```
C O M A   M E T E R   P O P S
O P A L   A B O V E   E R I E
M I L T O N B O I L   T E A L
I N T O N E S   T A K E O F F
C E A S E     T A T E R
      S A R A   E M O T E D
L O I N   M E R E   P A U S E
A T T U   P E T T Y   S N A P
M O C K S   D A T E   T A U T
B E H E L D   R A S P
      N U R S E   A D O R E
A U T O M A T   O P P O S E S
B R E L   P O A C H A D A M S
L A S T   E L I T E   O K I E
E L S E   R E R A N   S A T S
```

```
C O T E S   A S P I C   T A P
A V I L A   W A L D O   A V A
V A N I L L A B E A N   K I T
S L Y   T O Y E D   F L E S H
      H A L     R A I N
  B U I L D I N G B L O C K
D U R E R   A L O T   T O E
E T A S   O M I T S   O I L Y
S A T   W O O S   I N C A S
C H I C K E N N O O D L E
    S A N D   H E Y
H E L L O   S A U N A   M A Y
E V A   C A P I T O L D O M E
R E V   K L I N E   L E M O N
E R A   S E C T S   Y E A R S
```

```
D O J O S   A M I S S   S A D
I N A L L   C O O P T   A L E
C O D E O F H O N O R   F I N
T R E S T L E   S T A L E S T
      T E S T   Y E A T S
R A F T E D   E R N E S T
I V I E D   B R E E D   H U T
T I R E   C O M E T   I O T A
A D E   S P O I L   E L M E R
    E S C O R T   P A L E S T
V I S O R   E G O S
E N C L A V E   O L E S T R A
R C A   W I S E O L D H E A D
S A P   L O P E D   B O R G E
O N E   S L Y L Y   Y E M E N
```

```
R A D A R   A C E D   M U D
A C U T E   D A L E   T O M E
G R E A S E D P I G   E L B E
S E T   T A U S   R A F T E D
      A S P   T A I L O R S
S A N I T Y   K I D D O
T R A C E   T U N E   N E A T
A N D Y   R I D E S   P A P A
B O A S   E G O S   T A S E R
    T I M E S   M A N T R A
H O A R D E R   F O R
I N S E A M   S L O T   S R O
L I T E   B A N A N A P E E L
D O I T   E D A M   N O M A D
A N N   R A G E   S L I P S
```

```
L L A N O   D E I C E   C A F
O I L E R   E R G O T   O L E
S C O T C H B R O T H   F O E
T E E S H O T   T E A R F U L
      A L S O   N E E D Y
A D W A R E   U N D O N E
B E A R D   S T E E L   C O W
L A T E   R O W A N   C A V E
E R E   D I R E R   R A K E D
    R H A M E S   S E V E N S
O P C I T   T O T E
P E R C A L E   C A N A S T A
R A E   S O D A C R A C K E R
A S S   E L I H U   C R E A M
H E S   T A T A R   T E E M S
```

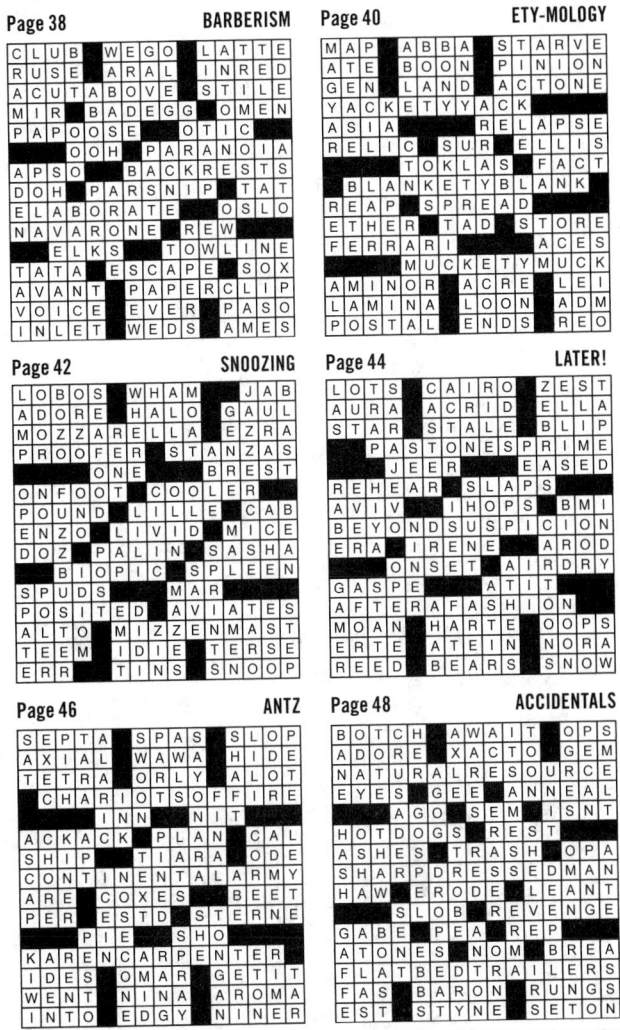

Page 38 — BARBERISM

```
C L U B . W E G O . L A T T E
R U S E . A R A L . I N R E D
A C U T A B O V E . S T I L E
M I R . B A D E G G . O M E N
P A P O O S E . O T I C . . .
. . . O O H . P A R A N O I A
A P S O . B A C K R E S T S .
D O H . P A R S N I P . T A T
E L A B O R A T E . O S L O .
N A V A R O N E . R E W . . .
. . . E L K S . T O W L I N E
T A T A . E S C A P E . S O X
A V A N T . P A P E R C L I P
V O I C E . E V E R . P A S O
I N L E T . W E D S . A M E S
```

Page 40 — ETY-MOLOGY

```
M A P . A B B A . S T A R V E
A T E . B O O N . P I N I O N
G E N . L A N D . A C T O N E
Y A C K E T Y Y A C K . . . .
A S I A . . . . . R E L A P S E
R E L I C . S U R . E L L I S
. . . T O K L A S . F A C T .
B L A N K E T Y B L A N K . .
R E A P . S P R E A D . . . .
E T H E R . T A D . S T O R E
F E R R A R I . . . A C E S .
. . . M U C K E T Y M U C K .
A M I N O R . A C R E . L E I
L A M I N A . L O O N . A D M
P O S T A L . E N D S . R E O
```

Page 42 — SNOOZING

```
L O B O S . W H A M . . J A B
A D O R E . H A L O . G A U L
M O Z Z A R E L L A . E Z R A
P R O O F E R . S T A N Z A S
. . . O N E . B R E S T . . .
O N F O O T . C O O L E R . .
P O U N D . L I L L E . C A B
E N Z O . L I V I D . M I C E
D O Z . P A L I N . S A S H A
. . B I O P I C . S P L E E N
S P U D S . M A R . . . . .
P O S I T E D . A V I A T E S
A L T O . M I Z Z E N M A S T
T E E M . I D I E . T E R S E
E R R . T I N S . S N O O P .
```

Page 44 — LATER!

```
L O T S . C A I R O . Z E S T
A U R A . A C R I D . E L L A
S T A R . S T A L E . B L I P
. . P A S T O N E S P R I M E
. . . J E E R . . E A S E D .
R E H E A R . S L A P S . . .
A V I V . I H O P S . B M I .
B E Y O N D S U S P I C I O N
. E R A . I R E N E . A R O D
. . . O N S E T . A I R D R Y
. G A S P E . . A T I T . . .
A F T E R A F A S H I O N . .
M O A N . H A R T E . O O P S
E R T E . A T E I N . N O R A
R E E D . B E A R S . S N O W
```

Page 46 — ANTZ

```
S E P T A . S P A S . S L O P
A X I A L . W A W A . H I D E
T E T R A . O R L Y . A L O T
. C H A R I O T S O F F I R E
. . . I N N . N I T . . . .
A C K A C K . P L A N . C A L
S H I P . T I A R A . O D E .
C O N T I N E N T A L A R M Y
A R E . C O X E S . B E E T .
P E R . E S T D . S T E R N E
. . . P I E . S H O . . . .
K A R E N C A R P E N T E R .
I D E S . O M A R . G E T I T
W E N T . N I N A . A R O M A
I N T O . E D G Y . N I N E R
```

Page 48 — ACCIDENTALS

```
B O T C H . A W A I T . O P S
A D O R E . X A C T O . G E M
N A T U R A L R E S O U R C E
E Y E S . G E E . A N N E A L
. . . A G O . S E M . I S N T
H O T D O G S . R E S T . . .
A S H E S . T R A S H . O P A
S H A R P D R E S S E D M A N
H A W . E R O D E . L E A N T
. . . S L O B . R E V E N G E
G A B E . P E A . R E P . . .
A T O N E S . N O M . B R E A
F L A T B E D T R A I L E R S
F A S . B A R O N . R U N G S
E S T . S T Y N E . S E T O N
```

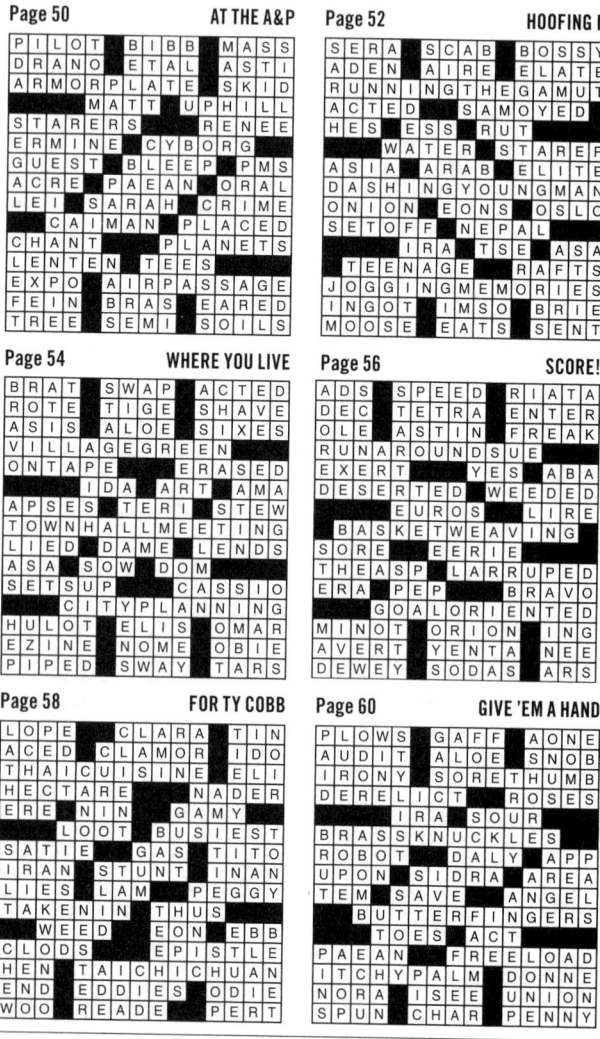

Page 50 — AT THE A&P

P	I	L	O	T		B	I	B	B		M	A	S	S
D	R	A	N	O		E	T	A	L		A	S	T	I
A	R	M	O	R	P	L	A	T	E		S	K	I	D
			M	A	T	T		U	P	H	I	L	L	
S	T	A	R	E	R	S		R	E	N	E	E		
E	R	M	I	N	E		C	Y	B	O	R	G		
G	U	E	S	T		B	L	E	E	P		P	M	S
A	C	R	E		P	A	E	A	N		O	R	A	L
L	E	I		S	A	R	A	H		C	R	I	M	E
		C	A	I	M	A	N		P	L	A	C	E	D
C	H	A	N	T			P	L	A	N	E	T	S	
L	E	N	T	E	N		T	E	E	S				
E	X	P	O		A	I	R	P	A	S	S	A	G	E
F	E	I	N		B	R	A	S		E	A	R	E	D
T	R	E	E		S	E	M	I		S	O	I	L	S

Page 52 — HOOFING IT

S	E	R	A		S	C	A	B		B	O	S	S	Y
A	D	E	N		A	I	R	E		E	L	A	T	E
R	U	N	N	I	N	G	T	H	E	G	A	M	U	T
A	C	T	E	D			S	A	M	O	Y	E	D	
H	E	S		E	S	S		R	U	T				
			W	A	T	E	R		S	T	A	R	E	R
A	S	I	A		A	R	A	B		E	L	I	T	E
D	A	S	H	I	N	G	Y	O	U	N	G	M	A	N
O	N	I	O	N		E	O	N	S		O	S	L	O
S	E	T	O	F	F		N	E	P	A	L			
			I	R	A		T	S	E		A	S	A	
T	E	E	N	A	G	E			R	A	F	T	S	
J	O	G	G	I	N	G	M	E	M	O	R	I	E	S
I	N	G	O	T		I	M	S	O		B	R	I	E
M	O	O	S	E		E	A	T	S		S	E	N	T

Page 54 — WHERE YOU LIVE

B	R	A	T		S	W	A	P		A	C	T	E	D
R	O	T	E		T	I	G	E		S	H	A	V	E
A	S	I	S		A	L	O	E		S	I	X	E	S
V	I	L	L	A	G	E	G	R	E	E	N			
O	N	T	A	P	E			E	R	A	S	E	D	
			I	D	A		A	R	T			A	M	A
A	P	S	E	S		T	E	R	I		S	T	E	W
T	O	W	N	H	A	L	L	M	E	E	T	I	N	G
L	I	E	D		D	A	M	E		L	E	N	D	S
A	S	A		S	O	W		D	O	M				
S	E	T	S	U	P				C	A	S	S	I	O
			C	I	T	Y	P	L	A	N	N	I	N	G
H	U	L	O	T		E	L	I	S		O	M	A	R
E	Z	I	N	E		N	O	M	E		O	B	I	E
P	I	P	E	D		S	W	A	Y		T	A	R	S

Page 56 — SCORE!

A	D	S		S	P	E	E	D		R	I	A	T	A
D	E	C		T	E	T	R	A		E	N	T	E	R
O	L	E		A	S	T	I	N		F	R	E	A	K
R	U	N	A	R	O	U	N	D	S	U	E			
E	X	E	R	T			Y	E	S		A	B	A	
D	E	S	E	R	T	E	D		W	E	E	D	E	D
			E	U	R	O	S			L	I	R	E	
B	A	S	K	E	T	W	E	A	V	I	N	G		
S	O	R	E			E	E	R	I	E				
T	H	E	A	S	P		L	A	R	R	U	P	E	D
E	R	A		P	E	P			B	R	A	V	O	
			G	O	A	L	O	R	I	E	N	T	E	D
M	I	N	O	T		O	R	I	O	N		I	N	G
A	V	E	R	T		Y	E	N	T	A		N	E	E
D	E	W	E	Y		S	O	D	A	S		A	R	S

Page 58 — FOR TY COBB

L	O	P	E		C	L	A	R	A		T	I	N	
A	C	E	D		C	L	A	M	O	R		I	D	O
T	H	A	I	C	U	I	S	I	N	E		E	L	I
H	E	C	T	A	R	E		N	A	D	E	R		
E	R	E		N	I	N		G	A	M	Y			
			L	O	O	T		B	U	S	I	E	S	T
S	A	T	I	E		G	A	S		T	I	T	O	
I	R	A	N		S	T	U	N	T		I	N	A	N
L	I	E	S		L	A	M		P	E	G	G	Y	
T	A	K	E	N	I	N		T	H	U	S			
		W	E	E	D		E	O	N		E	B	B	
C	L	O	D	S		E	P	I	S	T	L	E		
H	E	N		T	A	I	C	H	I	C	H	U	A	N
E	N	D		E	D	D	I	E	S		O	D	I	E
W	O	O		R	E	A	D	E			P	E	R	T

Page 60 — GIVE 'EM A HAND

P	L	O	W	S		G	A	F	F		A	O	N	E
A	U	D	I	T		A	L	O	E		S	N	O	B
I	R	O	N	Y		S	O	R	E	T	H	U	M	B
D	E	R	E	L	I	C	T			R	O	S	E	S
			I	R	A			S	O	U	R			
B	R	A	S	S	K	N	U	C	K	L	E	S		
R	O	B	O	T		D	A	L	Y		A	P	P	
U	P	O	N		S	I	D	R	A		A	R	E	A
T	E	M		S	A	V	E			A	N	G	E	L
			B	U	T	T	E	R	F	I	N	G	E	R	S
			T	O	E	S		A	C	T				
P	A	E	A	N			F	R	E	E	L	O	A	D
I	T	C	H	Y	P	A	L	M			D	O	N	N	E
N	O	R	A		I	S	E	E		U	N	I	O	N
S	P	U	N		C	H	A	R		P	E	N	N	Y

Page 62 — AGAINST THE GRAIN

F	A	L	K		K	E	N	O		S	E	L	M	A
I	D	E	A		E	L	A	L		A	V	O	I	D
B	R	E	R		N	O	N	E		M	E	N	S	A
B	A	R	L	E	Y	P	A	S	S	I	N	G		
E	T	A		R	A	E		T	A	S	T	E	D	
R	E	T	R	O		S	C	R	A	M		E	G	O
		A	D	E		R	E	F		A	R	G	O	
R	Y	E	S	E	N	S	E	O	F	H	U	M	O	R
E	A	C	H		G	U	M		S	E	T			
S	L	O		R	I	V	E	R		N	O	M	A	D
T	E	F	L	O	N		E	O	N		O	D	E	
		R	I	C	E	T	O	S	T	A	R	D	O	M
C	R	E	E	K		A	S	C	H		A	E	R	O
A	D	A	G	E		C	L	U	E		G	L	E	N
B	A	K	E	R		H	O	E	R		S	A	S	S

Page 64 — BOXING DAY

M	A	Y	S		K	I	D	D	O		S	H	A	W
I	G	O	T		O	C	E	A	N		T	A	C	O
F	R	U	I	T	P	U	N	C	H		E	L	M	O
F	E	L	L	A			R	A	G	W	E	E	D	
S	E	L	E	N	A			T	O	N	Y			
			G	R	O	U	N	D	R	O	U	N	D	
G	U	F	F		K	E	N			O	A	K	I	E
O	R	E	O	S		R	E	D		S	H	E	L	F
O	D	E	O	N		S	O	S			U	S	E	S
F	U	L	L	O	F	F	I	G	H	T				
			O	R	A	N		A	B	A	S	E	D	
C	R	Y	S	T	A	L			A	S	T	R	O	
H	O	O	K		M	A	S	T	E	R	C	A	R	D
E	L	K	E		E	N	D	E	D		A	G	O	G
F	L	O	W		R	A	I	N	S		P	E	L	E

Page 66 — CALLING EBENEZER SCROOGE

R	A	M	P		D	A	S	H		T	E	M	P	O
O	R	A	L		E	C	H	O		O	C	E	A	N
O	L	L	A		L	O	O	M		R	O	A	S	T
M	E	A	N	S	T	R	E	E	T	S		T	O	O
E	N	G		P	A	N		P	H	I	S	H		
R	E	A	D	E		S	C	A	R		T	O	U	T
			E	N	C		A	G	O		Y	O	K	E
T	I	G	H	T	R	O	P	E	W	A	L	K	E	R
A	G	R	O		U	N	O		S	M	U			
B	O	E	R		T	E	N	N		I	S	L	E	T
		E	N	A	C	T		A	S	S		A	L	I
M	A	N		C	H	E	A	P	T	H	R	I	L	L
A	S	T	E	R		N	I	K	E		E	D	I	T
T	H	E	R	E		T	R	I	P		D	U	C	E
H	E	A	R	S		H	E	N	S		O	P	E	D

Page 68 — TOYING AROUND

S	A	R	A	N		M	A	P	L	E		G	P	S
A	W	A	R	E		A	L	A	I	N		O	U	T
P	A	I	R	O	F	J	A	C	K	S		F	R	A
S	Y	N	E		L	O	S		K	I	L	L	E	R
			S	H	A	R		D	E	L	A	Y	E	R
C	O	R	T	E	X		S	E	R	E	N	A		
O	B	O	E	S		S	A	T	E	D		K	I	D
L	I	A	R		W	A	V	E	D		C	I	T	E
T	E	D		P	A	C	E	R		M	O	T	I	F
		B	R	O	T	H	S		M	O	L	E	S	T
S	A	L	U	T	E	S		F	O	T	O			
A	L	O	M	A	R		S	R	O		S	A	M	S
P	I	C		B	L	O	W	O	N	E	S	T	O	P
I	C	K		L	O	R	E	N		P	A	M	P	A
D	E	S		E	G	R	E	T		S	L	O	E	S

Page 70 — PAY UP!

C	L	I	P	S		S	T	E	P		S	H	A	H
P	A	D	U	A		M	A	X	I		P	O	G	O
A	D	O	R	N		A	X	E	L		L	A	O	S
	E	L	E	C	T	R	I	C	C	H	A	R	G	E
				H	O	T			H	A	T			
P	A	R	D	O	N		S	L	A	V		O	F	T
E	R	I	E		S	P	I	R	O		B	I	O	
D	I	S	C	O	V	E	R	E	D	C	H	E	C	K
A	S	K		P	A	G	A	N		A	S	H	E	
L	E	S		T	R	A	Y		S	P	L	E	E	N
			V	I	I			W	I	I				
J	U	N	E	C	A	R	T	E	R	C	A	S	H	
A	N	O	N		N	O	O	N		K	N	E	A	D
D	I	V	A		C	L	O	D		U	N	C	L	E
E	T	A	L		E	L	L	Y		P	E	T	E	S

Page 72 — "WELL, ISLE BE!"

B	A	S	R	A		B	R	A	U	N		S	A	O
O	B	I	E	S		R	E	P	R	O		C	P	A
W	E	L	S	H	R	A	B	B	I	T		O	A	T
S	L	O	T	T	E	D			F	I	T	C	H	
				R	A	S	P		D	A	N	C	E	S
S	P	I	R	A	L		A	W	E	I	G	H		
C	A	R	E	Y		S	N	E	E	R		P	I	T
O	V	I	D		S	I	D	E	D		D	I	N	O
W	E	S		H	E	R	O	D		K	I	N	E	R
		H	E	A	T	E	R		B	R	E	E	Z	Y
A	L	L	O	T	S			A	S	T	I			
P	A	I	N	T			A	U	S	T	R	I	A	
H	U	N		E	N	G	L	I	S	H	H	O	R	N
I	R	E		R	A	N	O	N		N	O	L	A	N
D	A	N		S	T	U	N	T		A	R	E	N	A

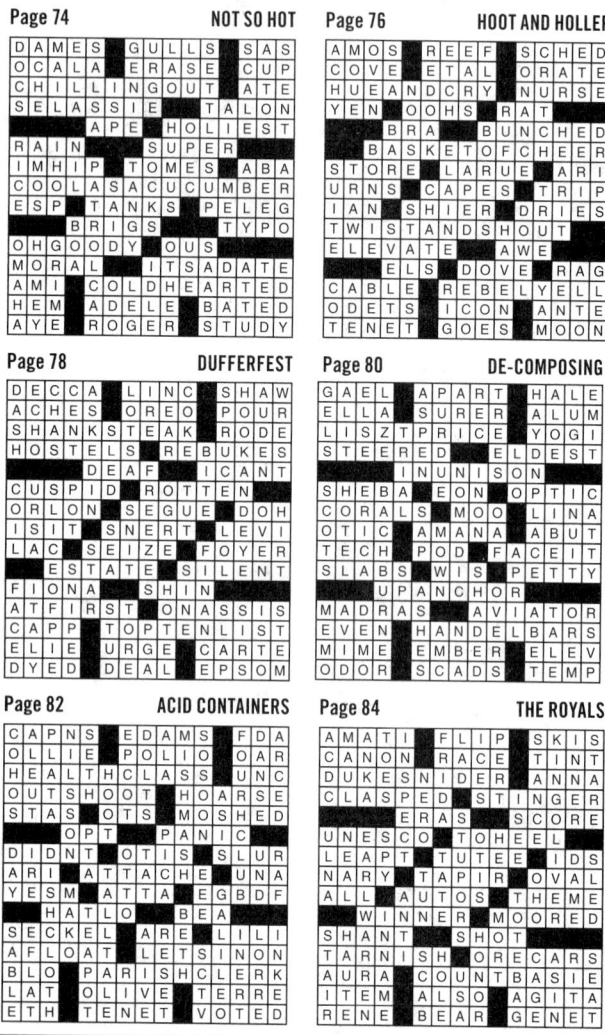

Page 74 — NOT SO HOT

D	A	M	E	S		G	U	L	L	S		S	A	S
O	C	A	L	A		E	R	A	S	E		C	U	P
C	H	I	L	L	I	N	G	O	U	T		A	T	E
S	E	L	A	S	S	I	E		T	A	L	O	N	
		A	P	E		H	O	L	I	E	S	T		
R	A	I	N				S	U	P	E	R			
I	M	H	I	P		T	O	M	E	S		A	B	A
C	O	O	L	A	S	A	C	U	C	U	M	B	E	R
E	S	P		T	A	N	K	S		P	E	L	E	G
			B	R	I	G	S				T	Y	P	O
O	H	G	O	O	D	Y		O	U	S				
M	O	R	A	L			I	T	S	A	D	A	T	E
A	M	I		C	O	L	D	H	E	A	R	T	E	D
H	E	M		A	D	E	L	E		B	A	T	E	D
A	Y	E		R	O	G	E	R		S	T	U	D	Y

Page 76 — HOOT AND HOLLER

A	M	O	S		R	E	E	F		S	C	H	E	D
C	O	V	E		E	T	A	L		O	R	A	T	E
H	U	E	A	N	D	C	R	Y		N	U	R	S	E
Y	E	N		O	O	H	S		R	A	T			
			B	R	A			B	U	N	C	H	E	D
	B	A	S	K	E	T	O	F	C	H	E	E	R	
S	T	O	R	E		L	A	R	U	E		A	R	I
U	R	N	S		C	A	P	E	S		T	R	I	P
I	A	N		S	H	I	E	R		D	R	I	E	S
	T	W	I	S	T	A	N	D	S	H	O	U	T	
E	L	E	V	A	T	E			A	W	E			
			E	L	S		D	O	V	E		R	A	G
C	A	B	L	E		R	E	B	E	L	Y	E	L	L
O	D	E	T	S		I	C	O	N		A	N	T	E
T	E	N	E	T		G	O	E	S		M	O	O	N

Page 78 — DUFFERFEST

D	E	C	C	A		L	I	N	C		S	H	A	W
A	C	H	E	S		O	R	E	O		P	O	U	R
S	H	A	N	K	S	T	E	A	K		R	O	D	E
H	O	S	T	E	L	S		R	E	B	U	K	E	S
				D	E	A	F		I	C	A	N	T	
C	U	S	P	I	D		R	O	T	T	E	N		
O	R	L	O	N		S	E	G	U	E		D	O	H
I	S	I	T		S	N	E	R	T		L	E	V	I
L	A	C		S	E	I	Z	E		F	O	Y	E	R
		E	S	T	A	T	E		S	I	L	E	N	T
	F	I	O	N	A		S	H	I	N				
A	T	F	I	R	S	T		O	N	A	S	S	I	S
C	A	P	P		T	O	P	T	E	N	L	I	S	T
E	L	I	E		U	R	G	E		C	A	R	T	E
D	Y	E	D		D	E	A	L		E	P	S	O	M

Page 80 — DE-COMPOSING

G	A	E	L		A	P	A	R	T		H	A	L	E
E	L	L	A		S	U	R	E	R		A	L	U	M
L	I	S	Z	T	P	R	I	C	E		Y	O	G	I
S	T	E	E	R	E	D		E	L	D	E	S	T	
			I	N	U	N	I	S	O	N				
S	H	E	B	A		E	O	N		O	P	T	I	C
C	O	R	A	L	S		M	O	O		L	I	N	A
O	T	I	C		A	M	A	N	A		A	B	U	T
T	E	C	H		P	O	D		F	A	C	E	I	T
S	L	A	B	S		W	I	S		P	E	T	T	Y
				U	P	A	N	C	H	O	R			
	M	A	D	R	A	S		A	V	I	A	T	O	R
E	V	E	N		H	A	N	D	E	L	B	A	R	S
M	I	M	E		E	M	B	E	R		E	L	E	V
O	D	O	R		S	C	A	D	S		T	E	M	P

Page 82 — ACID CONTAINERS

C	A	P	N	S		E	D	A	M	S		F	D	A
O	L	L	I	E		P	O	L	I	O		O	A	R
H	E	A	L	T	H	C	L	A	S	S		U	N	C
O	U	T	S	H	O	O	T		H	O	A	R	S	E
S	T	A	S		O	T	S		M	O	S	H	E	D
			O	P	T		P	A	N	I	C			
D	I	D	N	T		O	T	I	S		S	L	U	R
A	R	I		A	T	T	A	C	H	E		U	N	A
Y	E	S	M		A	T	T	A		E	G	B	D	F
			H	A	T	L	O		B	E	A			
S	E	C	K	E	L		A	R	E		L	I	L	I
A	F	L	O	A	T		L	E	T	S	I	N	O	N
B	L	O		P	A	R	I	S	H	C	L	E	R	K
L	A	T		O	L	I	V	E		T	E	R	R	E
E	T	H		T	E	N	E	T		V	O	T	E	D

Page 84 — THE ROYALS

A	M	A	T	I		F	L	I	P		S	K	I	S
C	A	N	O	N		R	A	C	E		T	I	N	T
D	U	K	E	S	N	I	D	E	R		A	N	N	A
C	L	A	S	P	E	D		S	T	I	N	G	E	R
				E	R	A	S		S	C	O	R	E	
U	N	E	S	C	O		T	O	H	E	E	L		
L	E	A	P	T		T	U	T	E	E		I	D	S
N	A	R	Y		T	A	P	I	R		O	V	A	L
A	L	L		A	U	T	O	S		T	H	E	M	E
		W	I	N	N	E	R		M	O	O	R	E	D
	S	H	A	N	T		S	H	O	T				
T	A	R	N	I	S	H		O	R	E	C	A	R	S
A	U	R	A		C	O	U	N	T	B	A	S	I	E
I	T	E	M		A	L	S	O		A	G	I	T	A
R	E	N	E		B	E	A	R		G	E	N	E	T

N	O	T	S	O		N	O	M	A	N		T	D	S
O	N	I	O	N		U	N	C	L	E		H	O	I
H	U	R	L	I	N	S	U	L	T	S		R	R	S
	S	E	I	N	E		P	E	A	T	M	O	S	S
		D	E	W	Y		A	R	E	A	W	A	Y	
P	O	P	S		H	A	W	N		R	C	A		
U	N	I		A	L	I		O	S	A	G	E	S	
P	I	T	Y		R	E	T	A	R		W	A	V	E
A	T	C	O	S	T		C	P	A		M	I	A	
		H	U	H		W	H	E	T		P	E	L	T
A	B	A	L	O	N	E		S	I	M	I			
L	E	T	L	O	O	S	E		O	A	S	E	S	
A	G	E		T	O	S	S	A	N	D	T	U	R	N
M	I	N		A	N	O	S	E		A	O	R	T	A
O	N	T		T	E	N	O	R		S	L	O	A	N

B	O	O	P		A	M	P	S		C	H	E	M	O
O	S	L	O		F	O	R	E		R	A	G	O	N
R	A	D	I	O	F	R	E	E	E	U	R	O	P	E
I	K	E		B	R	A	Y		L	E	A	S	E	S
C	A	N	T	S	A	Y		L	E	T	S			
			H	E	Y		G	O	V		S	H	E	D
S	H	E	E	R		L	U	B	E	S		I	C	U
T	E	L	E	V	I	S	I	O	N	P	I	L	O	T
E	R	A		E	G	A	D	S		I	R	O	N	Y
P	O	L	I		U	T	E		P	T	A			
			T	W	A	S		T	A	S	S	E	L	S
O	B	T	A	I	N		R	O	S	A		V	I	E
N	E	W	S	P	A	P	E	R	S	T	R	I	K	E
A	L	I	C	E		I	P	S	O		I	T	E	M
N	A	N	A	S		G	O	O	N		D	E	N	S

C	L	O	G	S		S	L	A	B		P	O	E	T
A	U	D	I	E		H	O	S	E		R	U	N	E
P	R	I	Z	E	F	I	G	H	T		E	T	T	A
S	E	N	A	T	O	R	S		H	E	S	T	E	R
				H	U	T			L	E	A	R	Y	
E	S	C	H	E	R		S	P	R	A	T	S		
B	L	O	O	D		F	E	R	A	L		I	A	M
R	O	O	T		C	I	V	E	T		E	G	G	Y
O	E	R		C	O	V	E	Y		C	O	H	E	N
		S	L	A	Y	E	R		M	A	N	T	R	A
S	A	L	O	N				P	O	M				
A	R	I	S	T	A		H	A	V	E	N	O	T	S
R	I	G	S		S	T	A	G	E	R	I	G	H	T
A	S	H	E		K	O	N	A		A	G	R	E	E
N	E	T	S		S	W	A	N			S	H	E	E	T

E	S	P	N		T	A	L	L		L	A	M	P	S
S	W	E	E		S	L	O	E		I	N	E	R	T
T	I	R	E		H	O	N	E		N	O	N	O	S
	T	U	R	N	I	N	G	R	A	D	I	U	S	
			O	R	E				T	A	N			
A	B	B	O	T	T		G	E	T		T	A	S	K
G	R	E	T	A		D	O	G	I	T		U	P	I
R	E	V	O	L	V	I	N	G	C	R	E	D	I	T
E	V	E		L	I	V	E	S		E	D	I	C	T
E	E	L	S		X	E	R		O	N	U	S	E	S
			H	I	E			A	R	C				
	S	P	I	N	N	I	N	G	W	H	E	E	L	
F	L	A	I	L		C	A	G	E		B	R	E	W
A	O	R	T	A		E	V	I	L		R	O	T	H
S	T	R	E	W		R	E	E	L		O	S	S	O

G	A	M	E		S	C	A	M		C	A	B	I	N
A	G	O	G		C	A	M	O		A	R	O	S	E
L	O	N	G	T	E	R	M	P	A	R	K	I	N	G
A	G	E		I	N	T	O		S	T	I	L	T	S
S	O	L	A	R	I	A		E	T	O	N			
		L	A	C		E	A	R	N		A	B	E	
S	P	O	O	N		A	L	T	A			L	E	A
W	I	D	E	A	N	G	L	E	L	E	N	S	E	S
A	N	D		O	N	I	N		L	E	O	N	E	
Y	E	S		U	T	E	S		D	E	R			
		E	N	O	S		S	A	V	I	N	G	S	
C	R	E	T	I	N		A	C	M	E		O	O	H
H	I	G	H	T	E	N	S	I	O	N	W	I	R	E
A	L	O	N	E		A	T	O	N		A	C	E	D
P	E	S	O	S		W	I	N	E		R	E	D	S

P	A	R	E	D		S	A	S	S		A	B	A	B
O	H	A	R	A		P	U	P	A		R	O	T	E
L	E	V	I	S		E	D	E	N		A	G	A	R
	M	E	C	H	A	N	I	C	A	L	B	U	L	L
				E	N	D			A	I	S	L	E	
D	I	V	E	R	T		M	O	M	M	A			
E	D	I	T		M	A	M	I	E			C	P	U
E	L	E	C	T	R	I	C	A	L	S	T	O	R	M
D	E	S		O	A	T	E	R		A	T	O	P	
			C	R	E	E	D		S	T	R	E	S	S
A	C	R	E	S				A	T	E				
C	H	E	M	I	C	A	L	S	Y	M	B	O	L	
H	I	V	E		A	M	O	K		P	A	R	I	S
E	V	E	N		S	I	R	E		E	L	A	T	E
D	E	L	T		K	N	E	W		R	E	L	E	E

Page 98 — SHOE!

```
B I R D S   S C A B   P O T S
A V A I L   O L L A   U N U M
S A N D A L W O O D   M I L E
E N G I N E   P O D   P O L L
        T A W   F I S H N E T
P R E S S K I T   E R A
H E L P   E D I T   S N A C K
D A L I   D E M U R   D R E A
S L A K E   R E N E   L E N T
        E E R   R E C R E A T E
C O N J O I N   R O E
O L E O   F O R   I C I E S T
U L A N   F L A T L A N D E R
T I R E   L A C E   S C E N E
H E S S   E N Y A   T A N D Y
```

Page 100 — HERE COMES THE JUDGE

```
G I A N T   M O M A   S C A R
P O L A R   A V O W   P A C E
S U I T O F M A I L   A S H E
        U R A L   S P R E E S
R E C I P E S   A S I D E
A T O N E D   S H A V E N
S H U N S   S H A D E   P H I
T A R S   M A R I E   D O I N
A N T   S E V E R   T A I N T
    J I L T E D   C R I N G E
S T E N O   C O A S T E R
P A S T E S   T H I S
L U T E   T R I A L H O R S E
A P E R   E O N S   E V I L S
T E R N   P O E M   S A B O T
```

Page 102 — HAVING A BAWL

```
A M I S S   C A I R O   B I G
R A C K O   A C R I D   A D A
C R Y I N G S H A M E   H I M
        P A R E E   S P A D E
S P A R T A   D A Y   E M I T
O H I O A N S   N E O N A T E
P E R P   T A S T Y
    W E E P I N G W I L L O W
        T R I T E   E V I L
P R O S A I C   R E P T I L E
R E P O   S K Y   R I D D L E
E V I T E   A M I G O
F I N   W A I L I N G W A L L
A L E   E L V I S   I N N I E
B E D   S L E E T   E S T E S
```

Page 104 — TAKE NOTES

```
P U R E   S P O T   V I S E S
I S I S   T A R O   I N T R A
C A B C H A R G E   A D O R N
        A G E   O P E D
P A P E R E R S   C R O W D S
I M A G E D   T O R E R O
C A R O M   H Y P E D   R D A
A I L S   P A L E D   S K I N
S N O   O I L E R   B E I N G
    R U D E S T   G R A N G E
H O P P E R   S T R A N G E R
A T I T   O E D
S T E A L   T E X A S C I T Y
N E C K S   B A I T   A C H E
T R E E D   A R C S   P E O N
```

Page 106 — WHAT'S YOUR SIGN?

```
L I M B S   A S I A   K A L B
A R I E L   B A N G   O L E O
N O S H O U L D E R   P L A N
A N T E   N E A R E D   A V E
        A S S   T E E T H E D
H O O D L U M S   D E W
E L M   A R I A S   P I K E S
S L I P P E R Y W H E N W E T
S A T E D   O N I O N   A L E
        E A R   O T H E W I S P
M I L K S O P   O D E
I R E   H O O K A H   A S E A
N A V E   M E N W O R K I N G
U N I T   I S E E   E E R I E
S I N S   E Y E D   D R E D D
```

Page 108 — CHOP-CHOP

```
P O N D   A T T Y   P O R T S
A M O R   R O B E   U R I A H
P A R E   G N A T   D E L T A
A N A X T O G R I N D   L E D
        E E N S   E L L E R Y
C A L L A   A T S E A
A L A   C L O S E S   O W E D
T O M A H A W K M I S S I L E
S E E R   D E E P E N   L I E
        B L I N D   O D D E R
G A S S E D   T R U E
A R E   H A T C H E T F A C E
M O L A R   A R A B   E R O S
E M I L E   R U N E   C L O P
S A G E R   P E E L   T O N Y
```

Page 110 — THE FAMILY JEWELS

P	I	N	D	A	R		H	E	D	Y		P	E	P
P	I	R	A	T	E		O	R	E	O		E	T	A
D	I	A	M	O	N	D	B	A	C	K		A	R	S
			A	N	T	E		S	I	E	R	R	A	S
S	A	R	G	A	S	S	O			O	L	D	E	
C	R	U	E	L		A	M	B	U	S	H	E	D	
A	L	B	S		P	E	K	O	E	T	E	A		
T	O	Y		R	E	C		O	R	E		R	L	S
		T	E	E	S	H	I	R	T		O	B	I	T
	F	O	U	R	D	O	O	R		A	R	O	M	A
A	D	E	N		S	A	N	D	A	R	A	C		
R	E	S	O	L	E	D		T	O	I	L			
L	S	D		E	M	E	R	A	L	D	I	S	L	E
E	S	A		N	I	C	E		T	A	S	T	E	R
Y	A	Y		S	T	O	P		E	S	T	A	T	E

Page 112 — FILLING THE BILL

R	A	S	T	A		S	T	A	I	R		B	I	C
O	R	I	O	N		E	A	G	L	E		I	C	U
B	I	C	Y	C	L	E	B	E	L	L		D	I	R
			I	A	M	S				L	I	F	E	R
R	U	B	B	E	R	S		P	L	E	N	A	R	Y
U	N	I	O	N	S		P	L	A	N	A	R		
B	L	O	A	T		P	R	A	D	O		E	P	A
L	E	F	T		W	R	O	T	E		S	W	A	N
E	D	U		P	A	I	N	E		C	H	E	S	T
		E	L	L	I	C	E		O	R	E	L	S	E
F	O	L	I	A	T	E		S	M	E	L	L	E	D
L	A	C	E	Y				P	I	N	T			
I	K	E		B	I	K	I	N	I	A	T	O	L	L
N	I	L		O	R	I	N	G		N	O	W	A	Y
G	E	L		Y	A	T	E	S		S	T	E	V	E

Page 114 — GETTING NUTTY

T	A	C	O	S		T	A	M	E	R		S	A	L
A	P	O	R	T		W	R	O	T	E		I	R	A
C	R	A	Z	Y	E	I	G	H	T	S		L	I	U
	S	T	O	R	M	S		S	E	T	T	L	E	D
			E	A	T				A	B	Y	S	S	
D	E	F	A	N	G		B	A	D	R	A	P		
E	L	U	D	E		C	O	M	E	T		U	S	O
N	I	N	O		S	A	X	O	N		S	T	U	D
T	A	N		E	A	V	E	S		P	E	T	R	O
		Y	A	S	S	E	R		S	L	A	Y	E	R
A	D	M	I	T				S	P	A				
V	I	O	L	E	T	S		C	A	S	T	O	R	
A	N	N		L	O	O	N	E	Y	T	U	N	E	S
S	E	E		L	O	R	E	N		E	T	A	I	L
T	R	Y		E	L	E	C	T		R	U	N	N	Y

Page 116 — BERG-ERS

C	A	S	S		S	E	R	B		L	E	G	A	L
A	S	T	I		C	L	U	E		E	V	A	D	E
C	L	A	N		O	L	D	E		V	E	R	S	E
H	A	N	K	G	R	E	E	N	B	E	R	G		
E	N	D		L	E	N		R	E	T	O	R	T	
			B	A	D		E	L	I	S		Y	E	A
A	S	T	E	R		O	X	E	N		E	L	A	N
S	T	E	V	E	N	S	P	I	E	L	B	E	R	G
C	A	R	Y		A	L	A	S		S	A	S	S	Y
A	R	M		S	C	O	T		R	A	Y			
P	E	P	P	E	R		R	U	T		S	P	A	
		A	L	L	E	N	G	I	N	S	B	E	R	G
N	E	P	A	L		A	L	L	Y		E	T	O	N
I	R	E	N	E		P	A	L	O		C	O	N	E
P	A	R	E	R		A	M	E	N		K	N	E	W

Page 118 — BREW CREW

P	L	I	E	S		H	O	P	I		S	L	I	D
E	A	G	L	E		O	P	U	S		Y	A	D	A
P	R	O	L	E		R	I	L	L		S	T	I	R
	D	R	A	F	T	S	E	L	E	C	T	I	O	N
			I	R	E				R	E	N	T	S	
E	N	T	I	T	Y		S	A	L	E	M			
B	O	O	N		A	C	R	E	S		T	A	U	
B	O	T	T	L	E	D	E	M	O	T	I	O	N	S
S	N	O		O	P	E	N	S		R	O	T	S	
			G	U	I	S	E		M	I	S	T	E	R
	S	P	I	E	S				R	E	S			
C	A	N	N	E	D	L	A	U	G	H	T	E	R	
A	U	T	O		E	A	R	S		T	O	P	E	R
P	L	E	A		S	W	I	T		A	R	E	N	A
E	A	R	N		I	N	D	Y		R	E	E	D	Y

Page 120 — AERIAL SHOW

P	I	A	N	O		R	O	E	S		C	A	W	S
O	R	R	I	N		A	S	S	T		A	G	R	A
R	O	C	K	E	T	J	S	Q	U	I	R	R	E	L
E	N	S		C	I	A	O		B	A	R	E	S	T
			M	A	C	H				M	E	E	T	S
A	T	W	O	R	K		H	U	S	S	Y			
B	A	I	L		K	O	R	E	A		M	A	D	
B	U	L	L	W	I	N	K	L	E	M	O	O	S	E
A	T	L		A	R	I	E	S		P	L	A	N	
			P	I	E	T	Y		C	R	E	E	P	Y
R	A	C	E	S				T	O	O	N			
A	L	E	R	T	S		O	I	L	S		I	S	M
B	O	R	I	S	A	N	D	N	A	T	A	S	H	A
A	N	T	S		N	E	O	N		E	L	L	E	N
T	E	S	H		G	O	R	Y		R	E	E	D	Y

Page 122 — COUNTRY STYLE

T	A	P	A	S		B	O	N	D		O	C	H	S
A	B	A	T	E		A	M	O	R		C	H	A	N
B	U	R	M	A	S	H	A	V	E		T	I	L	E
			L	O	I	N		W	H	A	L	E	R	
T	O	C	C	A	T	A		I	N	E	R	T		
A	T	H	E	N	S		I	N	S	T	E	P		
S	H	I	N	E		L	O	O	I	E		O	S	S
T	E	N	T		D	O	T	E	S		T	W	I	T
E	R	A		R	E	G	A	L		R	O	D	E	O
		C	H	I	V	E	S		G	E	N	E	V	A
R	E	L	I	C			D	E	S	E	R	E	T	
E	V	O	K	E	S		P	U	N	T				
C	A	S	E		T	U	R	K	E	Y	T	R	O	T
O	D	E	R		E	R	I	E		L	E	A	V	E
N	E	T	S		W	I	G	S		E	L	M	A	N

Page 124 — GOOD VS. EVIL

B	E	B	O	P		B	O	F	F			A	S	H
A	L	O	N	E		A	V	E	R		A	R	N	O
D	A	N	C	E		B	A	L	E		N	O	E	L
A	N	G	E	L	F	A	L	L	S		G	A	E	L
				E	R	R			C	H	E	R	R	Y
S	H	O	D	D	Y		A	F	O	U	L			
A	I	D	E		E	D	G	E		A	B	A	S	H
G	L	O	V	E		I	R	E		C	A	R	E	Y
S	T	R	I	P		B	E	D	E		B	L	E	D
			L	E	A	S	E		A	N	Y	O	N	E
P	O	D	D	E	D		F	R	I					
E	U	R	O		D	E	V	I	L	T	O	P	A	Y
S	T	A	G		O	R	A	L		W	R	I	T	E
T	E	N	S		N	I	L	E		I	C	E	I	N
O	R	K			S	E	E	D		T	A	R	T	S

Page 126 — TIEUPS

B	O	I	N	G		R	I	S	E		S	N	A	G
A	B	N	E	R		O	R	A	N		T	A	L	E
C	O	R	D	O	F	W	O	O	D		I	M	A	M
H	E	E		C	A	E	N		P	R	E	S	S	
			T	E	R	N		S	A	T	U	P		
T	H	R	E	A	D	O	F	A	P	L	O	T		
S	T	O	R	Y		E	A	T	S		A	K	A	
P	E	R	U		D	O	C	K	S		O	T	I	S
A	N	T		I	O	N	A		C	L	E	E	K	
S	T	R	I	N	G	O	F	B	E	A	D	S		
		E	N	T	E	R		A	C	R	E			
S	I	F	T	S		O	S	H	A		L	O	S	
O	D	O	R		L	I	N	E	O	F	W	O	R	K
A	E	R	O		A	R	C	S		E	R	O	D	E
R	A	M	S		M	E	E	T		S	Y	N	O	D

Page 128 — FOR THE BIRDS

A	T	A	T		S	O	F	T		F	I	T	T	O
L	U	C	E		E	P	E	E		I	C	O	N	S
O	D	O	R		R	I	T	E		N	E	S	T	S
H	O	R	S	E	F	E	A	T	H	E	R	S		
A	R	N	E	L			H	I	T			E	B	B
				M	O	B	S		C	U	R	S	O	R
C	P	A		T	O	Y	S			N	A	O	M	I
G	O	E	S	D	O	W	N	T	H	E	T	U	B	E
I	R	A	T	E			S	O	A	R		S	T	S
L	A	C	I	N	G		D	Y	E	R				
A	L	E		T	E	N			N	A	S	A	L	
			P	L	U	M	E	S	O	F	S	M	O	K	E
P	R	I	E	R		W	A	D	E		A	B	I	T
T	E	P	E	E		E	L	I	A		Z	I	T	I
A	P	E	R	S		R	E	N	T		E	G	A	N

Page 130 — PACKAGE DEAL

D	I	A	N	A		L	O	O	P		A	B	E	L
U	N	M	E	T		L	O	W	E		R	U	B	E
B	R	O	W	N	P	A	P	E	R		A	B	B	A
S	E	S	S	I	O	N		S	T	A	B	B	E	D
				G	L	O	W			G	I	L	D	S
B	U	S	C	H		S	E	R	V	I	C	E		
A	S	C	O	T	S		B	E	E	N		W	I	T
S	M	O	G		H	A	S	O	N		D	R	N	O
H	A	T		M	U	S	T		I	C	E	A	G	E
			C	L	I	N	K	E	R		A	M	P	E	D
R	E	H	E	M			R	E	E	L				
A	R	T	S	I	E	R		A	R	I	S	T	O	S
I	R	A	S		C	E	L	L	O	P	H	A	N	E
T	O	P	E		H	A	I	L		H	A	R	T	E
T	R	E	E		O	R	L	Y		S	W	O	O	P

Page 132 — WHAT'S YOUR TYPE?

C	L	A	M	S		H	E	E	P		D	O	D	O
R	O	G	U	E		O	V	E	R		E	V	I	L
A	B	R	O	N	X	T	A	L	E		S	E	N	D
M	O	O	N	S	E	T	S		D	R	I	N	K	S
				E	D	U			D	I	A	L		
A	B	A	C	I		B	P	I	C	T	U	R	E	S
S	L	I	T	S		R	O	T	E			A	L	E
T	E	N	S		T	W	I	N	S		I	B	I	D
R	E	T		S	H	O	O		R	A	I	S	E	
O	P	I	O	N	E	E	R	S		E	N	D	E	R
			R	O	C	S		P	E	R				
S	P	R	A	W	L		S	A	M	A	N	T	H	A
H	O	O	T		A	B	C	R	U	N	C	H	E	S
O	S	L	O		S	E	A	S		K	A	R	A	T
P	E	E	R		H	E	R	E		S	A	U	D	I

Page 134 — BUGGING OUT

```
A L D E R | G E E N A | C A R
H A I L E | O R B E D | O W E
S P E L L I N G B E E | B O W
O D D | O R E O | S T O K E
      S C A R | T O T A L E D
S A M P A N | G O R E N
I D I O T | A O N E | T R O T
B U T T E R F L Y S T R O K E
S E A L | O I L S | H U L A S
      E M O R Y | H O M E Y S
W E B S I T E | F I R S
A M A S S | E A R N | C P U
T I S | C R I C K E T B A L L
E L I | H A S T E | O R L O N
R E C | A S T O R | N A F T A
```

Page 136 — IN CODE

```
T O L E T | F A W N | G A S P
A G I L E | O B O E | A C H E
D R E S S B L U E S | I C O N
S E D A T E D | S A T E E N
      B E S T S | M E S S Y
H A Z M A T | O T H E R S
A V I A N | B R E W S | R H O
H O P E | M O N E Y | P O O R
A N Y | R O Y A L | C R A N E
O P E N E D | R H O D E S
C H U R N | R O S I E
H E R O E S | M A M M A L S
R I L L | L E G A L L I M I T
I D I E | O V A L | A L O N E
S I P S | W A L L | B E S E T
```

Page 138 — IN THE SADDLE

```
H A B I T | C P U S | P O L L
E L A T E | H A S P | E R I E
R O B E R T E L E E | C A N E
S T A M M E R | S C O O T E R
      S I R | T A S E R S
M O C | T I S | H E R B
A W A K E | H E A R | I R M A
S E M I | T I E R S | L O O P
K N O T | A L L S | C L O V E
      C O I L | H B O | M E X
A P P A L L | A N N
S E E R E S S | S E V E R A L
C A S S | P A U L R E V E R E
A L T O | I N T O | R E N E W
P E O N | N E A T | T R E A D
```

Page 140 — CROSSES TO BEAR

```
S O L A R | I D E S | S M O G
C R O N E | N E X T | P O P E
O N U S W A G N E R | E T T A
P E T A R D | T R E A C H E R
      R I D E | T E X | E D S
C H E A T E R S | T E A R
O A R | E R R O R | S I L A S
W H I T | S O L O N | R O B E
L A C E S | L E V E R | A L E
      B L O B | R E W A R D E D
S T U | O R C | R I T E
P A R T N E R S | S A L A D A
R U D E | W E I G H T A S E C
A P E S | E M M A | A T I L T
Y E N S | D E P T | T E A L S
```

Page 142 — CROSSING WORDS

```
S H A W | A M P S | I B S E N
T A C H | R A R E | L E A V E
A S T I | T R E E | L A M E D
S T O P T H E P R E S S E S
H O N S H U | N A T
      U R L | F R Y | C C C
S T R U M | O S L O | O A H U
L O O K B A C K I N A N G E R
O G L E | B A I T | B E E T S
P O L | P A L | S P A
      O U T | O S C A R S
L I S T E N T O R E A S O N
M A R A T | A U N T | R I T E
I M A G E | I N C A | O D O R
S A N E R | F E E L | N E R D
```

Page 144 — EEEEE!

```
A R K S | C O B | M O D E S
S U I T | O M A R | A R E N T
K L E E | M E S A | G R E T A
S E V E N E L E V E N | P E C
      L A T E | E S A | F R Y
D O P E S | T E L S T A R
A V E | T A T A | E E L E R S
M A T H | R E G A N | B E A U
N L E A S T | E P E E | Z I P
S E E H E R E | T E E N S
T I E | A U R | N A C L
R O E | G R E E N C H E E S E
A N G E R | C A I N | C L A D
P I E T A | T U N E | T A N G
S C R A M | X E D | S L A Y
```

W	O	O	D	S		B	L	O	K	E		H	E	M
W	O	V	E	N		A	U	D	I	E		A	V	A
W	H	O	L	E	S	A	L	I	N	G		R	E	D
			T	R	E	B	L	E	D		H	A	N	D
R	E	G	A	T	T	A			J	E	S	S	E	
A	X	I	S		H	A	L	F	N	E	L	S	O	N
G	I	G				E	R	O	D	E				
S	T	O	W		S	A	V	O	R		N	A	S	T
			A	D	A	G	E			L	I	E		
T	H	I	R	D	W	O	R	L	D		S	O	F	A
R	A	N	T	S			E	A	G	L	E	T	S	
A	N	T	S		M	C	E	N	R	O	E			
I	K	E		Q	U	A	R	T	E	R	D	E	C	K
T	I	N		A	L	F	I	E		E	G	R	E	T
S	E	T		S	T	E	E	N		D	E	A	L	S

B	A	S	E	S		B	U	R	B	S		A	S	A
A	D	E	L	E		O	P	A	R	T		N	U	N
R	O	A	S	T	M	A	S	T	E	R		G	I	T
E	S	T	A	T	E	S		S	T	A	T	U	T	E
			L	E	T	S			F	U	S	E	D	
A	N	K	L	E	T		T	W	E	E	T	Y		
B	O	O	E	D		F	R	O	N	D		O	I	L
L	O	B	E		C	R	I	E	D		T	U	N	A
E	K	E		F	O	O	D	S		F	U	N	G	I
		B	R	I	D	G	E		L	I	N	G	E	R
A	A	R	O	N		S	H	A	D					
S	K	Y	C	A	P	S		O	P	E	R	A	T	E
I	R	A		G	R	O	U	N	D	L	E	V	E	L
D	O	N		L	O	U	S	E		I	D	E	A	L
E	N	T		E	S	S	A	Y		S	O	R	R	Y

S	C	A	R	E		L	A	M	A		T	H	E	M
A	R	C	E	D		I	D	O	L		E	U	R	O
B	A	R	B	I	E	D	O	L	L		A	S	I	S
I	V	E		S	A	S		D	I	T	C	H	E	S
N	E	S	T	O	R			Y	E	A	H			
			U	N	L	E	T			B	E	S	E	T
F	L	A	P		E	T	H	E	R		R	I	C	O
A	I	D	E		S	T	O	R	E		S	T	O	W
R	E	A	L		S	A	R	G	E		P	E	N	N
R	U	M	O	R		N	O	N	C	E				
			H	E	A	D			T	A	T	E	R	S
R	I	C	O	T	T	A		E	R	R		L	O	T
I	R	O	N		B	Y	E	B	Y	E	B	A	B	Y
P	A	R	E		A	N	K	A		S	I	T	I	N
A	N	D	Y		T	E	E	N		S	C	E	N	E

P	O	W		C	A	M	E	L		P	U	F	F	
O	R	A	L		O	L	I	V	E		E	R	I	E
S	C	R	U	B	P	I	N	E	S		R	A	R	E
S	A	N	T	A		G	R	A	P	P	L	E	D	
E	S	S	E	N	E	S			G	A	L			
				C	L	E	A	N	E	N	E	R	G	Y
S	C	A	M		I	N	D	O		E	X	I	L	E
C	A	N	I	S		T	H	O		D	E	C	A	L
A	L	I	S	T		R	O	D	S		D	A	M	P
R	I	N	S	E	C	Y	C	L	E	S				
			T	A	O			E	X	I	S	T	E	D
P	R	E	A	M	B	L	E		L	A	I	N	E	
H	I	L	T		W	A	S	H	B	O	A	R	D	S
I	D	L	E		E	L	S	I	E		R	E	E	K
L	E	E	S		B	O	O	E	D		D	D	S	

M	E	O	W	S		A	B	R	A	M		M	O	W
G	E	T	I	T		M	E	A	L	Y		I	T	A
B	E	T	S	Y	P	A	L	M	E	R		S	T	L
			P	E	R	I	L		S	O	C	C	E	R
P	L	A	Y		E	N	Y	A		N	E	H	R	U
E	O	N			U	M	S		L	A	S	S		
K	A	N		I	N	A	P	I	C	K	L	E		
E	M	I	G	R	E	S		G	A	L	I	L	E	E
		E	A	R	T	H	W	O	R	M		M	A	L
E	R	O	S		S	E	A			A	R	K		
R	E	A	P	S		S	N	C	C		A	N	N	E
R	A	K	E	I	N		G	R	A	S	P			
A	L	L		M	A	R	L	A	M	A	P	L	E	S
N	E	E		O	B	O	E	S		C	L	E	E	K
T	R	Y		N	E	E	D	S		K	E	N	N	Y

A	M	E	S		F	A	C	E	D		H	I	Y	A
N	O	V	A		A	B	A	S	E		A	D	E	N
D	R	I	L	L	C	O	R	P	S		M	E	L	T
E	A	T		A	I	D	E		T	A	M	A	L	E
S	N	A	P	P	L	E		M	I	T	E			
			L	E	E		P	A	N	O	R	A	M	A
H	E	M	A	L		B	A	T	E		T	R	E	X
I	R	A	N		H	I	R	E	D		H	E	A	L
P	I	N	E		O	B	E	Y		P	R	A	T	E
S	E	X	T	U	P	L	E		C	R	O			
			I	S	E	E		C	R	O	W	B	A	R
S	L	I	C	E	S		S	H	A	M		A	V	A
L	I	N	K		F	I	L	E	F	O	L	D	E	R
O	N	C	E		O	D	I	S	T		O	G	R	E
B	E	A	T		R	A	T	T	Y		W	E	T	S

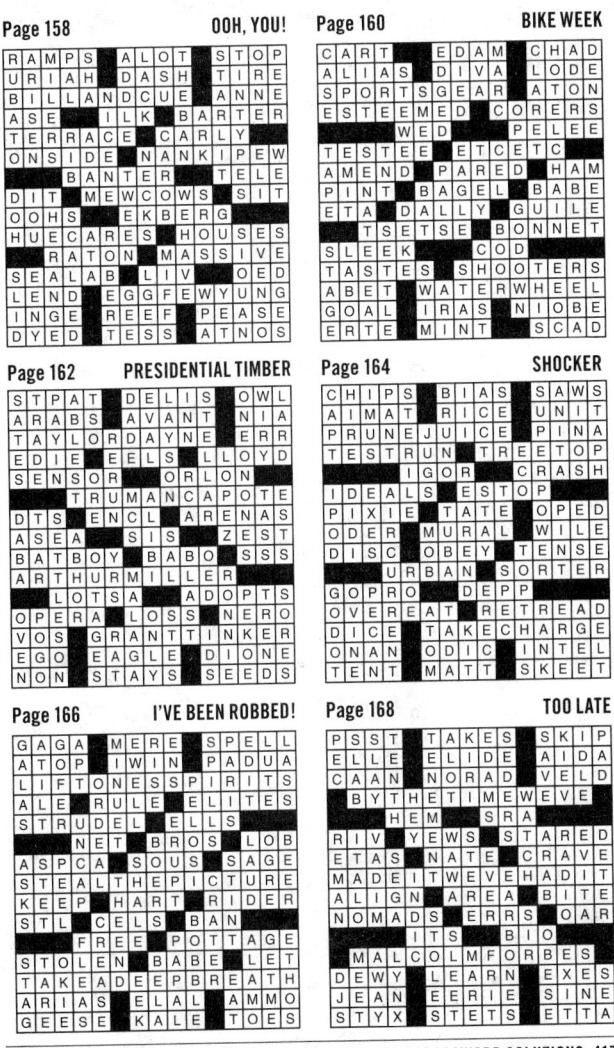

Page 158 — OOH, YOU!

```
RAMPS ALOT  STOP
URIAH DASH  TIRE
BILLANDCUE  ANNE
ASE ILK  BARTER
TERRACE  CARLY
ONSIDE NANKIPEW
  BANTER   TELE
DIT MEWCOWS  SIT
OOHS   EKBERG
HUECARES  HOUSES
  RATON  MASSIVE
SEALAB LIV   OED
LEND EGGFEWYUNG
INGE REEF  PEASE
DYED TESS  ATNOS
```

Page 160 — BIKE WEEK

```
CART   EDAM  CHAD
ALIAS  DIVA  LODE
SPORTSGEAR   ATON
ESTEEMED   CORERS
   WED     PELEE
TESTEE  ETCETC
AMEND  PARED   HAM
PINT  BAGEL  BABE
ETA DALLY  GUILE
 TSETSE   BONNET
SLEEK    COD
TASTES  SHOOTERS
ABET WATERWHEEL
GOAL IRAS   NIOBE
ERTE MINT   SCAD
```

Page 162 — PRESIDENTIAL TIMBER

```
STPAT  DELIS   OWL
ARABS  AVANT   NIA
TAYLORDAYNE   ERR
EDIE  EELS  LLOYD
SENSOR    ORLON
  TRUMANCAPOTE
DTS ENCL  ARENAS
ASEA  SIS    ZEST
BATBOY BABO   SSS
  ARTHURMILLER
  LOTSA   ADOPTS
OPERA LOSS   NERO
VOS GRANTTINKER
EGO EAGLE  DIONE
NON STAYS  SEEDS
```

Page 164 — SHOCKER

```
CHIPS  BIAS  SAWS
AIMAT  RICE  UNIT
PRUNEJUICE  PINA
TESTRUN  TREETOP
   IGOR   CRASH
IDEALS   ESTOP
PIXIE  TATE  OPED
ODER  MURAL  WILE
DISC  OBEY  TENSE
  URBAN   SORTER
GOPRO    DEPP
OVEREAT  RETREAD
DICE  TAKECHARGE
ONAN  ODIC  INTEL
TENT  MATT  SKEET
```

Page 166 — I'VE BEEN ROBBED!

```
GAGA MERE   SPELL
ATOP IWIN   PADUA
LIFTONESSPIRITS
ALE RULE  ELITES
STRUDEL  ELLS
  NET BROS   LOB
ASPCA SOUS  SAGE
STEALTHEPICTURE
KEEP HART  RIDER
STL CELS  BAN
  FREE  POTTAGE
STOLEN BABE  LET
TAKEADEEPBREATH
ARIAS ELAL  AMMO
GEESE KALE  TOES
```

Page 168 — TOO LATE

```
PSST  TAKES  SKIP
ELLE  ELIDE  AIDA
CAAN  NORAD  VELD
  BYTHETIMEWEVE
    HEM   SRA
RIV YEWS  STARED
ETAS NATE  CRAVE
MADEITWEVEHADIT
ALIGN AREA  BITE
NOMADS ERRS   OAR
   ITS  BIO
  MALCOLMFORBES
DEWY LEARN  EXES
JEAN EERIE  SINE
STYX STETS  ETTA
```

Page 170 — PRESIDENTIAL NICKNAMES

```
A S A ░ A B O M B ░ U N F I T
M A L ░ C O R E R ░ N E A T O
A B E V I G O D A ░ L A M A S
S L U E D ░ S N O O P E R S ░
S E T T I N G ░ D O C ░ ░ ░ ░
░ ░ ░ C A L R I P K E N J R ░
C R A B ░ B O O ░ S C O U T ░
A I R E ░ S P Y R I ░ T O N E
S P I N S ░ A U G ░ O N E S ░
░ T E D D Y W I L S O N ░ ░ ░
░ ░ ░ ░ S O N ░ T R E S T L E
C H A S T E N S ░ B U Y I N ░
L I T H E ░ I K E T U R N E R
O D I U M ░ N E V I L ░ A G O
P E T E S ░ G E E N A ░ N E L
```

Page 172 — WHERE'S ED?

```
V A S E S ░ C A D S ░ J A W S
O G I L L ░ A B U T ░ E M I T
T E D K E N N E D Y ░ D O R A
E N L ░ D E A L ░ L O C K E T
S T E N G E L ░ V I A L ░ ░ ░
░ ░ ░ E E R ░ M I S T A K E N
S A N D S ░ B E S T ░ M E T E
A B A B ░ F R A T S ░ P E A R
M E N U ░ L A N A ░ H E L L O
S T A N D O U T ░ H U T ░ ░ ░
░ ░ ░ T O W N ░ M A N T R A S
A N G L E E ░ A U N T ░ A B A
T O R I ░ R E D S K E L T O N
O N A N ░ E R I K ░ R E E V E
M O D E ░ D E N Y ░ S O R E R
```

Page 174 — BELLS

```
H A H A ░ A R I ░ A S K E D
O V A L ░ L A S E ░ S T A R R
B I L L ░ B I N G C H E R R Y
O D O R ░ I S T O O ░ R O S S
░ ░ ░ I F N I ░ I C O N ░ ░ ░
D I N G D O N G S C H O O L ░
O M A H A ░ O T I S ░ L E M
S H O T ░ S T S ░ S A V E
T I M ░ A S T I ░ S A N E R
░ P I N G P O N G P A D D L E
░ ░ ░ A T O P ░ U E Y S ░ ░ ░
B R A G ░ O O Z E S ░ A M O K
R I N G O F F I R E ░ C O H N
A L T E R ░ F O R T ░ K A N E
S L I D E ░ N E A ░ S T O W
```

Page 176 — PETRIFIED FOREST

```
G A L L O ░ W H O S ░ P E S T
A V O I D ░ O I L Y ░ E L I A
B O U L D E R D A M ░ B I N S
E N D ░ S A T E ░ P T B O A T
░ ░ ░ R A S H ░ S H E L T I E
C A V O R T ░ A M O R E ░ ░ ░
A L I C E ░ I R A N ░ B L U B
N E C K ░ E N T R Y ░ E A R L
E X E C ░ A L I T ░ S A R G E
░ ░ ░ O G R E S ░ P A C K E D
G A N N E T T ░ M A T H ░ ░ ░
O R A C L E ░ M A R C ░ S O U
T O M E ░ S T O N E H E N G E
U S E R ░ T O R E ░ E M I L Y
P E R T ░ S P E D ░ L U T E S
```

Page 178 — WRECKERS

```
D E L V E ░ T R A I L ░ D A H
O A S E S ░ R O N D O ░ E R A
T R U S T B U S T E R ░ A I R
░ ░ ░ T A R E S ░ S E L L E R
V I S I T O R ░ ░ A B L Y ░ ░
I M A G E S ░ P A S T O R ░ ░
C A F E ░ K O R E A ░ E A T
E R E ░ H O O S I E R ░ A S A
S I C ░ O R B E D ░ S K I P
░ ░ R I N G E R ░ A C C E D E
░ ░ L E A D ░ ░ C H A I R E D
E N C O R E ░ T E E N S ░ ░ ░
A S K ░ A T O M S M A S H E R
S U E ░ K A R A T ░ R O U T E
H E R ░ E L E N A ░ D R E A D
```

Page 180 — THE FICKLE FINGER

```
B O A R ░ S A W S ░ A S T E R
E D N A ░ T R I O ░ M A I N E
L O T S ░ I L L S ░ A C C R A
T R I C K L E D O W N ░ K O P
░ ░ ░ A N T S ░ I D Y L L S ░
M A P L E S ░ P A R A D E ░ ░
E R I S A ░ R O M E ░ S P E D
S I C ░ D E E P E S T ░ I D O
S A K S ░ V E E S ░ R A N G E
░ ░ L A P E L S ░ P A R K E R
░ C R E T A N ░ S O D A ░ ░ ░
H I C ░ S T I C K L E B A C K
A C H E S ░ M A I L ░ I R O N
W H I T E ░ A B L E ░ A N T E
S E P A L ░ M O L D ░ N O S E
```

Page 182 — I'M PUZZLED!

```
H A S T E | S T A M P | F T C
O R L O N | C A M E L | R H O
S O U N D B A F F L E | E O S
E S E | P I N T | A L E R T
R E S U L T S | R E S E T |
  N A E | T O G E T H E R
A R T S Y | E R M A | A R L O
L U R E | C L U E D | L O A D
D I E T | L E N O | D O W N S
O N E T R A C K | U R N |
  S L A N T | B R E E Z E S
R A T E S | M A G S | A L A
I C U | C A N D L E S T I C K
D E M | A M U S E | E E R I E
E S P | L A T E R | R E E D S
```

Page 184 — CHUMP CHANGE

```
W I L D E | S M O O T | U P S
A R I E L | P A R C H | N I A
D R E S S | I R A T E | R E S
    P E N N Y L O A F E R S
A R N O | A S S | R A C E
T O O T I N | A R C A D E S
L A T I N | S I D E R |
  N I C K E L D E F E N S E
  E V I A N | D I A L S
M E T E R E D | T O G G L E
O D A Y | S E W | H E A T
D I M E N O V E L I S T |
E T A | E V I T A | A C U R A
L O L | M E L O N | P A N E L
A R E | O N E N D | S P O D E
```

Page 186 — GROUP THEORY

```
H A Z E D | S H A M | L A Y
A S I D E | P E R U | G O R E
R I N G B E A R E R | A B E L
P A G E A N T S | A N N E A L
O N S | T I E | S L A G |
  B E D | S T I P P L E D
M E S A S | H O R S | L O V E
E C O N | S A D A T | A R I A
S H O D | O D A Y | K N E L L
H O T W I R E S | N I K |
  I V E S | Y A W | T I P
S H A D E S | S O N A T I N A
T O R T | P A C K A N I M A L
E A C H | O B O E | I R E N E
P R O | T A T S | S E X E S
```

Page 188 — PUT-DOWNS

```
M I S T S | I M A M | R E D S
A D O R E | R A C E | I D E A
J O D I E | O R C A | P I L L
S L A M D A N C E R | S T E T
  Y E W | S A W N |
S W A P | R A M S | H O U S E
L I M A | O R E | S O R T E R
A D I N | B E A S T | T I E R
T E C H I E | N E A | E L M O
S N E A D | S T A N | R E E L
  N A P E | M C A |
S H A D | R A P S E S S I O N
N A I L | O B I T | C A R R E
O L D E | P E T E | O N I N E
B O A R | S E A R | T A S E R
```

Page 190 — TUNEFUL TETRAD

```
R E C A P | S O A V E | T E D
E R I C A | O R L O N | I N E
C R O O N E R B I N G | P A M
  R A C E S | | A T M O
S T E N C H | S A S S O O N
P I C | H O O C H M A K E R S
A T O N E | P O R E R S |
T O N E | B I R D S | I B I S
  S P I N E L | S N A R E
V I N T A G E A U T O | R A T
I N T E N D S | I M P I S H
A R E A | | S I N A I |
B O S | B A S E B A L L S C Y
L A T | A D O R E | I L I A D
E D S | D O N A T | A S S T S
```

Page 192 — ERRORS

```
A M O R | S C A R | D E A L T
S I M I | E R I E | E L V E R
E D A M | R O D E | C L A V E
A I R I S A W E L B A | G E E
  N O G | S E E | Y A R D
B A C I L L I | D E C O R |
O D E | A I N T | H Y D R A
H E I R C O N D I T I O N E R
R E L E E | S T E M | E N O
  I N D U S | S N E E R E D
I S N T | K E G | S R A
R A G | E R E A P P A R E N T
I N F U N | P Y L E | T R U E
S T A N D | E L I E | H I K E
H A N D S | D E E D | S K E D
```

Page 194 — SWIT(C/H)EROO

```
T H E T A S # V E T O # T H E
A E R O B E # E A R N # R U S
S H R U B N U R S E S # I M P
# # R O S S S E A # R A V I #
A L L # T O T E # D E E D E E
S E E # T R A # G L A S S E S
H E A D # # # D E E R E # # #
# S H R I M P A N D S A V E #
# # # O C E A N # # # L E V Y
S E R P E N T # S T S # R A E
O N E I D A # A T O P # O N T
I R A N # C A V E D I N # # #
L A S # S H R E W D R I V E R
E G O # H E A R # L A T I N A
D E N # E M M Y # E L E C T S
```

Page 196 — TO, BUT NOT FRO

```
C A R O B # A S A P # I N A N
A B O D E # W E V E # D O D O
H E A D T O H E A D # O S L O
N E D # T W I T # C L E A N #
# # T O E T O T O E # T I S #
S O F A R # # # R U S S O # #
I R A S # H A I R T O N I C #
P A C T S # O R E # A R O M A
# S L E E P O V E R # T S P S
# # T R I P E # # # G E E S E
Q U O # E A R T O E A R # # #
U N F E D # E L A L # T A E #
I T A L # H A N D T O H A N D
L I C K # E A S E # S E T O N
T E E S # W H E N # H Y E N A
```

Page 198 — THAT AIN'T HEY!

```
B R A S # J I B S # J A C K S
L A V E # E D E N # U B O A T
A V E R # A I R E # R A S T A
S E R V I N G T R E Y # M E G
E N T I R E # T A R S I # # #
# # # L E T G O # T I N C A N
P A L E # T U B S # G O R D Y
A L E # R E L O A D S # E D S
N O T S O # L E G O # L Y R E
T E U T O N # S A O N E # # #
# # # S U T R A # D I V E S T
M V P # B A S T I L L E D E Y
E E R I E # C O R E # R I A L
S I E V E # O D O R # E T T E
S L Y E R # T O N S # T H O R
```

Page 200 — RACK'EM UP!

```
E S T E S # S L A B # S H A R
G U I L E # N O R A # T O B E
O L D S C R A T C H # R U E S
S K E E T E R # # # H A S T E
# # # O N E S # D E T E S T #
A F F O R D # P R E F A B # #
S O R E # V A U L T # # R O D
P R E D A T E # B E S I E G E
S E E # L I N U S # R A R A #
# # S T I N T S # T E R K E L
S P A R K Y # H A H A # # # #
N O F E E # # # D O S A G E S
I D E A # M E M O R Y B A N K
P I T T # O V E R # A B I D E
S A Y S # P A T E # S E N S E
```

Page 202 — CLEAN IT UP!

```
C A S S # M A T S # B O S N S
A S T O # A R A L # U N T I E
S C R U B P I N E # G I A N T
S E A # O L D # D E B O N E S
I N T U N E # # # T E N # C O O
S T A N D # F A T H A # # #
# # C I V I L W A R B U F F #
S O I L # O S L I N # L E F T
T A K E A S H I N E T O # # #
E R E # S T Y N E # R O V E D
# # I S O # M O D E L A # # #
P A N C A K E # O O P # S A N
A T E I N # W A X P O E T I C
T R E N T # A M E S # G E N E
S A R G E # N Y N Y # O D E R
```

Page 204 — HI-LO

```
# L A W N # D R E A D # S I D
T I B I A # R U D G E # P R O
M O U N T A I N D E W # I A N
I N T O T A L # Y E A R E N D
# # # N E A L E # R A D I I #
P O L A R # # A L I S T # # #
I K E # E S P R I T # S U M P
P R A I R I E S C H O O N E R
E A R N # R E H E E L # I N A
# # # A R E N O # D A T U M #
P E N N E # T H E F T # # # #
S Q U E A L S # E R O T I C A
A U K # V A L L E Y G I R L S
T U E # O V O I D # E R I E S
S S S # W E E P S # Y E S M #
```

Page 206 — TWIRL SERIES

R	I	P	U	P		C	A	S	H			R	A	P
A	M	U	S	E		R	I	T	E		D	E	L	L
B	A	N	D	L	E	A	D	E	R		R	U	L	E
E	N	T	A	I	L	S		P	E	T	U	N	I	A
			C	A	S	T			A	M	E	N	D	
S	A	M	P	A	N		H	A	R	E	M			
O	D	E	O	N		L	E	V	I		A	L	A	S
D	E	A	L		R	O	B	O	T		J	U	N	E
A	N	T	I		I	R	O	N		F	O	L	I	C
			C	E	D	E	S		R	E	R	U	N	S
	A	C	H	E	S			S	L	I	D			
T	H	U	M	P	E	R		E	M	E	R	I	T	A
L	I	M	A		R	E	L	A	Y	R	A	C	E	R
A	N	O	N		I	M	O	K		E	V	E	N	T
W	A	R			N	O	S	Y		R	E	S	T	S

Page 208 — STOCK SPLITS

S	T	A	P	H		A	L	S	O	P		C	A	P
I	N	D	I	A		C	A	L	V	E		A	C	E
S	T	A	G	S		D	R	I	E	R		J	A	R
			S	T	I	C	K	E	R	S	H	O	C	K
T	O	P	T	E	N			S	T	E	E	L	I	E
A	W	A	Y		C	A	P	T		L	E	A	D	
P	E	N		T	I	R	E		O	I	L			
	S	T	A	R	T	I	N	G	B	L	O	C	K	
			E	Y	E		N	A	I	L		H	E	S
	D	U	E	S		K	E	G	S		A	E	R	O
I	N	V	O	I	C	E			P	A	N	F	R	Y
S	T	O	P	T	H	E	C	L	O	C	K			
A	R	K		S	I	N	A	I		T	A	S	K	S
R	U	E		O	D	O	R	S		U	R	I	A	H
M	E	D		K	E	N	Y	A		P	A	T	T	Y

Page 210 — IN THE PAPERS

M	A	D	C	A	P		S	P	A	R		T	A	G
A	V	I	A	T	E		E	U	R	O		O	L	E
V	E	R	T	E	B	R	A	L	C	O	L	U	M	N
E	R	G	O		B	E	L	L		T	E	R	S	E
N	Y	E		A	L	A		T	O	U	T			
			P	E	R	I	O	D	P	I	E	C	E	
A	R	E	N	T		D	Y	E		T	R	O	D	
M	A	X	I		P	R	E	S	S		B	I	R	D
P	R	E	K		H	E	S		W	E	E	D	Y	
S	E	C	O	N	D	S	T	O	R	Y				
			L	A	S	T		N	E	E		M	A	G
A	R	O	A	R		S	T	E	P		W	E	L	L
D	E	F	I	N	I	T	E	A	R	T	I	C	L	E
E	L	F		I	M	O	N		O	I	L	C	A	N
N	O	S		A	P	P	S		S	P	L	A	Y	S

Page 212 — DISNEY AND DAT

M	A	T	C	H		B	A	M	A		P	A	R	
A	R	E	S	O		S	E	P	A	L		A	V	E
D	O	N	A	L	D	T	R	U	M	P		P	I	N
A	M	O		D	I	E	T		M	A	D	E	D	O
M	A	N	A	S	S	A		M	A	C	E	R		
			M	I	C	K	E	Y	M	A	N	T	L	E
B	R	U	I	N		L	O	I	S		A	A	A	
R	A	N	D		T	O	M	B	A		S	P	I	T
O	V	I		T	E	L	E		M	E	E	T	S	
	M	I	N	N	I	E	D	R	I	V	E	R		
		V	E	R	N	E		N	O	T	A	B	I	T
U	N	I	C	E	F		I	D	O	L		I	C	U
N	A	T		D	A	I	S	Y	M	I	L	L	E	R
U	S	E		O	V	A	L	S		F	A	G	I	N
M	A	D		F	E	N	S		E	D	E	N	S	

Page 214 — ABDOMINABLE

L	E	D	O	N		T	I	P		A	C	T	U	P
A	M	O	R	E		A	C	E		C	H	U	T	E
P	O	T	B	O	I	L	E	R		R	I	M	E	D
A	T	E	I	N	T	O		P	R	E	A	M	P	S
Z	E	D	S		I	N	S		E	S	P	Y		
			O	A	S		I	L	L		E	T	A	L
S	I	G	N	S		M	O	I	S	T	U	R	E	
O	S	U		S	T	O	M	A	C	H		C	I	A
H	O	T	S	T	O	V	E		O	S	K	A	R	
O	N	C	E		P	A	R		G	O	T			
		O	T	B	S		S	K	I		A	S	T	I
S	H	U	T	E	Y	E		A	R	T	F	O	R	M
C	A	R	L	A		B	E	L	L	Y	F	L	O	P
O	L	S	E	N		A	L	E		R	E	E	V	E
W	E	E	D	S		N	I	L		E	D	S	E	L

Page 216 — HIT ME!

W	E	L	D	S		S	L	I	M		B	A	U	M
A	L	E	U	T		C	A	N	E		U	L	N	A
S	L	O	M	O		A	I	L	S		B	L	I	P
	A	S	B	L	I	N	D	A	S	A	B	A	T	
			L	E	N	T		W	A	W	A			
R	E	R	U	N	S			G	A	S	B	A	G	
E	R	I	C		A	M	B	E	R		E	C	O	
M	I	C	K	E	Y	M	O	U	S	E	C	L	U	B
	U	S	A		R	E	A	M	S		R	O	T	E
	S	A	N	T	A	S			C	R	E	W	E	L
			I	T	A	S		W	O	O	D			
	G	E	T	O	N	T	H	E	S	T	I	C	K	
D	I	R	T		D	E	A	L		A	T	O	N	E
O	R	A	L		N	E	L	L		T	E	N	E	T
E	L	S	E		O	R	E	S		E	D	G	E	S

Page 218 — AFTER WORDS

```
P O S E D   I D E A     R A M
A B O V E   N E A R     T I L E
L I F E S A V E R S     A V I S
S T A R T L E D     O S A K A
      R A N   M A N T L E S
A L A M O   T O U P E E
D E L A Y S   A N T   T A I L
D I E T   A R T I E   E L M O
S A S H   L E E   R E S T O N
    L O V E R S   S T O N E
S T R E W E D   P I T
C R A T E     J A N I T O R S
R O V E   S H O C K V A L U E
I V E S   P O N E   A R E N A
P E N   A V I D   L O G E S
```

Page 220 — IN THE FICTION AISLE

```
N I M B Y   C H I C   C O R D
A D O R E   H E R O   O M A R
R O M A N C E L A N G U A G E
C L A N   A S P   T A N N E D
    D I R T   F O R T
A L E   M Y S T E R Y M E A T
B I N G O   E A T   E R G O
A T T U   C E N T S   I R A N
S H E A   O L E   T N O T E
H O R R O R S T O R Y   R E D
    A N N E   C O R N
E V I N C E   A T A   E V A C
W E S T E R N S A N D W I C H
E R I E   E R I N   A L O H A
R O S E   D A N E   T Y L E R
```

Page 222 — HOTEL AMENITIES

```
G A B O R   S K I S   L I C K
A L L I E   C A R T   E C O N
P O O L P L A Y E R   N E M O
S E T S A I L   S A L T B O X
    N E A T   P O O R
B O S S E S   A L P O   E B B
E M A I L   A L I E N   A R E
H E F T   R I L E D   A K I N
A G E   L E D I N   S T E E N
N A H   O D E S   S T A R R Y
    A T O M   H O P I
M A R I T A L   C A P S T A N
E L B E   P A P E R P L A N E
O D O R   L I S A   L I M O S
W A R S   E R I N   E D E N S
```

Page 224 — SPREADING THE WORD

```
A R A L   S T E W   D E L L A
T I G E   N A V E   E L I A S
A V E S   U T I L   P L A N S
R E N T A B I L L B O A R D
I N T E L     S A S
    R A P I D   D E S E R T
C P U   M I T E R   O D I E
H A N D O U T L E A F L E T S
A G U E   Y A N N I   N E T
R E M A P S   Y E S N O
    L E A   E X I L E
H I R E A S K Y W R I T E R
C O R E A   P O O R   D A D A
A M A S S   I N G E   E L I S
D E N T E   C A I N   S Y N E
```

Page 226 — THREE VIRTUES

```
A D O R N   S L I D E   A S P
L E M A T   P O L E R   U P I
F A I T H H E A L E R   T I N
A N T E   A N N   M A L O N E
    H A L T   N A M E D
A S P I R E   L I O T T A
S T A K E   G O O N   T E N
H O P E A G A I N S T H O P E
E W E   N I N A   R E N E E
    R E C U T S   L E A S E D
I M P E L   P E E R
G A L L I C   W O N   A M E S
A L A   C H A R I T Y B A L L
V A N   K I T E S   A L L I E
E Y E   S C E N E   M E T E D
```

Page 228 — BENCHWARMERS

```
N O T S O   S H I P   F U L L
E R E C T   P A R R   A S I A
S C R U B N U R S E   R E F I
T A I L   O R K   F A I R E R
    L U M   R A I N
  R E S E R V E C L A U S E
M O O R S   E A V E S   R E O
O R G S   M A L E S   E B A N
M A E   C A G E R   A M A S S
A L T E R N A T E P L A N
    J E A N   S I N
R E N E W S   T I S   A L T A
E X E C   S U B S T A T I O N
S P A T   A R A L   R E M I T
T O T S   S I R E   I D O L S
```

```
COILS . BASE . SOHO
UDDER . ARIA . AMEN
PIEFILLING . HERE .
SEAT . OLD . LLANOS
. WACO . SEAR . . .
NICOTINEPATCH . . .
IRONS . DAYS . WHO .
BORG . SCOPE . HAIL
ISM . MILL . SONNY .
SHAMELESSPLUG . . .
. OREM . LAYS . . .
BARREN . RAN . EGOS
EXIT . COUNTYCORK .
ELLA . EDIT . DANCE
BEER . DENY . STEAD
```

```
ALPS . FOOL . WRAP
ROUT . HINDI . HIRE
COPA . ASCOT . ODIN
. PARTTHEREDSEA . .
. HEY . ROE . . . .
MARTYR . CLAM . AMA
AREA . WRITE . GAP .
COMBTHEEVIDENCE . .
ASI . RASPY . LEER .
WET . ERTE . PRISSY
. SAD . TOO . . . .
. CUTTHEMUSTARD . .
DANA . ALINE . WORE
EVIL . TATER . OVEN
FETE . SLED . LEWD
```

```
MARC . LASSOS . CHE
OLEO . ALMOST . RAP
DINNERTABLE . ALE .
. CEDES . ORACLE . .
TASER . RHO . NUKES
HIPPIES . BRAKE . .
EMOTER . POOL . RRS
FER . RACED . JUL .
TET . FEST . ESCAPE
SARDI . COERCED . .
SPAGO . STU . TAKES
PARENT . ARABS . . .
AVE . TAMMANYHALL .
DEN . ALBERT . ERIE
ERA . LEASES . DELT
```

```
OPEDS . SATIN . DAS
FLEET . OPERA . ORE
FORWARDPASS . WIN .
. REOS . TONES . . .
TAGTEAM . GRAPPLE .
OXNARD . SIESTA . .
OMITS . SHAVE . YTD
TAME . CHINS . OMAR
SNO . PLANT . THESE
. CORALS . FEINTS .
OLDTIME . DENOTES .
PONCE . ROAD . . . .
ASA . STEERTSKCAB .
REP . TOTEM . TETRA
TRU . SOCKS . ONSET
```

```
OHGOD . GROG . ACDC
BEALE . LEAR . RUIN
STRIPTEASE . ARNO .
. VIAND . NIBLET . .
RECALL . CAD . ORE .
IGO . ACCORDION . .
CRUST . ARIA . EENS
HENIE . GIS . UNSET
ETTA . SENT . POLAR
. EMBARGOED . ITA .
CUR . ANS . TRIPOD .
APPEND . NICAD . . .
SPAT . BRUSHFIRES .
TERN . ABLE . TOORA
SRTA . RILE . STEEP
```

```
MAVS . SPASM . SACS
OBIE . TAUPE . MULE
DUSTJACKET . ADEE .
EST . ORE . WARRIOR
LEATHERS . LET . . .
. INS . TALLYHOS . .
PULES . PARI . POME
ARAB . COMIC . ARIA
PAIR . APED . GNATS
ALDERMEN . HOT . . .
. AVE . SLAPSHOT . .
JACKSON . ARR . OPE
ACRE . VESTPOCKET .
DEER . EVOKE . AERO
ADES . REWED . DYAN
```

Page 242 — HUNKS O'CHEESE

```
S M A R T | F R Y | M O W E R
S I D E A | L A O | O L I V A
R O A D B L O C K | T A C I T
      S A O | K E M O | K A T
O F F E R U P | L A R C E N Y
M A L A D I E S | N E R D
E L Y | S R O S | D I S C S
G L I B | E P I C S | B L O C
A S N E W | S L O P | I R A
    G L A M | S U R F A C E D
D O W A G E R | T I L L E R S
O R E | E D I T | N O T
E I D E R | C A R T W H E E L
R O G U E | E X O | E E L E D
S N E R D | R I B | R A K E S
```

Page 244 — ZIPPING ALONG

```
R U N | M A G I C | U T A H
A M O S | A R E S O | M E G A
B A R R E L R O L L | B A E R
A S S O R T | E L D E R
T S E | R E A D | A I R S A C
    B E D L A M P S | H U R
S I D E D | B R O S | S E G A
O M A N | M I T R E | L E I S
F U S S | L I N E | L I T E S
I S H | G R O U N D E D
A T B E S T | N O R M | M A P
    O M A H A | A M O E B A
T H A I | F L Y S W A T T E R
W A R T | U S U A L | B E A T
O D D S | L O P E S | D M C
```

Page 246 — EASY GOING

```
S P I R E | T A C T | S A C
T Y S O N | H U L A | T A D A
A R N A Z | O D E R | O D O R
G E T M Y D R I F T | M I R E
        M A N | A S C E N T
G O P H E R | S O N A R
O S L O | K H A N | S U I T S
O H A I R | A B E | H I T I T
S A Y S O | L E S S | S I R E
    T O P E R | P R E S E T
S H A S T A | O R E
C O L A | I V O R Y C O A S T
A S T I | R I P A | E V I T A
P E E L | E D E N | S E D A N
E R R | D I N G | S N A R K
```

Page 248 — ICK!

```
C U B I T | O M I T | S T I R
A R E N A | C O R A | P A R I
P I C K U P T H E P I E C E S
T S K | T O E S | M A I N E
    T E N T | C H A R T E R
S T R A N D | P O E M
E R I N | C O M M A | T A U
L I C K O N E S F I N G E R S
F O E | C O R E Y | I N G E
    L O T S | C O N D O R
M A C R O N S | D O D O
A U R I C | B O N E | K I A
S T I C K T O O N E S G U N S
S O S A | A V O N | S A R D I
E S P N | M A T E | A L T O S
```

Page 250 — FOR MEN ONLY

```
O L E A N | B E E N | S T A B
R O L L E | A L A I | T O M E
B U L L A R T I S T | E M M A
S T E E L E | E E R | A F A R
      G E N L | D I A M O N D
R O B E | T U T | C L E O
U N U | E M I T | A R L E N
S E C T | R E T R O | S E R A
T A K E N | T H A N | R I P
P A I R | E S E | T Y N E
S C A R L E T | H I H O
L I S I | D O I | D E M A N D
E L S E | C O C K A M A M I E
P I E S | A R E A | A T O N E
T A R T | P A S T | N O S E D
```

Page 252 — ROMAN AROUND

```
P A A R | B A T S | M A D A M
L I R A | A R E A | A D A G E
A D E N | E L A L | L A V E R
T E N C H R O M O S O M E S
O S T I A | N O N
    D R A I N | T E N D O N
A D A | D I G I T | A R G O
F I F T Y I R O N H U B B A R D
A C R O | T E A S E | T E E
R E O P E N | S W E A T
    T O O | R E S T S
O N E H U N D R E D S P A N
A M A N A | S O I L | T A P A
R A N I N | E R O S | E R I K
T R A D E | T A T A | R E N E
```

```
OPTED  AVAST  MIL
REESE  RASTA  ACE
BRASSMONKEY   NIA
STROKES   PLANES
    LEOS   OVERT
ASSIST   NEARER
BOONE  ULNA   ISA
BRONZEMEDALISTS
ATT   SPAS  TOMEI
 HISSES   TRUSTS
PASTE   DEMO
ERASES   ENDGAME
REY   STEELGUITAR
ONE  TAPED  ALIST
TAR  ORALS  LATTE
```

```
PARER  WHAM   SCAT
ABODE  HULA   COLE
CUBICMETER    ASIA
STEELER    SKIMMER
     UTEP   SPINY
ACCUSE   EROTIC
NOISE  FRODO   DUH
NOVA   NICAD  SUPE
ELI   BORED  RASTA
 CRAVEN   BETTOR
AMPED   TARS
HARNESS   PAISANO
EMIT   COMICSTRIP
AIDE  URIS   TONNE
DEED  MESH   SPOON
```

```
ACID  SERIO   STOP
DONE  AWAKE   HOPE
DUKESNIDER    IBET
ALI   CANI   PEON
MENLO   GILHODGES
SEDERS   AID   GRO
VET   AMP    CAST
 WARRENSPAHN
STAR   IVY    ORE
TOR  AVE   SCAMPS
YOGIBERRA    ATALE
LADS   AGED   LAN
CAME   WILLIEMAYS
UTES  ADLER   AGEE
PEST  LEYTE   PARD
```

```
CHILE  EPIC    REG
HEMAL  LAVA   SOLE
IRONMAIDEN    EDIT
NONCOM  USA   ASTI
   ERICA   ROTTEN
STP   ECO   ADOBE
TAIL  EYED  FEWER
AREA  SODOM  LAZE
BOCCE  TARE  TRIP
 ERASE   ENA   TOO
ANGORA   PEALE
ROOS   CHE  CATSUP
AMOS   HEATERHOSE
BADE  EASE  MISER
YRS   TREE  SCARE
```

```
PART  SCAR   CAFES
OPUS  CONE   HELGA
MESA  ALTI   OREOS
EXTRAPOINT    KIX
LEI   RAN   HEATER
OSCAR   SOAR  LIFE
 SIR   PIUS    MAX
TRAVELERSCHEX
ROO   EDEN    THE
ETAL   CASS  ISLES
MODELA   UPS    AXE
 STUPIDPETTRIX
OMITS   RAIN  HOLT
CADET  MINT   ISEE
TIERS  ASEA   NAST
```

```
CLEF  WASPS   OPAH
HEAR  ASCAP   NILE
INSOLITARY    LAIR
RYE   OVER   GOINTO
PALAVER    PLANO
  PER   SHAKESUP
UNSER  CLASS   ORE
SOTS  BRASS   SLIT
EPA   DRAKE  CLOSE
DEGREASE    DOE
 PUNCH   SENDOFF
ELAPSE  SWAG    RIO
DARE   LONERANGER
ANTE  ERODE   YANG
MAYS  TOWER   ENDO
```

M	A	S	C		D	E	I	S	M		D	A	R	C
A	T	W	O		O	N	C	U	E		O	D	O	R
H	O	O	P	D	R	E	A	M	S		N	O	D	E
A	N	O	T	E			N	U	S		U	R	I	S
L	E	N	S	C	A	P		P	U	P	T	E	N	T
				O	M	A	N			P	A	S		
C	O	N	C	R	E	T	E		C	H	I	L	D	
O	R	A	L		N	E	V	I	S			O	R	E	O
P	E	N	A	L			E	S	C	A	P	A	D	E
			S	A	G			R	I	A	L			
B	O	R	S	T	A	L		S	T	O	M	A	C	H
A	L	A	R		L	O	O			H	E	C	H	E
S	I	M	I		L	O	C	K	W	A	S	H	E	R
E	V	E	N		O	S	H	E	A		T	E	E	D
S	E	N	G		P	E	O	N	Y		A	S	P	S

E	T	A	L		A	L	P	H	A		G	A	F	F
G	A	L	E		R	E	T	A	G		U	R	A	L
G	R	A	N	D	P	I	A	N	O		F	A	R	E
S	A	R	D	I			S	N	U	F	F	B	O	X
			E	R	L	E		A	T	E				
	G	R	E	A	T	W	H	I	T	E	W	A	Y	
C	H	A		R	I	C	H			A	R	O	S	E
H	O	V	E		C	H	E	S	S		G	R	E	W
O	M	E	G	A		E	N	I	D			S	A	S
C	O	L	O	S	S	A	L	O	L	I	V	E		
			T	O	L			B	O	N	E			
D	J	A	K	A	R	T	A		G	N	O	M	E	
R	A	B	E		B	I	G	B	R	O	T	H	E	R
E	V	E	N		E	M	I	L	E		E	N	T	O
W	A	T	T		T	A	N	T	O		R	O	S	S

H	E	I	R	S		P	E	T	A	L		B	A	S
A	T	R	I	A		L	A	R	G	E		U	R	N
S	T	A	G	F	L	A	T	I	O	N		C	I	A
H	A	S	A	F	I	T		T	A	K	E	R		
			R	O	O	M		T	I	P	P	L	E	
E	G	G	S	O	N		A	Z	A	L	E	A		
C	R	O	O	N		C	L	E	F	S		S	E	T
H	A	L	T		M	O	T	E	T		O	S	L	O
O	D	D		P	A	R	E	S		T	A	E	B	O
			E	L	A	T	E	D		P	E	T	R	E	L
P	A	N	E	L	S		S	M	E	E				
A	C	H	O	O			A	S	S	A	I	L	S	
S	R	I		M	E	E	T	J	O	H	N	D	O	E
T	I	N		A	L	T	H	O		O	N	L	O	W
A	D	D		R	I	S	E	R			T	E	E	N	S

M	I	D	A	S		A	C	T	S		P	R	O	D
A	B	O	U	T		S	L	O	E		L	E	N	O
L	I	N	D	A		C	O	N	E		A	S	I	N
S	T	I	N	G	O	P	E	R	A	T	I	O	N	
				C	A	T			L	E	N	N	Y	
T	O	R	T	E	S		T	O	P	E	D			
I	V	A	N		E	I	D	E	R			S	E	C
V	I	R	T	U	A	L	M	O	N	O	P	O	L	Y
O	D	E		H	O	S	E	R			I	R	A	S
			R	U	L	E	D		A	S	C	E	N	T
S	H	E	E	R				T	I	E				
C	A	L	C	U	L	A	T	E	D	R	I	S	K	
A	L	F	A		I	D	E	A		E	T	H	A	N
M	E	I	N		D	E	A	R		N	O	O	N	E
P	Y	N	E		O	N	L	Y			E	N	D	E	D

W	E	R	E		E	V	O	K	E		G	L	U	M
I	C	E	R		R	I	P	O	N		R	O	S	A
S	H	O	O	T	E	M	U	P	S		A	D	E	N
P	O	S	S	E			S	P	I	T	F	I	R	E
				A	G	O		E	L	I				
	S	C	R	A	M	B	L	E	D	E	G	G	S	
G	E	A	R		G	I	L			E	L	L	I	E
A	R	N	O		S	T	U	R	M		M	A	L	E
P	I	T	A	S			R	A	E		A	S	A	P
S	C	A	T	T	E	R	B	R	A	I	N	S		
			O	L	A			A	N	D				
L	A	C	E	W	I	N	G			L	E	V	E	E
O	R	A	L		S	C	O	O	T	E	R	I	N	G
N	I	N	A		H	I	L	D	A		A	L	D	O
G	A	E	L		A	D	D	E	D			S	A	S	S

S	P	L	A	T		S	L	A	G		P	A	P	A
O	R	A	T	E		W	I	N	O		A	W	O	L
F	A	B	E	R	G	E	E	G	G		S	A	N	D
A	M	S		R	A	P	S		E	N	T	I	C	E
			C	A	S	T		S	T	A	R	T	E	R
S	M	O	O	C	H		D	O	T	T	Y			
L	A	R	U	E		H	O	L	E		C	R	A	G
A	L	E	C		F	A	D	E	R		H	O	R	N
M	E	S	H		I	G	O	R		S	E	L	M	A
			P	I	N	E	S		I	N	F	E	S	T
C	O	L	O	R	I	N		A	M	O	S			
A	B	A	T	E	S		S	L	A	P		A	P	T
R	A	T	A		H	A	I	L	C	A	E	S	A	R
O	M	I	T		E	L	L	E			K	L	I	N	E
N	A	N	O		D	I	O	N			E	S	S	E	X

```
M A N U P   E L A L   H O E D
A L O N E   D A N E   A C R E
G O O D N I G H T S S L E E P
S T R O N G E R   C O A C T
        E O S   G L O   N T H
M A R T Y R   S E E N
O R A N   A N T I C   O T S
B E T T E R M O U S E T R A P
S A S   S H A R P   S A R A
  P U N T   E M P L O Y
R A P   I M A   E V E
E R A S E   O V E R A L L S
B E S T S E L L I N G B O O K
U N T O   S E A T   E L I S E
S T E W   C A F E   D E N S E
```

```
M A K I N   T W O S   M O P S
A L E N E   H E L P   A B E T
G I A N T P A N D A   M O N A
M E N   W A N T   C E M E N T
A N E M O N E   A E R O
    O R E   S T A R T S U P
S T A N K   S L O G   H U L A
O A R S   L A I N E   C L A N
D U C T   A N T E   V A U N T
A T H E I S T S   D I V
    R O T O   N I C E T R Y
H U M M U S   S E A T   R E P
O N E A   T I T A N O S A U R
U T E S   O V A L   R H I N E
R O T H   P Y N E   Y A T E S
```

```
S T A N D   M A N O R   E B B
A B L E R   A S I D E   T R U
C A P T A I N S L O G   H I S
  G R I T   R A V I N E
B A Z O O K A   L A C E D
A D O R N S   T O K E N S
B O N E S   P A V E D   P I S
E R I S   H O K E Y   T A S K
L E N   S I R E N   P A N S Y
    G L I D E R   M A D E U P
C A B I N   S A R A L E E
A T O N C E   G A Z A
B R A   E N G I N E B L O C K
A I R   R O U N D   L A T H E
L A D   E S S A Y   E B S E N
```

```
S U G A R   H E S S   K E G S
A R E N A   A R I A   I V A N
G A R A G E B A N D   T O T O
E L M   D A I S   S U C K E R
    C O S T   R A S H E S T
S M E L L Y   N I C H E
C A R O L   H O C K   N A P S
A S I S   S A T E S   S L O T
T H E E   A R M S   T I A R A
    T A U P E   T E N N E R
L A T E N C Y   B A S K
A D R A T E   P E R T   L A G
D O I T   P A R L O R G A M E
E R T E   A B E L   U N I O N
N E E R   N A P E   N U R S E
```

```
D O R A   F A L A   E P C O T
A P O P   A L A S   S A L V E
R E N T A C O O P   T R U E S
T R I   M E T   C H O K E R S
H A N D E L   G A R N I
    O X I D E   S I N G E R
S N O W   F I N S   A G A T E
E O N S   T R E A T   L O N E
A V A I L   E R I E   O L A F
L O N N O L   A L A M O
    G O G O L   R A T T A N
S M I R K E R   S I R   O D E
C A N O E   B U N N Y H O O P
A C T O R   I N I T   A T R A
M E L D S   T O P O   S H E L
```

```
C L A M   F O G G   B A S A L
R A G E   E M I R   O C A L A
O V E R   R A G A   U R I A H
C I N C I N N A T I R E D S
E N T E R       E V E
    R A M B O   Y E L L A T
A S H   T A L I A   A O N E
C L E V E L A N D B R O W N S
T A R E   S K A T E   S A T
S Y S T E M   S M U T S
    M I A   A O R T A
H O M E S T E A D G R A Y S
K I T E R   O L D E   D I P S
O R I N G   L I E N   I S E E
H E S S E   L A N G   D E B S
```

Page 290 — JACKIE

```
PCB   GADS   EGGIER
AHA   ELIA   MIMOSA
ROBINSON   BRANCH
ERECTOR   MEAN
EDSEL   SERF   RCA
     EBBETSFIELD
SPAS   BLAH   ELCID
WILT   CUBAN   LANE
INTEL   RENO   SPED
PEEWEEREESE
ERR   ALES   LAMAS
   SPAD   SPANISH
RICKEY   FORTYTWO
INTERN   ALOE   ZAP
VARESE   BOPS   INS
```

Page 292 — SANDWICH SHOP

```
TABLA   SHEAF   HAS
IDEAL   TOSCA   ARK
MEATBALLSUB   MRI
ESTEEM   TERA   TOE
   NEST   NARROWS
LIES   TIM   SEER
ANG   EDAM   SEPIA
LOGO   LAGOS   LEDS
ANGLE   LIRA   DES
REAM   CAL   BOSN
EMIGRES   LOCO
VAN   ASTA   MOTHER
IND   CHICKENHERO
AGE   HENRI   DELIA
NOR   ESTER   ORDER
```

Page 294 — LETTERWOMEN

```
OSCAR   PASTA   GAL
NIOBE   ALTOS   ISO
ELLACINDERS   APT
STATOR   ANTE   CIT
   ENOS   TERRACE
BETS   NAT   STAR
ARI   IRAS   STATE
LIAM   CABOT   SNOW
DCCAB   NOLA   GOO
ALOT   OER   BILK
PARLORS   SARA
IRR   KEAN   WANGLE
ERE   EMMALAZARUS
TAR   NOOSE   ENACT
AYE   DRATS   DAMES
```

Page 296 — TOPSY-TURVY

```
SABOT   BLOB   AJAX
ARENA   LIAR   SORE
INVERTAFRACTION
LOY   MIST   RUSSO
   SALT   FLATTEN
SPLICE   ORATE
ALUM   KNIFE   GEE
DUMPAGIRLFRIEND
ESP   TOWEL   BLOG
   STAID   PRISSY
SESTETS   SEED
PALES   OPED   TKO
OVERTURNARULING
SEWN   SOUR   CAVIL
ESSO   NOSE   EMOTE
```

Page 298 — BAGGING FOWL

```
FERAL   SKED   SHAD
AMINO   AIDE   EELY
SITTINGDUCKCALL
TREETOAD   ATRIA
EON   WAR   DEN
TAVERN   BAMA
OLIN   ARGOT   PAT
GOLDENGOOSENECK
ATE   XENON   COHO
PEEK   TBONES
AMA   EDS   SHO
SOLAR   STEWARDS
COLDTURKEYSHOOT
OREO   MAYA   EMILE
TENS   PEEL   RELET
```

Page 300 — ALL-NEW

```
SHORT   SPAS   DENS
OUTER   TATA   OLIN
SCIFINOVEL   NINO
OKS   BARE   TOTTER
   HUNK   DILBERT
FARINA   DONEE
IMAGE   SAVE   FROM
LECH   SINES   RAGA
EXEC   PECS   REPLY
   USAGE   CASTES
ASARULE   MOTH
MARRED   OUCH   FEW
PULE   ITSTOOLATE
EDEN   NILE   LEMON
DINT   GPOS   EVENT
```

Page 302 — JOINT SESSION

```
AGATE CHIAS AWL
RETRO HYMNS CHI
KNEESLAPPER TEM
IRAS ATEAM BEEP
NESTOR LIKUD
ELBOWMACARONI
ELSIE TRUED
FRI ANNUL TEA
RUNES SNEAD
ANKLEBRACELET
BLARE RESETS
POLS ALGAE INRI
EGO SHOULDERPAD
ART AMASS DEICE
LES SANTO DENTS
```

Page 304 — NOT!

```
RIPS GAGS ONION
IDLE RULE RINGS
NEAP EDEN INTRA
SAYITAINTSOJOE
ESSAYS ALA
PEA STE SKI
SATIE NEMO STAT
THATDOGWONTHUNT
AMPS PEER HONEY
GEE TAR ESE
PER TREXES
ICANTBELIEVEIT
SHARD AVON INGE
HORSE BEAK TIER
UPPER ARMY EARN
```

Page 306 — QUARTERBACK OPTIONS

```
SHED ACHE CELEB
MAZE SLOT OXIDE
AGIN SORT SITIN
RUNTHEGAUNTLET
TEE ONS ICE
ANT JOCOSITY
STAID MECH SHE
HANDOFFTHEBATON
ECO ARTS ATOMS
MONALISA JIM
SON SAT TBA
PASSTHEMUSTARD
HUMUS AVON AMID
AMORE HIRT OPAL
GASES ALES SANE
```

Page 308 — YOUNG 'UNS

```
HALF MOIRE HAD
ISAAC ORSON URI
CHICAGOCUBS SIT
INADAZE CHAT
REHEAT SUR APSO
ANA DES TOFU
TOV ISSUE REPRO
ILENE TSE ASPIC
OAKEN SALON INT
IPSO SAG ESE
DATA RIM TEASET
INTL WHEREAS
AGE DEADENDKIDS
RIN ELVIS EERIE
YES BLEAT DANE
```

Page 310 — LOWER AND LOWER

```
ROBS GALA SNIPS
EURO ENID TAROT
STANDONCEREMONY
EIK ERIE ORANGE
TEENAGE PUNT
OLE RAG HALF
AMINO SEVER LOO
SITOUTTHESEASON
IRA TARAS FROND
SELL LAB PRE
EELY SHEARER
STRATO LAOS ARE
LIEDOWNONTHEJOB
ALLEN INTO LADE
PEONS LEAN SHEL
```

Page 312 — ATHLETIC WOES

```
STASH THOR SHAG
HENIE RONA TALL
EXTRA EPIC ELIA
STRAINEDPEAS
ACS LET ABYSS
LAICAL TOADY
EPSOM OOPS SLO
CRAMPEDQUARTERS
ALP PIUS HEALY
RHINE SIPSON
ASHES CAN ENE
TWISTEDLOGIC
TINS BOAR TATER
INGE ROMA IRONY
CEES ORAL SPODE
```

Page 314 — AT THE BAGEL SHOP

S	I	F	T	S		C	A	R	A		D	E	L	I
I	N	L	E	T		O	V	A	L		E	R	I	N
A	D	O	R	E		P	O	P	P	Y	C	O	C	K
M	O	O	S	E	J	A	W			E	A	S	E	S
		D	E	L	E			S	A	L	L	Y		
C	A	P	L	E	T	S		V	O	L		O	P	S
A	L	L	Y		A	S	I	D	E		P	E	A	
T	O	A		S	A	L	T	A	I	R		E	S	T
C	H	I		E	L	O	A	N		I	N	C	A	
H	A	N		A	T	O		S	I	G	N	S	I	N
		G	L	A	N	D			T	A	S	E		
D	E	L	H	I		U	N	A	M	U	S	E	D	
O	N	I	O	N	D	O	M	E		E	L	A	T	E
R	O	D	S		E	R	A	S		S	A	M	O	A
A	S	S	T		W	E	S	T		T	R	E	N	D

Page 316 — HISS MAJESTY

U	S	D	A		S	T	E	P		S	A	L	A	D
S	P	E	C		T	E	L	L		T	W	Y	L	A
C	A	N	I		A	C	L	U		O	G	L	E	D
	M	Y	D	O	G	H	A	S	F	L	E	E	C	E
			R	U	E	S			L	I	E			
B	L	E	A	T	S		M	O	O		Z	E	T	A
A	D	L	I	B		F	A	R	S	I		W	A	Y
D	O	W	N	O	N	O	N	E	S	N	I	E	C	E
E	P	A		X	A	X	I	S		A	D	L	E	R
N	A	Y	S		N	Y	C		S	T	I	L	T	S
			E	S	C			A	T	I	T			
B	L	A	C	K	E	Y	E	D	P	E	A	C	E	
L	I	B	R	A		O	L	D	E		R	U	T	H
I	N	L	E	T		G	A	I	T		O	J	A	I
P	E	E	T	E		A	N	N	E		D	O	L	T

Page 318 — JUST DUCKY

S	T	R	U	T		D	A	D	A		A	S	A	P
A	B	A	S	H		E	B	O	N		R	I	L	E
L	A	M	E	E	X	C	U	S	E		I	T	L	L
		P	E	R	T			W	E	S	T	I	E	
F	A	C	T	O	R	Y			S	T	I	N	G	
A	D	O	R	N		S	A	M	P	A	N			
I	D	L	E	D		M	A	C	O	N		G	A	P
R	U	D	E		L	I	V	I	D		O	B	I	E
E	P	S		K	I	T	E	D		C	R	U	S	T
			T	R	I	T	E	R		H	A	L	L	E
S	T	O	O	L			S	P	E	L	L	E	R	
T	I	R	I	N	G			P	A	L	M			
E	L	A	L		L	U	C	K	Y	L	I	N	D	Y
E	D	G	E		E	T	T	E		A	D	O	R	E
R	E	E	D		N	E	S	S			B	O	G	U	S

Page 320 — ONE FOR ALL, ALL FOR ONE

A	T	H	O	S		S	I	R	S		E	T	A	L
C	O	U	N	T		P	R	O	P		S	A	V	E
H	O	N	E	O	F	F	A	M	E		A	L	I	A
E	N	T	I	R	E		S	E	A	G	U	L	L	S
			D	E	L	L		O	R	E		C	A	T
R	O	S	A	R	I	E	S			S	A	T	O	
O	P	T		N	E	A	R		R	I	L	E	Y	
M	A	A	M		E	D	G	E	S		C	O	R	A
A	L	L	O	W		S	A	L	T			R	I	P
	L	E	A	D		N	A	R	C	O	S	E	S	
S	A	W		L	O	S		Y	E	A	R			
I	N	A	S	T	A	T	E		E	L	D	E	S	T
T	I	L	L		B	O	N	E	P	L	A	Y	E	R
O	S	L	O		L	U	T	E		I	R	E	N	E
N	E	S	T		E	T	O	N			T	E	D	D	Y

Page 322 — MEAT MARKET

S	A	B	R	A		A	U	R	I	C		S	E	T
A	S	T	I	N		P	R	A	D	O		T	R	I
C	H	U	C	K	Y	E	A	G	E	R		R	O	M
		E	L	I			L	E	A	S		I	D	O
E	S	T	R	E	E	T		S	L	I	P	P	E	R
D	A	B	S		L	O	W		S	C	U	T		
G	O	O		D	R	I	P			A	R	E	A	S
A	N	N	A		S	T	E	A	K		L	A	M	A
R	E	E	D	S		E	L	L	A			S	A	L
	W	I	T	S		D	E	L		M	E	T	S	
I	N	A	N	I	T	Y		S	I	B	E	R	I	A
M	E	L		F	E	E	S		N	O	M			
O	A	K		F	L	A	N	K	E	R	B	A	C	K
U	T	E		E	L	S	I	E			G	E	N	O	A
T	O	R		N	A	T	T	Y			E	R	N	S	T

Page 324 — THE STARTING GUN

S	T	R	A	P		S	L	A	M		T	A	C	T
O	H	A	R	A		P	E	P	E		A	S	H	E
W	A	V	E	D		A	V	E	R		S	T	A	N
R	E	A	D	Y	M	I	X	C	E	M	E	N	T	
			L	E	S			W	A	R	T	S		
A	B	A	S	E	S		E	R	V	I	N			
L	O	N	E		O	D	E	O	N			S	O	P
S	E	T	A	W	E	D	D	I	N	G	D	A	T	E
O	R	E		I	C	E	I	N		A	L	T	O	
	A	D	O	R	E			C	A	N	T	O	N	
A	M	I	N	O			D	A	M					
G	O	D	O	W	N	T	H	E	T	U	B	E	S	
A	U	L	D		A	H	E	M		S	O	L	I	D
T	R	E	E		N	E	R	O		E	L	A	T	E
E	N	D	S		A	M	E	N		D	O	L	E	S

Page 326 — OX TAILS

```
S P U R T   A B E T   A P S E
P A S H A   S A G E   V E E S
A P P O M A T T O X   A N D S
M A S S A C R E   T R I A G E
      B R O       A L L E N
D O U B L E   S E X I S T
E R N I E   L E V E L   Y A K
A E O N   R A V E D   A B B A
F O R   Z I N E S   P R O B E
      T R U M A N   D R E X E L
E T H E L       L A O
B R O G U E   C O N T E S S A
S I D E   C H I C K E N P O X
E T O N   H U T U   A D O R E
N E X T   O D E S   M O T E L
```

Page 328 — WOOFERS

```
C U B S   P A R E   M E T E R
A S E A   I R O N   O L I V E
M A R K S P I T Z   N I N E S
E G R E T S   C Y S T   E N T
L E A S E     M I A S
      W A S H E D U P   P U G
A R R E S T E E   K R O N A
R O I L   F E A T S   A L T I
A S I D E   R E L A T I O N
B A S E M E N T L A B
      R E P O     A S H E S
D A M   R I S K   A S H O R E
E L E N A   H E L L H O U N D
M O R E L   E L S A   A S I A
S T E E D   S P U N   T E E N
```

Page 330 — NO 17's, 36's, OR 57's

```
S C A B S   M A I D   S L O B
L A G E R   A C R E   C A V A
I F I R A N T H E C I R C U S
T E N T   A T E   K N E E L S
      R A V E     C A S E Y
S C A P E   C R E A M
G O O N S   S A I L   S A E
A N D D O N T C O M E B A C K
L G E   B U T T   C L I N E
      D H A B I   C R U D E
R E P R O     T R U E
E L A I N E   B R O   B I D E
B U T F E W A R E C H O S E N
E D I T   E V A N   R O L E O
L E O S   S E N D   S K E D S
```

Page 332 — BARRIERS

```
L O W I N   C A P E   H O S S
A V I L A   A N O N   E P I C
W A L L S T R E E T   D A T E
S L Y   C H E W   R A G L A N
      F E A T   C E L E S T E
R E P E N T   L O A T H
E V E N T   H I N T   O H N O
D I S C   L A C E Y   P E E P
S L O E   E R I S   S P A R E
      S C O T T   S T E P O N
R A D I A T E   B O O R
I G O T T A   L E A P   A D D
P A N T   R A I L R O A D E R
U T N E   D U L L   F L A K E
P E A R   S K I S   F A M E D
```

Page 334 — WHAT'S NEW?

```
S W O O P   F I S H   W I S H
H I L D A   I N T O   E L M O
E L D E R   E D E N   L I O N
      S O R R Y T O O L A T E
A D S   D A Y   L A U D E D
R A I S I N   S L U R P
C I T E S   F O A L   P I A
E L E C T R I C C U R R E N T
D Y S   I N K Y   E E R I E
      D I N K S   P A N I C S
A L I E N S   A I D   L E T
D O N T G E T F R E S H
D U D E   O R A L   F I V E S
I S I S   F I N E   O V E R T
N E A T   F O G S   R E T R Y
```

Page 336 — LAUGHING IT UP

```
S K I D   E M B E D   C O P A
L I L I   G I L D A   A L E C
A W L S   G L A D H A N D E R
M I S C   N A B   L A I N E
      I R O N   H E I R E S S
H A P P Y G O L U C K Y
E X I L E   A S H E   P I T
E L S E   S O C K O   F U M E
P E A   R O U E   P O P I N
      M E R R Y G O R O U N D
R E F I L E S   O P E D
A C E L A   A V E   F I S T
J O L L Y R O G E R   I D E A
A L O E   O H A R A   S L A P
H I N T   C O R N S   H E R E
```

```
B E A S T   A M O K   J I M A
A C T O R   P E T E   U R A L
C H I T A   R A I N   L O L L
H O T S Y T O T S Y   I N L A
        N A N   O C A S E Y
E M P T O R   T O N I C
M O L A R   R I P   T H R O W
M A U D   A B U   I O N O
A N G L E   Y E S   S L O M O
      I N S E T   P A D D E D
S P I N E T   I L L
C I N C   I K I D Y O U N O T
U N D O   R I M E   O H A R A
T O I L   U L N A   N O L A N
S T A N   P O O L   S H A N K
```

```
S C O W   F I B S   S P L A T
H A R E   O B I E   P A I G E
A N G L I C I Z E   A R G O T
R O A D S I D E D I N A H
D E N S E   T E N   S T E M
      E P A   D A S   I V E
T H O S   O R B   S U N N I S
Y O U D I R T Y C H E E T A H
L U T I S T   O O O   T O N Y
E S O   P E P   X E R
R E F S   N R A   A B I E S
    P L A T I N U M M Y N A H
S P L A Y   M I N I S T A T E
O R A T E   A S I S   E N I D
N O Y E S   L E T S   S E T S
```

```
L A M A R   G E T A T   C A T
A R E N A   A M P L Y   A R I
C I T Y S L I C K E R   R E M
E A R   C I T E   A R O S E
      O V A L   E C O N O B O X
F L A I L A T   A N N O
A U R A   C O U N T Y F A I R
T S E   R N D   N R A
S T A T E V I S I T   S C A T
      A X O N   D O M A I N S
P A T N I X O N   N O E L
A L I S T   I A G O   L A G
R I B   F E D E R A L C A S E
E V E   E R E C T   A P R I L
S E T   E A S E S   H O Y A S
```

```
O P U S   A M I S S   A Y E S
F E T A   D A R L A   T O R I
F R E N C H H O R N   M U N G
      S H E E N   T O O T I N
T A C   A R R   M A R S H E S
A L L U R E   W E A L T H
B L U N T   C A N N Y   O K D
L E T S   S O F I A   A S E A
E N C   R A V E N   M I T E R
      H E A L E R   F O M E N T
S A H A R A N   N A N   L E S
A D O R E D   P A T T Y
D A M N   B E A C H H O U S E
A G E E   A S T R O   L E A K
T E R R   R E H E M   K Y L E
```

```
S C A M P   M O P S   T A P A
O L L I E   A S I A   U T E S
N E A R S I G H T E D N E S S
Y O N   T O D A Y   O N I C E
      P E T A   S E E N I T
S C L E R A   T O P S Y
P O O R   A E D E S   A V A
A R O U N D T H E C O R N E R
R E P   O U T E R   I T E M
      A L O N E   M E S S R S
C A N T O S   D O L E
O B O E S   S A U T E   A F B
C L O S E B U T N O C I G A R
C E N T   I R O N   T R O V E
I D E S   D E M O   S A G E R
```

```
C U P   R U D Y   S H A R K S
O S O L E M I O   H E T E R O
B A L L P A R K   A P E M E N
      O A S   G E A R   A M A
    I S M   B E L L P E P P E R
H A H A H A   I S T O
E M I   E L S I E   H E A R D
I S R   B I L L N Y E   T O E
R O T O R   O L S E N   T W A
      Y E L P   L E S H A N
B O L L W E E V I L   H E N
A H A   A S I N   C O T
N A N T E S   B U L L R I N G
A R C A N E   E S T E E M E D
L E E R E D   S E R F   E D S
```

```
L O A N S   H O O P   S P A M
A T B A T   A L B A   I L I E
S I E N A   D I O R   T A D A
  S T A R T O V E R   S T A N
      R U N E   O R I E N T
H A S T E N     S T I N G
A C T E D   S H I E D   L A B
I R A N   R O U N D   P A N E
L E N   F O A M S   R A S T A
    D R O O P   V E R S E D
A S S E R T   A C I D
L A T E   B A L L P O I N T
I T I S   E N D O   U N I O N
V I L E   E Y E S   T O N T O
E E L S   R A R E   S N E E R
```

```
W A K E N   A L M A   C A P E
A S I D E   L I O N   O M E N
T H E Y U L E L O G   H E A T
T E L S T A R   D E F E N S E
        I T S   L E N D E R
P A C K E R   P R E Z
A L L I E   G R I N   E T T U
Y O U L L P A Y F O R T H I S
S T E T   E P E E   A T O N E
      Z E E S   M E A N E R
S P A R E R   T A O
T I L I N G S   M O R A I N E
R A I N   Y U L B R Y N N E R
O N E S   N E I L   A N G E R
P O N E   T R E E   N E A R S
```

```
S A N E   R O W S   E Q U A L
A M O R   O B I T   L U N G E
A B L E   C O L A   M I D I S
B L A C K K E Y S   I C O N S
S E N T I N     H A R K
      R E S T   Y A K K E D
C R A C K   H I D E   I L I E
H U R L   N A N A S   C E R F
A S I A   E Y E D   S K E E T
D H A R M A   S A R A
    K O P S   I N S I S T
T A L K S   T R I C K K N E E
A R I E S   R O D E   I D L E
P L A N E   O V E R   F I L M
S O R T S   P E A S   F E S S
```

```
B A S S   P E A K   S A F E R
L U T E   A X L E   E L U D E
A G A R   R A T A   E L Z I E
S I L V E R M I N E R   Z E D
T E L E X     U S E B Y
      S T R I P   E D A M E S
A M A   R E T R O   N A N O
S U B W A Y C O N D U C T O R
A L B A   H U L O T   H S T
P E E W E E   D Y N E S
    Y A N K S     R O S S I
M G R   S E W E R W O R K E R
A I O L I   A R E A   D A T E
T R A I L   M I N I   I T I S
A D D L E   P E E L   D E N T
```

```
S T R O M   S A F E   G R A M
O H A R A   P R O D   R E F I
F A B E R G E E G G   O B I T
T R E S T L E   G E S T U R E
      H A R P   O T T E R
W E B C A M   R E P R O
E U R O   E A T A T   M S G
S L I P P E R Y A S A N E E L
T A M   A B I E S   A C R E
    E M B E R   A F G H A N
S T A M P   S A N A
M U D B A T H   S T E E L I E
I D L E   R E D H E R R I N G
T O E D   A L O E   O M E G A
E R R S   P I E S   E A S E D
```

```
S O L T I   D A R C   E G G S
A V I A N   U S E R   A R E A
S O U P F O R Y O U   R E S T
      O B O E   D O N A T E
S P H E R I C   M E T E D
L O O N I E   M A K E R S
A L L O T   R A V E N   H A M
K E D S   C A N O N   C A V E
E R S   B O R O N   L A K E S
    B A R T E R   G E N E R A
S T A R E   A R T I S T S
E R R O R S   A X I S
P E R U   T I M E T O L O S E
I V E S   E V I L   F O R A Y
A I D E   W E D S   F O R G E
```

Page 362 — SQUARE ONE

H	I	S	S		W	H	I	P	S		B	Y	E	S
I	R	A	Q		H	A	C	E	K		I	O	T	A
Y	A	L	U		O	P	E	N	I	N	G	D	A	Y
A	S	T	I			A	P	R			A	M	A	S	S
			R	I	M	E			S	O	D	A		
S	T	A	R	T	I	N	G	P	R	I	C	E		
O	A	T	E	S			L	E	E	R		C	I	D
O	P	E	L		L	A	U	D	S		P	O	G	O
T	A	U		T	I	G	E		H	O	N	O	R	
		P	R	I	M	A	R	Y	C	O	L	O	R	S
	U	B	E	R		E	R	G	O					
A	M	U	S	E			L	S	U		P	A	I	D
F	I	R	S	T	C	L	A	S	S		O	B	O	E
A	N	N	E		H	I	T	I	T		N	I	N	E
R	E	S	T		A	P	E	R	Y		Y	E	A	R

Page 364 — WATCH IT!

L	A	R	G	E		W	E	T		R	O	A	D	S
A	L	A	R	M		I	D	O		E	N	D	O	W
S	O	C	I	O		Z	I	N		C	A	I	N	E
S	T	E	M	T	H	E	T	I	D	E		E	T	A
			M	I	E	N	S		A	D	J	U	S	T
I	T	A	S	C	A			T	H	E	E			
P	E	R		O	R	A	T	E			S	P	I	T
S	E	C	O	N	D	H	A	N	D	S	T	O	R	E
O	S	H	A		E	X	T	O	L		L	O	X	
		T	H	E	M			N	U	G	E	N	T	
F	U	S	S	E	R		B	U	D	G	E			
I	N	E		F	A	C	E	L	I	F	T	I	N	G
R	I	P	E	N		R	A	T		E	S	T	O	P
S	T	A	V	E		O	U	R		S	T	E	N	O
T	Y	L	E	R		P	T	A		T	O	M	E	S

Page 366 — FAD WEAR

M	I	M	I	C		S	P	R	A	T		L	O	L
A	M	A	N	A		T	A	E	B	O		E	R	E
C	O	O	N	S	K	I	N	C	A	P		I	D	A
			H	I	N	T			R	U	S	E	S	
S	A	N	D	I	N	G		F	E	A	T	U	R	E
P	R	E	Y	E	D		B	A	N	T	E	R		
O	C	H	E	R		C	O	K	I	E		E	T	C
K	E	R	R		E	R	R	E	D		A	S	E	A
E	D	U		S	T	O	O	D		S	L	U	R	P
		J	O	H	A	N	N		C	H	A	I	S	E
S	H	A	P	E	L	Y		C	O	U	N	T	E	R
P	A	C	E	R			F	A	C	T				
E	L	K		B	E	L	L	B	O	T	T	O	M	S
A	V	E		E	T	A	I	L		E	A	S	E	L
R	E	T		T	A	S	T	E		R	U	S	T	Y

Page 368 — CODE RED

S	A	R	A	H		O	F	F	E	R		P	D	A
O	P	E	R	A		R	O	D	E	O		R	U	N
L	U	C	I	L	L	E	B	A	L	L		I	N	G
			O	I	L	S			L	A	N	C	E	
H	O	M	A	G	E	S		S	P	E	N	C	E	R
A	P	A	C	E		E	N	L	A	R	G	E		
S	I	R	E	N	S		O	A	T	S		H	A	H
I	N	K	S		T	R	I	P	E		L	A	D	E
T	E	M		S	E	A	S			S	T	O	R	M	S
		C	R	E	A	T	E	S		A	C	R	E	S
M	A	G	I	L	L	A		L	E	M	O	Y	N	E
O	H	W	O	E			M	I	C	A				
T	M	I		C	O	N	A	N	O	B	R	I	E	N
T	A	R		T	R	I	C	K		L	I	N	G	O
O	D	E		S	E	X	E	S		E	P	S	O	M

Page 370 — GIFT RAP

E	L	A	M		O	G	L	E		R	E	N	T	A
P	E	P	A		U	R	A	L		E	G	G	E	D
I	C	E	R		S	I	N	K		F	R	O	M	E
C	H	R	I	S	T	M	A	S	P	I	E			
			A	H	E	M			U	N	T	I	L	
S	P	I	C	E	D		N	I	L	E		N	I	P
P	O	O	H			T	A	M	E	R		T	E	A
A	N	N	I	V	E	R	S	A	R	Y	S	O	N	G
I	I	I		E	N	I	A	C			O	T	O	E
N	E	Z		I	D	O	L		A	F	F	O	R	D
			S	E	I	N	E		A	L	O	T		
		B	I	R	T	H	D	A	Y	S	U	I	T	
D	E	N	S	E		A	E	O	N		O	N	T	O
A	R	I	E	S		T	A	R	O		A	D	A	M
G	R	A	N	T		E	D	E	N		P	O	L	E

Page 372 — TWO THUMBS DOWN

S	P	A	R	S		A	L	B	U	M		F	R	O
O	R	S	O	N		S	O	U	S	E		L	E	X
B	U	S	T	O	F	H	O	M	E	R		O	L	E
I	N	A	H	O	L	E			C	A	P	O	N	
G	E	M		K	A	N	T		S	E	T	H		
			M	E	X		O	V	E	R	T	O	N	E
A	C	T	O	R		T	R	E	X		R	U	E	D
S	O	U	L		R	A	T	T	Y		A	S	H	E
T	O	R	I		I	C	U	S		I	C	E	I	N
A	S	K	E	D	F	O	R		T	N	T			
			E	R	I	E		E	V	E	S		V	I	P
N	O	Y	E	S			A	S	T	A	I	R	E	
A	L	L		B	O	M	B	S	H	E	L	T	E	R
V	E	E		A	D	O	R	E		P	I	A	N	O
E	G	G		R	E	P	O	S		S	T	E	E	N

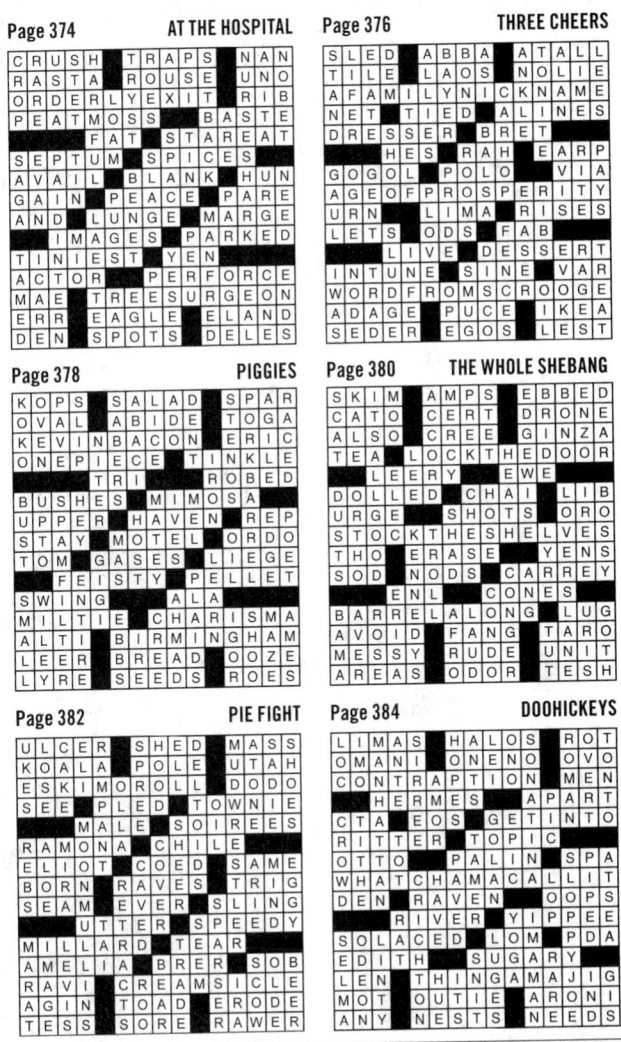

Page 374 — AT THE HOSPITAL

C	R	U	S	H		T	R	A	P	S		N	A	N
R	A	S	T	A		R	O	U	S	E		U	N	O
O	R	D	E	R	L	Y	E	X	I	T		R	I	B
P	E	A	T	M	O	S	S		B	A	S	T	E	
			F	A	T		S	T	A	R	E	A	T	
S	E	P	T	U	M		S	P	I	C	E	S		
A	V	A	I	L		B	L	A	N	K		H	U	N
G	A	I	N		P	E	A	C	E		P	A	R	E
A	N	D		L	U	N	G	E		M	A	R	G	E
	I	M	A	G	E	S		P	A	R	K	E	D	
T	I	N	I	E	S	T		Y	E	N				
A	C	T	O	R		P	E	R	F	O	R	C	E	
M	A	E		T	R	E	E	S	U	R	G	E	O	N
E	R	R		E	A	G	L	E		E	L	A	N	D
D	E	N		S	P	O	T	S		D	E	L	E	S

Page 376 — THREE CHEERS

S	L	E	D		A	B	B	A		A	T	A	L	L
T	I	L	E		L	A	O	S		N	O	L	I	E
A	F	A	M	I	L	Y	N	I	C	K	N	A	M	E
N	E	T		T	I	E	D		A	L	I	N	E	S
D	R	E	S	S	E	R		B	R	E	T			
			H	E	S		R	A	H		E	A	R	P
G	O	G	O	L		P	O	L	O		V	I	A	
A	G	E	O	F	P	R	O	S	P	E	R	I	T	Y
U	R	N		L	I	M	A		R	I	S	E	S	
L	E	T	S		O	D	S		F	A	B			
			L	I	V	E		D	E	S	S	E	R	T
I	N	T	U	N	E		S	I	N	E		V	A	R
W	O	R	D	F	R	O	M	S	C	R	O	O	G	E
A	D	A	G	E		P	U	C	E		I	K	E	A
S	E	D	E	R		E	G	O	S		L	E	S	T

Page 378 — PIGGIES

K	O	P	S		S	A	L	A	D		S	P	A	R
O	V	A	L		A	B	I	D	E		T	O	G	A
K	E	V	I	N	B	A	C	O	N		E	R	I	C
O	N	E	P	I	E	C	E		T	I	N	K	L	E
			T	R	I		R	O	B	E	D			
B	U	S	H	E	S		M	I	M	O	S	A		
U	P	P	E	R		H	A	V	E	N		R	E	P
S	T	A	Y		M	O	T	E	L		O	R	D	O
T	O	M		G	A	S	E	S		L	I	E	G	E
		F	E	I	S	T	Y		P	E	L	L	E	T
S	W	I	N	G		A	L	A						
M	I	L	T	I	E		C	H	A	R	I	S	M	A
A	L	T	I		B	I	R	M	I	N	G	H	A	M
L	E	E	R		B	R	E	A	D		O	O	Z	E
L	Y	R	E		S	E	E	D	S		R	O	E	S

Page 380 — THE WHOLE SHEBANG

S	K	I	M		A	M	P	S		E	B	B	E	D
C	A	T	O		C	E	R	T		D	R	O	N	E
A	L	S	O		C	R	E	E		G	I	N	Z	A
T	E	A		L	O	C	K	T	H	E	D	O	O	R
			L	E	E	R	Y		E	W	E			
D	O	L	L	E	D		C	H	A	I		L	I	B
U	R	G	E		S	H	O	T	S		O	R	O	
S	T	O	C	K	T	H	E	S	H	E	L	V	E	S
T	H	O		E	R	A	S	E		Y	E	N	S	
S	O	D		N	O	D	S		C	A	R	R	E	Y
			E	N	L		C	O	N	E	S			
B	A	R	R	E	L	A	L	O	N	G		L	U	G
A	V	O	I	D		F	A	N	G		T	A	R	O
M	E	S	S	Y		R	U	D	E		U	N	I	T
A	R	E	A	S		O	D	O	R		T	E	S	H

Page 382 — PIE FIGHT

U	L	C	E	R		S	H	E	D		M	A	S	S
K	O	A	L	A		P	O	L	E		U	T	A	H
E	S	K	I	M	O	R	O	L	L		D	O	D	O
S	E	E		P	L	E	D		T	O	W	N	I	E
			M	A	L	E		S	O	I	R	E	E	S
R	A	M	O	N	A		C	H	I	L	E			
E	L	I	O	T		C	O	E	D		S	A	M	E
B	O	R	N		R	A	V	E	S		T	R	I	G
S	E	A	M		E	V	E	R		S	L	I	N	G
			U	T	T	E	R		S	P	E	E	D	Y
M	I	L	L	A	R	D		T	E	A	R			
A	M	E	L	I	A		B	R	E	R		S	O	B
R	A	V	I		C	R	E	A	M	S	I	C	L	E
A	G	I	N		T	O	A	D		E	R	O	D	E
T	E	S	S		S	O	R	E		R	A	W	E	R

Page 384 — DOOHICKEYS

L	I	M	A	S		H	A	L	O	S		R	O	T
O	M	A	N	I		O	N	E	N	O		O	V	O
C	O	N	T	R	A	P	T	I	O	N		M	E	N
			H	E	R	M	E	S		A	P	A	R	T
C	T	A		E	O	S		G	E	T	I	N	T	O
R	I	T	T	E	R		T	O	P	I	C			
O	T	T	O		P	A	L	I	N		S	P	A	
W	H	A	T	C	H	A	M	A	C	A	L	L	I	T
D	E	N		R	A	V	E	N		O	O	P	S	
			R	I	V	E	R		Y	I	P	P	E	E
S	O	L	A	C	E	D		L	O	M		P	D	A
E	D	I	T	H		S	U	G	A	R	Y			
L	E	N		T	H	I	N	G	A	M	A	J	I	G
M	O	T		O	U	T	I	E		A	R	O	N	I
A	N	Y		N	E	S	T	S		N	E	E	D	S

Page 386 — NUMBER PLEASE

```
H E L M S # S I F T # A P S O
A B O U T # A S I A # T H U D
H O U S E B L E N D # H O P I
A N T E N A V E # S C E N E S
# # # C R O # # I N E R T # #
P E P S I S # C A N T A B # #
A P R I L # S A V O Y # O E D
L E I S # H U R O N # M O R O
L E M # B I D E N # D I T T O
# E G R E S S # A R C H E D #
# # S A M O A # B W I # # # #
C L O W N S # A I R B A L L S
R I V E # L U C K Y B R E A K
I C E S # O K I E # L E A S E
P E R T # W E D S # E A S E D
```

Page 388 — YES!

```
P A T E S # B O C K # E S P N
A R E N A # O N T O # L U T E
B Y A L L M E A N S # I R A S
L A S # T E R I # H I T E S T
O N E L E G # R E E D I T # #
# # # E D A M # F R E S H E R
L A Y S # L A F F # S T I N E
I W O # N O D O U B T # N Y E
S O U C I # R O S A # E G A D
A L B A N I A # E R M A # # #
# # E V E N S O # R O U S T S
L A T E S T # A P E D # H I T
A B C S # A B S O L U T E L Y
N E H I # K E E P # L A B E L
E L A N # E A S E # E R A S E
```

Page 390 — WAX AND WANE

```
R A C E R # A J A R # B A H
A L O N E # D U B A I # U T E
F O R T Y W H A C K S # S S A
T E A R # H O N # E T C H E R
# # # E P I C # T H R O W A T
R E W A R M # H E I G H # # #
E R A T O # S H U L A # A C E
B O Y S # W H O R L # S C A M
S O N # S I R E S # R I K K I
# # # E N T R E # G O T S E T
R O S E R E D # S L E D # # #
U P B E A T # I K E # O S H A
N E O # W A Y N E N E W T O N
E R R # S P A R E # K N E L T
S A O # S W I T # E S T E S
```

Page 392 — ANT FARM

```
D A L I # P R O F S # C A L L
I G O R # R I L L E # O R E O
A N T E B E L L U M # B E E R
L E T # A S E A # O N W A R D
S W O O N E D # A L O E # # #
# # # M A T # T W I N B E D S
L E A N N # C A A N # D R Y
A N T I A I R C R A F T G U N
M I O # D E E D # L I E G E
E D N A B E S T # T E L # # #
# # # D O C S # V A N E S S A
S C H O O L # O O P S # T A M
L O O P # A U N T I E M A M E
A L O T # R A C E R # A V O N
P A T S # E W E R S # R E A D
```

Page 394 — BURGER TOPPERS

```
P S S # C O P # V A C # T B A
A P T # A L A M E D A # E E N
C O O # P I G I R O N # E D D
K N O W O N E S O N I O N S #
E G G O # # # I N M A T E # #
R E E N G A G E # S E E G E R
# # # O S O L E # # G E A R #
C U T T H E M U S T A R D # #
# V A N E # # R A R E R # # #
C L I N G S # N O T A T I O N
R I V E R A # # # I N G E # #
G E T I N T O A P I C K L E #
C U R # P E O N I E S # P A D
R L S # E L M T R E E # O L E
T A E # D Y E # E R E # T A D
```

Page 396 — WATERY CONCLUSIONS

```
S H A L T # G O T H # S P A M
B E L O W # A B B A # T O N I
A R T N O U V E A U # A R K S
# # # P R E Y # L I T T L E
T O P S A I L # # T I M E R #
E R R O R S # M O N I C A # #
A G E N T # S I L O S # N E D
S A S S # S A L A D # S T A R
E N S # H O N E Y # S I E G E
# # B U I L D S # M U R A L S
C L U B S # # T I S S U E S #
L A R O S A # # M A M A # # #
I D E A # C L E M E N C E A U
N E A T # T I R E # N O T I T
G N U S # S E E R # A W A R E
```

```
PIERS | COPA | STAT
ARTIE | AVER | WINE
MATTE | MERC | ALTA
  QUARTERPOUNDER
    EEL     REEDY
STRODE | BADGE |
ARIA | MARIE | BIT
  HALFHEARTEDNESS
LYE | ARIES | ARLO
  GLAND | LUNGES
ALCOA |   ION
  FULLSPEEDAHEAD
TROD | ORAL | OASES
RIVE | TIRE | OVINE
ADEN | SEND | KENYA
```

```
FOIST | ASAP | ROAD
ENRON | NILE | ECHO
  STARTINGPITCHER
TONE | NIN | ATEAM
  HIKE | RECORDS
SURETY | GATOR |
ONEAL | LINC | SHO
  MIDDLEOFTHEROAD
ETS | VATS | MALLE
  SHEDS | RIVETS
REPAIRS | BARI
EVILS | SUM | SPAS
  FINISHINGSCHOOL
ETON | OVAL | PENNE
RENE | TYPE | ADDED
```

The Self-Employment Survival Guide

Mokena Community
Public Library District

APR 3 0 2018